THE
INTRICACIES
OF
SOUL
RELATIONSHIPS

THE INTRICACIES OF SOUL RELATIONSHIPS

Relationships, Soul Connections and Twin Flames

An Anthology of Soul Readings by

JUDITH KÜSEL

Published by Judith Küsel
info@judithkusel.com
www.judithkusel.com

First Edition 2023

THE INTRICACIES OF SOUL RELATIONSHIPS
An Anthology of Soul Readings by Judith Küsel

ISBN Paperback: 978-0-796-12038-0

Printed by Castle Graphics, Cape Town, South Africa

Table of Contents

Introduction

Heart Opening

An intense heart opening is currently taking place as the shift intensifies.

The heart will be cleaved open to reveal the core of the soul and the eternal truth, which is revealing whatever is still within us that needs to be resolved and left behind forever – that which is keeping us from completely stepping forward into the new, higher dimensional frequency bands, and a new way of living, and of course, **Loving**!

Over the past few weeks, I've been wondering what has been happening, as things I thought I had resolved a long time ago were coming up again, persistently. I was at a loss about how to deal with this, even though I had experienced an intense unprecedented breakthrough while working with the White Flame in the highest degree, and had been told to bring this to Humanity.

I was brought back to love and loving relationships, particularly the Twin Flame Relationship, which has not worked out for me. I have long since made peace with this, and indeed, love is never absent. Other souls always step in to fill the void, and these can be multiple, not just one! Such is the Universal Law. Certainly, in my case, many others have stepped in, and powerfully so.

I was reminded of the core truth, namely that Love is eternal and can never just be turned off like a tap. The soul lives on, thus souls are always eternally with each other, in love and with love, for in truth the **Soul** is **Love**.

At its core truth, there is not a single soul who is not **Love**, and does not incorporate **Divine Love**. It is impossible!

It may appear that some people are lacking this on the earthly plane, especially in the 3D, but this is an illusion. They merely choose to play out certain actor's roles, but in the truth of their soul, Divine Love is present, which always makes its presence felt, through the entire incarnation of the soul. As souls have free will and choice in the 3D, they often reject unconditional Divine Love, closing their hearts, cutting themselves off from their own souls, which creates pain and suffering.

I was shown the *Core Soul Fires*, and how Love is truly eternal. So even if it seems as if they are parted in this lifetime, souls cannot part nor be apart, for in reality all is ONE. We all embrace Divinity within us, and stem from the Self-same Source. Twin Flames originate from the same Soul Fires, so cannot be separated, although they may choose to be apart during an incarnation.

It is also most important to understand that most Souls on Earth do **not** have their Twin Flame incarnated. The souls agree to this before incarnating, and some of the Twin Flames who did not incarnate, serve as higher guides and are always with the incarnated one during their sleep state. Again, nothing is ever missing!

At this moment, we are undeniably being faced with this eternal truth. When we open our heart centre, and get back to the **Core Truth** within, **Divine Truth**, we can only expand in **Love**.

This truth is all the more *powerful* at this time, because, by Divine Dispensation on the 5 July 2020, when the Old Earth ceased to be and the New Earth was fully born, **all Karma** was lifted off souls on Earth. We were freed from the karmic wheel.

This is immense!

Note that you have free will and choice. You can choose to hold onto the old for dear life, all the unforgiveness, and shame, blame and guilt, or you can choose to finally let go, and thus free yourself and others.

There will come a time when you are reminded of the love you felt for the Twin Soul concerned, in eternal form. It will be there. It will show up in this time period. Why? It is because we are now leaving everything we have ever created in the 3D behind, including all the negative patterns we may have created during previous incarnations. Nowhere is this truer than with the Twin Flame.

I was shown my twin this morning, in his glorious innocence, and perceived the truth of his soul. It is not that I have never seen this before, it was just that I was able to see him from an elevated perspective, as I have shifted immensely in the last few months and years, in all aspects, and have been totally transformed. Indeed, many past experiences now feel as if they happened light years ago!

The Divine then showed me that all souls will be freed, and in the New Earth will experience love in such an expanded form that it currently cannot even be comprehended. This is what I was being prepared for!

In that moment of realization, I was speechless. Such unconditional love welled up within me that I understood – the highest love is when we finally attain wholeness within ourselves, and thus perceive wholeness reflected in the other. One is loved as **soul**, and not for anything else other than the **soul**. It becomes a **merging of soul within soul**, yet neither loses its wholeness in the process, but rather expands into a greater Spiral, a Torus of Creation itself!

When I was shown this, I could only completely surrender everything into Divine Hands. I am unable to fully express this profound revelation in words.

All I can say, is that, if you think you know all about Love, the Power of Love will open more gates, and more portals, and you will discover that, in reality, you know no-thing, and what remains to be experienced and discovered about Love, is infinite! There is no end and no beginning. One starts to step into the vastness of the Power of Love, which goes beyond description!

I am sharing this today, because so many have had a deep misconception about what True Love is. Some seek love so desperately, when in truth all paths lead within, and only when we truly experience the deepest love inside, for ourselves and the Divine, can this expand to another soul, even a Twin Flame.

The *Gnosis* lies within.

This is something you need to find out for yourself. For all paths lead back to yourself and your Maker, and the Infinite Core Truth. You will only be given the truth to the degree that you are open to receive it, and to surrender to the greater power of Love. I have been asking for many months and years to be able to experience the deepest and the most profound Love, never knowing where this path would lead me, just like my Quest for the *White Flame*.

Now everything is coming together, for it is time to step fully into the New Earth and New Embodiment, and to leave all the old false beliefs behind, the old false programming and fragmentation, the brokenness, forever!

This will soon be felt more intensely than ever – the waves upon waves upon waves of the deepest clearing of all that is still hindering the full heart and soul opening of Humanity at large.

You will be cleaved open to the core of your soul, where you cannot hide anymore, and the Truth will find you and set you free, in all ways and forms, so that you can step through the Golden Gateways, into the New Earth.

The transformation that is imminent cannot be put into human words, and indeed we will lose the need for words, and return to telepathy – heart to heart, mind to mind, and soul to soul communication!

I have spoken!

Judith Küsel

The Readings

You are first and foremost a soul, who has taken on a physical form during this incarnation on Planet Earth. Your soul is infinite and therefore has immense talents, abilities, and knowledge accumulated from many thousands of lifetimes, in many dimensions and in many forms of life all over the Cosmos.

My soul readings put you in touch with your own soul. I give you your Soul Name, your Soul Group name, your galaxy of origin, your tonal chord and soul colours. I will give your soul purpose, talents, gifts and abilities.

When we are born onto this planet, we slip into forgetfulness, unable to remember why we are here, often feeling a deep void, or having the constant sense that there must be more to life than just this. Some simply feel lost, and some would love to know more, in order to empower themselves on all levels by living their highest soul purpose. My soul readings answer that and more.

I record these readings in writing. As such, a wealth of information comes through, which you will need to digest and read through time and again. I receive feedback from all over the world daily about how these readings have positively impacted people's lives in many ways.

The Twin Flame soul readings are very popular. They concentrate more on relationships, and determine if the Divine Other is your Twin Flame or not. Often, ways of relating were established over many lifetimes, which have not always served our higher soul growth and good. My readings will identify these, and assist you with creating new and more loving patterns to bring greater love and insights into your life and relationships.

The Soul Readings are about you – why you are here, your soul purpose and mission, and the specific talents and abilities that you anchor into this planet.

Note: I do not channel, I am not a psychic, or a medium, nor do I use astrology, or numerology or any such tools. I tap into the Super-consciousness field, and *transmit* the soul records held at the Divine Source.

This is the first in a series of books addressing various key topics of interest, composed of extracts from the thousands of readings I have done over the years. As such, they often contain original and unique information, not necessarily available elsewhere.

They are my gift to you, in your quest for soul empowerment and enlightenment.

CHAPTER 1

Sexual Energy, Purity and Sacred Sexuality

(Part 1)

Extracts from Soul Readings

SOUL GROUP: The Shining Ones

"It is also to be understood that with your soul, and your womanhood in particular, because you work with the keys and codes of cellular activation, every time you have sexual intercourse, you are allowing someone into your cellular memory bank field. So, all their residue and emotional baggage, will be dumped into your energy fields at a cellular level. This could lead to many physical problems in the sexual area later in life, and this needs to be understood. So, rather clear those energy fields of all past lovers or anyone from the past, whoever entered there, and be extra careful to not engage sexually, until complete love and trust is there, and the partner comes in total love, trust and respect, without their own ego, and unresolved issues.

This needs to be like a red light going off as a warning signal. For you cannot afford to sabotage yourself on this level, and it would be better to go and love yourself and keep your energy fields crystal clear, rather than to engage with someone who is neither mature enough nor ready to meet you as an equal with great love, trust and respect."

———

SOUL GROUP: The Light Bearer Souls

"It almost seems that in this lifetime, she forced the issue of having sex with a man in this physical body, because she felt she was losing out on something, and then nearly fainted, for in truth, Human beings have forgotten that the sexual energy, does not need a physical body to express itself in its highest and most beautiful form. Some who have sunk lower than the animals, just have sex for the sake of it, and it becomes a performance game of manipulation, which causes so many woes.

In truth, in the beginning everyone knew the bliss and ecstasy of true Sacred Union, but then one mated for life, and knew how to use sexual energy correctly and in beautiful, soul enhancing, and soul-beautifying ways. Sexual union took place in such a sacred manner, which created the third fire and flame, becoming the Divine Masculine in union with the Divine Feminine, as co-creators. However, when people have sex for self-gratification, for self-service, with multiple partners, the sacredness of it all is totally lost, and they cause their own downfall."

SOUL GROUP: The Spiraling Creative Ones

"There was a lifetime prior to this one, where you lived in France, during the First World War, and grew up in an occupied area. You then somehow became involved with a female doctor, who had disguised herself as a man. She enticed you to become her lover, and this experience introduced you to lesbian sex. After the war this behaviour became a way of survival for you, and you joined a group of lesbians who were also forced to put the pieces together again. Some were married or had men, just to produce children, but in reality they hated them. *Much of your own confusion in this lifetime stem from this, along with your deep-seated fear of being used and abused sexually in any way at all, by either sex.* The gay relationships in the lifetime prior to this, have intensified the confusion, the sense of often not really knowing if you were male or female. However, in truth your soul is *feminine*, and therefore has always incarnated as female, and never male."

SOUL GROUP: The Ones who Serve in Unlocking

"If an angry or bad-tempered man enters you in a sexual relationship, he will add to the overload in your central nervous system, but also block your sexual area completely, with this negative energy. So be aware, and do not allow anyone to enter who is not filled with love, coming with truth, and true feelings of love and respect. Your soul is so sensitive that any infringement of this will add to your ill health, causing you to feel deeply depressed, for your body and especially your womb, is a sacred temple and must be entered with respect, with pure love, and with true love intentions."

***

SOUL GROUP: The Energetic Sounding Ones

"It is also good to clear the base, sacral and solar plexus chakras, and then the lower vertebrae, for energy can get very blocked up there. Your womb area, your sacred sexual centre is very clogged, with so many negative hooks, cords and ties from all the men you have ever had any kind of sexual exchange with, as they have left a karmic residue and imprint in you. This needs to be severed, if they did not come in pure love, with a true intention to love unconditionally. So be aware of this.

There might indeed be some connection with the grandmother, as it was her own soul journey, and choice during that lifetime. Some of it is genetic, yes, and here you can ask for *genetic lineage clearing*, but generally each soul is responsible for their own physical form, often not understanding that the sexual areas and the womb are sacred. Any woman who really knows this, will not allow anyone into that area, who is not of the same energy frequency, and does not share complete trust, respect and love. When self-respect is lacking and just anyone is allowed in, deep soul wounds make themselves felt, for women *feel* through that area, and inherently know if a man is just using them, or just pumping anger or whatever emotion, into them. So, the reasons are many, and it is already known, that during the war years there were many rapes and events hidden as family skeletons, so deeply buried in the trauma – scars that need clearing and do not only stem from that grandmother, but from others as well, men included."

***

SOUL GROUP: The Loving Ones

"You incarnated mainly to work through these karmic ties, and to open your heart more, no matter what. This concerns gaining a greater understanding that a woman's heart energy centre is closely linked to her womb and sexual energy centre, her vagina. If the heart is totally open to its very core, if trust and respect are fully present, then the 7 gateways of the womb are also fully open, and consequently there can be a full, honest and heartfelt acceptance of the male inside. However, with distrust and disrespect, the heart and womb close. Sex without love, is hurting oneself.

In ancient times you were highly trained to understand this, and did a daily anointing ceremony of the heart and womb. This was a deep, profound meditative state one entered consciously, inviting the Goddess to open up each of the thousand petals of the heart and soul, filling them with beautiful unconditional love. This was then extended to every single cell, atom, all the bodily parts, especially the womb, and then flowed into the emotional, mental, spiritual and soul bodies.

The womb was filled with love energies, rose quartz crystals and other tools and singing bowls attuned them to the heart frequencies, as healing energy moved into it, the heart and all energy centres. This was a beautiful and heartfelt ceremony, and kept one firmly centred in the heart with unconditional love for oneself, the Goddess, and for others. One could do and be no other than love!"

SOUL GROUP: The Luminous Ones

"So, this soul needs to do plenty of self-healing and self-validation work, practising loving herself totally, completely, utterly, until she overflows and can open up her heart, soul and her whole body in total loving trust to her twin flame. If this is absent, there will be a closure of the heart and her sexual areas, which will make sexual union okay, but not extraordinary. For if the heart withholds in any way, then sexual energy will also be blocked, because if there is any distrust and fear of pain and disbelief in love from the partner, it won't work, since the heart energy centre is vital to this soul. The more she opens, the more the heart energies flow, the more she is congruent to her own higher soul calling and to the greater soul frequency she is – for she is pure love.

When she is in this higher state of Love, then she is so loving, so totally present in love that she can love in an expanded form. Her sexual energy will then soar and escalate, and she will easily recall how, in her first incarnation, her twin and her participated in the *ancient twin flame sexual sacred rites,* with the resulting sublime and utterly blissful union, the shared ecstasy where both are whole and complete within themselves, with an added bonus of two complete people merging and then entering the third whole, and igniting the third flame. When one is not equal to the other, the sexual flame will burn more than ignite, and thus there will be extreme pain."

———

SOUL GROUP: The Knowing Ones

"In one incarnation the two of you were born into the same family, it may sound strange, but both your parents were involved elsewhere, and you were half-brother and half-sister but very close, indeed so close that you became lovers from early on. In Greece this was a familiar practice, as it was in Egypt, so at that time it was nothing out of the ordinary, and happened because of the close bond between you and you both being more or less the same age. Nevertheless, when your parents discovered this, and the church intervened, you were both married off to other partners and were both miserable and continued to be lovers until you left the planet. You met clandestinely, often in caves or the high mountains, or anywhere where you could not be seen."

———

SOUL GROUP: Those who serve the Divine

"These two have incarnated here before in the lands of Lemuria. They had *one form*, being *androgynous*, and then as Atlantis was rising in power, and had both male *and* female forms, they felt like they were missing out on something vital, which of course is the sexual energy force. So, they requested to be *split* into a male and female form, which caused untold heartache between them, for since the split they drifted apart, and with the sexual energy came the lusting after other partners to experience orgasms, all the while moving away from each other, until the relationship completely broke down."

———

SOUL GROUP: The Precious Ones

"She also has to be very careful who she gets involved with, when her hormones start going haywire! If she allows just any boy into her sexual area, they may well jam her frequencies and vibrations, and she will become depressed with distorted energies. So there needs to be an understanding that one must be careful to only allow those in who are of the same high frequency, and not lower, especially because of who and what she is at a soul level."

SOUL GROUP: The Graces

"In this lifetime you will have to release all vows of chastity, obedience and poverty. You wore chastity belts, during those convent lifetimes, and were often punished in certain lives for even thinking lustful thoughts, or something similar, which was rather bizarre. So, then all of this must be released, for they closed off your sexual energy flow, so you may have problems reaching orgasms in this lifetime, or have troubles related to your sexual centres, which will need to be released from those "belts", and the associated repressive convent programming."

SOUL GROUP: The Intricately Creative Ones Who Work with Love Light Frequencies and Vibrations

"She is a volunteer soul, and will often feel attracted to men, but in essence she is so highly evolved in frequency bands, that very few men can match that vibration, without completely draining her energy fields. Thus, she should be very discerning as to whom she lets into her energy fields, especially sexually. Some men will feel supercharged after sex with her, because they will feel the higher frequency charge she receives. Some will then want that for themselves, and will zap her energy away, so protection and caution is needed.

Such highly evolved souls as you are different, and you really are 7th dimensional – so imagine the frequency difference between you, when someone still very much in the 3rd Dimensional world, comes into your most intimate area. That is a vast discrepancy, and with your super sensitive energy fields, your finely attuned state can drop to a state of total imbalance and depression, if you are not careful. This does not mean that you cannot have a relationship with a man –rather it is best that you are mindful to attract someone on your frequency band, knowing there are very few, but then, you want to have the best, don't settle for mediocre."

SOUL GROUP: The Light bearers

"You also have to be careful about with whom you have intimate relationships, as there are very few souls on this planet at the moment from your own soul group, as they are so very highly evolved and advanced, that most cannot hold onto the heavy 3D form. Your own body was especially designed to hold the higher light frequencies, and if you allow someone into your energy fields and especially your sexual area, who is of lower vibrations, they will jam your energy fields, and make you feel used and depressed. So just guard against that happening, and rather ask your angels and guides to bring only those to you who match your frequency bands, so you are in higher alignment with your soul and calling."

SOUL GROUP: The Intricate Web Beings who bring the Light Quotient into All that Exists

"As you conformed to society, and forgot more and more of who and what you truly are, for the first time you experienced sexual relationships. In your own home galaxy, you are an *androgynous* being, so this was a novel experience which brought great heartache, because your soul is just not geared towards anything which is a counter-balance, anything or anyone that disrupts or disturbs your natural equilibrium. You also allowed disturbed people to be intimate with you, because of your tendency to pick up lame ducks, and soothe their pain away, which you then absorb into your physical and emotional bodies, suffering severe overload.

You need to refrain from sex for a while, and truly clean and cleanse your womb area, including all the negative energy, cords and ties and hooks, which men planted there. It causes blockages in your thyroid, as your inner systems are screaming to be heard. Deep down you knew that something was not *kosher*, but you suppressed that, like everyone else was doing, so you had to do it too.

Once done, get back into your heart and soul, and know that you have come to do light energy work. You can literally transmit the higher cosmic energies and frequencies and then beam them into *Mother Earth*, into places which need healing, and into people, animals and plants."

––––––––––

SOUL GROUP: The Infinite Star Beings of Light

"Sometimes it is good to just sit quietly opposite each other, without speaking, without words, really gazing into each other's eyes, for they are the windows of the soul. Then just gently from the heart centre, breathe love in and out, first to yourself, until your whole body and auric field is filled with pure unconditional love for yourself, and then start connecting to each other's base chakras, allowing this loving energy to enter there and circulate between you. Then the sacral, solar plexus, until you reach the crown, where you allow the rainbow fountains to just sprinkle forth there like a million stars, and now let that become a mighty rainbow stream of energy, pull that down through all your chakras, through your base chakra and project this into his base chakra, working up, and then allow the stream of light to come from his crown charka into yours again, and repeat this until the energy is streaming in and out of you like a might river of love and light, clockwise and then anti-clockwise. Then feel how you start merging energy bodies, how you become *one single energy field*. How does it feel to be totally **One**, and held within a beautiful unconditional loving pulsating rainbow of love energy field?

In that moment, you truly are meeting each other as souls. As energy, for the soul is pure energy. You do not need words – for they often mislead and hurt. You do not need even to touch – you are already **One**, inside and out."

––––––––––

SOUL GROUP: The Infinite Light Beings

"Remember how the ancient sexual rites were practised within the priesthood, with very strict rules, not to prohibit sexual intercourse, but rather to understand the sexual energy, and to use it in the greatest possible way for the higher good of all. Thus, the partners were hand-picked, after having had soul readings and then only those partners who were *Twin Flames,* after strict training on how to use the energy correctly. These ancient rites were known in what we remember as *Paradise* – but the *Fall of Humanity* came when they abused these rites, and started using them for self-gratification, and later on for black magic, and thus were expelled from Paradise, having to relearn this when the soul was ready to receive – with absolute purity and purity of intent, and *only* after having gone through immense initiations in the inner planes.

The soul will first have to endure these inner initiations to return to innocence, if she wishes to have this gift and the release from all karmic bonds. Deep down she knows this and that is why there is reluctance to practice this with the current partner, with the history of what happened between them."

SOUL GROUP: The Energetic Ones

"All soul memory banks of persecution, of anger you felt as a woman in being used sexually, and as a chattel, the whole spectrum of these past lives, must be released, so that your womb, solar plexus area, throat and upper chakras can be cleared, for so often you could not give voice to the anger, the helplessness you felt inside. You need to truly work on this, and just allow the release to come, and move into the state where you really just feel love flooding these areas, so that your natural energy flow can be returned, and therefore also the energy flow of the Goddess energies.

In this lifetime every time a man entered your womb, you subconsciously had memories activated from those other lifetimes. So, be sure to also clear that area of **feelings** you often felt during intercourse, or when you felt that a person(s) did not enter you with great love in their hearts. Because you are so super-sensitive in this area, you will automatically hone into the true state of mind and heart of your partner, which will bring forth a chain reaction in your womb, for you will **sense** and **feel** what is **inside** of him – even if he does not speak a word. So, then the more this area is cleared, the lighter and brighter you will become, and as a result your transmitting power will open up. You will start reconnecting with your own core soul, and the truth of who and what you are, and then will find that your third eye opens up, with transmitting abilities.

In that lifetime you just loved work, although the training entailed abstinence from sexual intercourse for certain periods, and then only occurred with a *carefully chosen* partner with great love, on the same frequency band as oneself energetically. In your case you have to be extra careful, as a man of lower vibrations, or not of the same intent and wavelength, could damage your transmitting abilities if let into the sexual or womb area, thereby causing havoc with your own energy field. It was common knowledge that you had to be diligent, and to guard against the base animal nature, which just wishes to procreate in lust, so you were taught to cultivate the Higher Soul Self and Higher Mind, and to be extremely discerning with sexual partners and in this case, completely so. Rather focus on an external mission than engage with the wrong partner, for it was recognized as a responsibility to render the greatest possible service, in the purest way possible. It was no accident that many priestesses preferred to be a virgin, rather than allowing a man who was not on the same frequency band, or not higher service-orientated into their energetic fields. This was the highest path of purity, and such priestesses were immensely powerful in their own right. In that lifetime you stayed on that path and never swayed, remaining a virgin because of this knowledge."

SOUL GROUP: The Ones who Know

"This soul is one with a very interesting record of working with crystals, crystalline forms and crystal skulls in ancient times, long before Atlantis and long before what was founded by *Quetzalcoatl*. At the time of the *Lion Kingdom*, millions of years ago, they worked with the creation of the **original** crystal skulls, not the ones which have now manifested, or were still in the hands of shamans from Mexico.

In those days there was a special priesthood, who worked with distinct crystal deposits, which are now buried under the sea offshore from Mexico, and the Americas. There were huge crystal deposits very deep underground, and the quartz used for these skulls was the finest quality, not cut, but rather fashioned. The priestess, in this case you, went into a deep trance, and a higher dimensional state, that of the 13th (at that time the civilization was in the 7th), and visualized what the crystal skull would look like. You had a crystal-clear picture in your mind, and also saw how it would be used in the ceremonies of the 12 tribes, and the 12 Crystal Pyramids, each on a different colour ray. You then projected this image to the crystal chambers and the crystal *Elementals*, **inside** the crystal and asked them to work with you, thus together you created such a skull.

They would then take your mind picture into themselves, while you went into the highest trance state, opening your heart and sexual energy centre, the sacred womb, infusing your energy into the crystals by *dissolving* into them – in other words, you disintegrated completely (your physical form) and became **one** with the crystals and elementals, as together you created and birthed the *Crystal Skulls*. Thus, when it manifested into form, it was perfectly shaped, without the use of any machines, human hands, or instruments cutting or shaping it.

You emerged out of the trance state, reassembled your physical form and woke up to your normal state again, and there on a plinth your crystal skull would be – beautiful and perfect in every way."

―――――――――

SOUL GROUP: The Caring Ones

"This soul comes out of a long association at soul level with the *Druidic tradition* and the *Bardic Order of the High Lords and Ladies of the Celtic Rounds,* which is a type of Order associated with a deep caring for the land, music, and poetry, and the inner order of humans, inner harmony and healthy beingness, which translates into that deep caring at soul level for the lands, animals, plants and thus all living creatures, as well as other people.

In the first lifetime, in what was the Celtic Order, long before Avalon was born, she was one of the *Celtic High Order of Bardic and Healer Priestesses* who looked after the fertility rites, and also performed ceremonies for hand fasting, pregnancy and child birth, acting as the caretakers of the tribes, and the women were the rulers of the lands. They also chose their partners, or had multiple partners, and the country was well run and populated. This was ensured by fertility rites, and the rites of passage, as they were in charge of the general well-being of the tribe itself.

Some of these women in the *Bardic Order* played the harp to heal the minds of others, as it vibrates at frequencies which bring in higher healing. They sang songs in the ancient language to fairy folk too, to encourage them to work with the people and help with the crops and land fertility.

They gathered in the stone circles, in the dolmens and in the greater circles of the land.

There priestesses were also in charge of the wild horses, and were their custodians, for they brought these horses with them from Lyra and the Bear Constellation. The horses were considered sacred and belonging to the Goddess and all rites were dedicated to the Goddess, whom they served.

This soul returned to those parts that she felt drawn to, because there lies the remnant of this ancient land, the remainder has sunk under the sea west of the Island, along with the temples of the Goddess. In her sleep state she often visits those abodes, and then feels slightly disorientated on waking up at times. This is because her *soul shape-shifts naturally*, often even during waking hours, although she is not always aware of this.

She was drawn to this man first and foremost because he was a partner from the *Druidic Order of Men* in that lifetime, with whom she as a Priestess performed certain fertility rites. She was trained to do this during the spring and winter solstices, according to certain astrological charts, within one of the stone circles in spring, and inside one of the underground caves or shelters in the winter. These rites were done over 7 days, under strict conditions. For the rest of the year there was no physical contact with each other, as these rites were considered sacrosanct, with a deep honoring of the Goddess, through the man, with him gifting her with the seed of his manhood. With regards to the serpent energies, they were used in a different manner, but in the sexual rites this was termed the *Dance of the Serpent Flame*, considered so potent and sacred, only those trained in these sacred and secret rites could partake in them. It was then believed that the dance of the serpent and what it ignited, it would add to the fertility of the people and land.

The fact that she is remembering these experiences with this man, is a deep ignited memory bank. Concerning the idea of tantric sex – these rites were similar to the tantric ones, but are by no means tantric in nature, but were rather ancient. The priestesses and priests were trained specifically in them, and performed them twice a year in a very secret and profound manner. It is the memory of this that stirs deep inside.

However, in this, and in previous lifetimes, she often tended to misuse this power, thus the perceived failure in relationships. This is all is about the higher healing of the Goddess energies, and most of all, of women at large. For the fall of that civilization came when men began to resent the sexual power of the priestesses, and then sought to revenge themselves on them, by withdrawing more and more into the mind. They then tried to control women by withholding sex, or by bargaining with it. When this happened, the power swung to the males, and later they enslaved women by forcing them into marriage, bondage and slavery, or raping or selling them to other men. In essence then the healing of all of this has now come to the fore. Deep down she is realizing this, and is yearning then for the right man – or the Divine Other, because deep down she knows that once upon a time, there was a higher and more profound union, and this is what she remembers, particularly with this man.

In other lifetimes they did meet again when he either forced her to marry him for partnership reasons like her dowry, to gain wealth, or as a bargaining tool. In one lifetime she was his daughter, and he literally sold her to the highest bidder. So, in this lifetime he appears as the perfect business partner, but with intense sexual baggage. *What he fears more than most is his own impotence – for he fears to lose his manhood in intercourse.* He had a liaison with a woman, who ridiculed his manhood, so he could not perform any longer, however this is more of a psychological problem than a physical one. This woman was there to teach him love – that without love, sex is empty, and of no worth.

Sex merely for pleasure or for self-gratification, loads karma onto the soul. The sexual energy was always considered a gift of the Gods and Goddesses to be used in a sacred and sanctified manner – for it is the power of the *Tree of Life* itself. This was understood the first time they had a union, and as a priest he was highly trained to honor and understand this. So, in essence this is a journey of his own soul, and he has to heal on multiple levels here, to reclaim and to honor his own manhood.

In essence these two souls were drawn to each other, to heal on many fronts. It has to do with deep soul woundedness in the sexual area, but also the pain of souls who used each other for control and bargaining tools in the past. There is a lot of emotional baggage to heal on both sides and they can help each other here, without having sexual intercourse.

Thus, you really are in the right spot – your soul chose to reconnect with your other soul parts there. Basically, this really is not about finding a man – but your soul, and reconnecting deeply and profound with your own Goddess parts. It is only when you do so, that something deep and profound within yourself will shift, and the memory will return of the initiations you endured as a Priestess, into the sexual rites. When you start remembering that, you will understand that they were in essence that deep and profound connection to the Goddess herself – in that one *became* the Goddess – one became all that She is. Thus, one incorporated the energy of the Goddess into oneself, in order to gift the man with union with the Goddess herself, like he gifted her with the fullness and deep penetration of the God himself, because he became the male Godhead himself."

SOUL GROUP: The Illumined Ones

"She also needs to cut all negative cords and ties with her ex-husband from her energy fields, as being with him for a while, blocked certain energies in her sexual area, causing the numbness in her left (female) side. She should have acupuncture on her meridians and nadis to unblock them. Her sexual area needs to be cleared of all negative cords and attachments there – ask Archangel Michael to clear them and also her throat area as she often does not speak out when she should, or feels that she cannot voice what is inside. This has to do with both lifetimes above, the one when she could not voice her jealousy so was chosen to be a sacrifice for others, and the other when pretending to be a man, unable to voice her womanly feelings. So, there is a need to learn to speak up fearlessly to share her innermost heart and soul with others, and to stand in her power and strength."

SOUL GROUP: The Anointing Ones

"Her soul group has not been involved on this planet like many of the other soul groups, and she is a *volunteer soul* and thus will always feel that she does not belong. She functions at multiple levels, thus can span dimensions quite easily, as she is a multi-dimensional being and a cosmic soul, and is used as a *Transmitter Channel*. The higher cosmic rays and frequencies are transmitted through her, and when involved in sexual activities, she channels this energy into the Earth's energy grids, and anchors them in. However, there is a proclivity of this soul to misuse these powers, not understanding that there is both a proper and a destructive use for them. To truly reconnect these sexual energies, one must do so with the understanding that sexual energies should be considered **Sacred**. So there has to be a heart and soul connection on multiple levels, for the energies to be channelled in a correct manner, otherwise the sexual act becomes an act of self-gratification. It is best then to reconsider what your motives are for having sex – *is it to be adored and loved in that way, or for self-gratification?* Do you wish to learn to step up in frequency, to gift men in a beautiful way with the loving grace of unconditional love, and to channel energies released during orgasms in the correct manner?

This entails not releasing them through the base chakra, but pouring them up and out of your crown chakra, back into your heart, and then into the heart of Planet Earth. You can learn to do this, for this channel knows how to do this, and works with this constantly. You both are essentially on the same assignment, so have to learn to embrace this, and to teach others. As female transmitters you are healing the planet from deep within, and can open up massively clogged up areas, while pacing yourselves. Humankind has forgotten how to do this. One must remain focused, and truly pray to be used as a crystal clear, truthful and authentic *Transmitter Channel.* Ask to attract the appropriate souls with whom you can engage in this act. Many men use sexual energy as a stress relief, or as a means for self-gratification, and do not know how to connect with their heart and soul, in emotional intercourse. Once you are able to teach them to open up their hearts and souls without attaching to them, you will conduct energies into their heart and soul and **heal** them, which becomes a Divine act of higher service.

Understand that at this relevant time, a balancing of the masculine and feminine energies is essential, as previously power-based men abused this, by having sex, but **not** connecting their heart to their penis, so our call here is to teach them how to open their hearts and souls, to give themselves totally within the sacred sexual act. Once the heart is open, then the energies transmitted during sexual intercourse with **specific souls** (you are *one* of them, and there are 12 in all), they are brought into balance and restored.

Your soul took it upon itself to restore this balance, and you are now asked to step more and more into your **Higher Soul Self.** So go into retreat, truly reconnect with your own soul on multiple levels, do not engage in sexual intercourse for at least three weeks, and ask to be **initiated** into the **Ancient Sacred Sexual Rites.** You may call upon your teachers in these planes, *Merlin, Apollo* and *Aphrodite* to assist you. Your overall direction will come from **Archangel Gabriel,** who is in charge of the sexual chakras, and so guides the opening up of the heart and soul, to be ready for sex, and the proper use of the channel. During this time, you will undergo the various stages of the **first** initiation of **12**, with the **13**th as the final.

At the time of this reading, this channel has already passed through the first 4. You all agreed to this mission to bring in the beautiful balance and higher healing between masculine and feminine energies and more importantly, a Higher *Healing* into the Earth's Energy Grids, where men blocked the portals in their attempts to block the *spinal cord* of the planet's energy centres.

You are both *Cosmic Souls* with the power to do just this and more, yet you need the Masculine Energy Consciousness to blend in with your Feminine Consciousness, to facilitate the energy becoming powerful enough to open up these centres.

Your twin flame has not incarnated, and the man you are asking about is a **Soul Mate,** from the same star system. You thus share an attraction for each other. He gifted you with the awakening of your **Heart centre,** so you can step into this initiation. However, other men will now step into this role, who will be guided to you and will fulfil the act of initiation, once you have gone through the first initiation of being on your own, without sexual intercourse during those three to six weeks (depending on how you are assimilating the initiation, and how you are coping).

Your greatest gift to the world at this *time is this beautiful and profound gift to help men back to their beautiful hearts and souls, by having sex with them,* in truth and with integrity, and then to gift the planet with the opening up of the energy portals. Remember at all times that sexual energy used in a correct and sacred manner is there to raise the **Consciousness,** for it is therefore the *same* energy in a different form, and when used cosmically in the correct manner, and under supervision from Archangel Gabriel, will bring an ultimate union between the Divine Masculine and Divine Feminine, to **all** of Creation, and with the raised consciousness, will open the energy grids and portals to bring them into the same beautiful heart-centred balance."

SOUL GROUP: The Graces

"So, let us go back to Atlantis. You were very happily settled there and came from the Pleiades, bringing that innocence they have. Atlantis opened the whole planet for colonization from the Cosmos, and some new elements settled there, which eventually led to its destruction, as this group from Mars returned, (as it had before). Earth always associates Mars with wars, and the God of War, and Mars indeed holds this energy, since it was nearly blown up in the Wars of the Heavens, after its sister planet, between Mars and Jupiter, blew herself up, and total chaos reigned.

You fell in love with a man from Mars, and then your happy life in Atlantis totally changed into one of tears and woe. He had that type of brooding quiet and intense energy, which was the total opposite of your bubbling, effervescent self. So total opposites do attract each other, and you married him, although loving friends warned against him, you paid no heed. The sex was great at first, but soon turned into something sadistic and truly kinky, and something within you rebelled, but he had you in a whip hold, literally. In that lifetime you detached yourself from your physical form, for the first time ever, and often watched yourself from above – something you tend to do even now, if something happens you cannot cope with. It was like he could do whatever he liked with your physical body, and you just looked on like a spectator. Later on, when Atlantis was in trouble, he took you back with him to Mars, which you hated. Then a very dear friend, a man who truly loved you, visited and persuaded you to free yourself, and to return to Jupiter, where you healed. This man is your *twin flame*.

However, in other lifetimes, you often fell into the old patterns of Atlantis, and somehow attracted men who misused you – now abuse and misuse might sound like more or less the same thing, but there are many forms of it, and it is not always physical or sexual.

This was all meant to happen in this lifetime, so that you could finally break the pattern, and dissolve the marriage contracts, the state agreements, and whatever else you took in vows, signed contracts, etc., in those lifetimes in Austria, Atlantis, and elsewhere. It is best to call in *Archangel Michael* and ask him to please assist you with the releasing of them along with rings and regalia, for you will need to clear it all. It would also be good to go to a hypnotherapist, to take you back to the moment of the fall down the stairs, so that you can heal the associated ingrained soul memory bank, so that your hip and leg might heal (this is not fortune telling – merely a suggestion that might help). However, there are so many soul memory banks attached to this planet, concerning sexual abuse (hard to pinpoint here, but the man/men often used you sexually as a plaything, and in games of political manoeuvring, spying, etc.). This has severely clogged up your lower spine, connected to the coccyx area, uterus, vagina etc., and you need to release stuck energy there. If something is associated with misuse, trauma or pain, the soul memory banks are carried over in those parts, until cleared. So, seek out a healer to help release all of this, and cut the negative cords, ties, hooks, etc. from that area, work with the base, sacral and solar plexus and throat chakras, for all are linked. Your throat chakra is blocked, from being unable to voice your truth."

SOUL GROUP: Resonant Ones who Sing Praises to the Divine

"At this moment it is important to understand that there are many suppressed emotions in her base chakra region, which is essentially connected with nurturing, how to sustain life or the life-giving Force, fear of not having enough, or lacking the means to support herself, and standing firmly grounded on Mother Earth. There is also some added trauma, or memory banks connected with the sexual organs, resulting in the boils. What is it that you find intolerable?

Here, understanding must dawn on this soul that this is the **first time** she has incarnated here, and in her sphere of soul, there is no distinct male or female form, but it is *angelic* and *androgynous*. Thus, sexual intercourse is foreign to her, and she may feign enjoyment of it, to feel accepted somehow, and also to still her own fears of sustaining herself. Essentially these two are connected.

Know this Little One, there is nothing wrong with you – you are perfect, whole and complete, and deep down you *know* this. You will not understand the meaning and depth of true Oneness, while trying this out with men in your life. Rather first understand that your body is a *tuning fork,* and must be nurtured and honoured. It is best to refrain from sex, until you have learnt to use your beautiful qualities in higher service to Humankind, in bringing that *Sound Healing* back to the planet.

Your twin flame is with you all the time, and helps you and in actual fact you are never separated – you are fulfilled and filled to the brink. You get your "sexual" energies from your spiritual and soul energies tuning into the cosmic music, and dancing as one, that is where your true bliss lies, experiencing ecstasy, bliss and euphoria – not in union with just any man.

There are indeed very few men who would be free and able to match your vibrational frequencies. You can do well without it all – if you do have intercourse with them, they pull or deplete your sexual energies constantly, so you feel depressed, as if something is wrong, when they are feeding on your energies, and you can no longer sing, as they unconsciously take away your energies, like a vampire. You need to cut those negative cords and hooks from your entire womb area, in order to feel much more complete and lighter, so you can again dance to the music of the cosmic spheres.

Once you have healed and accepted yourself completely, vibrating at your true soul frequency, becoming more luminous and beautiful, then the right man will be attracted to you, on the same wavelength of your song frequency. Until then, it is wise to refrain from all of this, to fine-tune your soul and its natural abilities.

You will find that this man plays the violin, and is much older, but is a very gentle and dreamy soul, who will be more interested in a deep and abiding friendship rather than being intimate. You will feel safe and much loved with him and eventually, should you choose to, you could have intercourse with him. But do learn to **flow** with the beautiful cosmic music of love, rather than just having sex for the sake of doing it, and thereby harming yourself."

SOUL GROUP: The Golden Ones

"Sex wears off eventually, and then one has to find the deep bonding somewhere deep inside. That is not to say that you cannot find each other sexually – you can, for in that lifetime in France you were a high initiate into the *Ancient Sexual Rites*, the *Hieros Gamos*. (*Hieros gamos* or Hierogamy ("holy marriage") is a sexual ritual that plays out a marriage between a god and a goddess, especially when enacted in a symbolic ritual where human participants represent the deities. Wikipedia)

It will do well for both of you to study the *Gnostic inner knowledge*, but also *White Tantra*, if you truly wish to bond at much deeper levels. For when you truly understand that one does not need to even touch, to bond in a deep manner, with the Divine sexual energy, then you will be able to go deeper into the soul connection and experience the Divine in this way.

You have three souls who are wishing to incarnate through you, and you have soul bonds with all, although some have never incarnated here before, and seek you both as parents, knowing you will help them to bring their unique and beautiful genius to Planet Earth. They are Sun children from the 7th Galaxy of the Central Sun."

SOUL GROUP: The Inquisitive Ones

"For see here – a woman was created with all her power in her sexual energy centre as held in the womb area, where she stores her emotional memory bank, and it is here that she feels the most, and is the most vulnerable.

Therefore, when a man forcefully enters her, he violates this sacred space, and she feels misused, with deep rooted anger, fear and resentments which will fester. Know that this area has gone awry for women in the last few thousand years when in Atlantis all became distorted, so the greater healing of Humanity lies in the healing of the womb and sexuality. This is not an aggressive healing, rather that of the heart energies, for the womb and heart are connected, as they in turn are linked to the *pineal* and *pituitary* glands, and to the *serpent* or *kundalini energy*. One cannot flow without the other, they all need crystal clear channels, for the woman to feel safe enough in herself, for a man to enter her. If she distrusts him, or feels she is just being used for his own gratification, or that he is not honoring her sacred space, she will withdraw from him emotionally and physically, and will not share all of herself, being absent during the sexual act, on a soul level. She literally goes up into the astral and watches without feeling as, to her, this is merely a mechanical process.

Her **soul** presence withdraws. When he is fully present with her, he wins her respect and trust, with deep love and a loving presence, she feels her **soul** honored and acknowledged, and in turn will share the deepest, most hidden parts of herself. Then she is open sexually, her vagina is open, intercourse is painless, as she takes him into herself, more and more, until she literally wraps herself and all that she is, around him. She receives him with a deep love, the innermost parts of her soul, gifting him, as she receives **all** of him inside her. She stays present all the time for she is **soul-fully** there."

SOUL GROUP: Those who live the Tau

"You might also find this true when having sex that you feel that you are not in your body, or where you need to be. This comes from knowing about sex in your true soul state (where it is unnecessary to procreate, as said), and thus you are sometimes puzzled as to why people want this so much! So, it will take a great opening up of your own heart and soul, and that of whoever you engage with sexually, before you will truly be able to experience something deeper. It will have to be a person who is in tune, and on the same wave length, or else you will shut them out at some level.

This is mainly due to the scientist within you, who wants to record what the experience feels like physically, as you tend to view this as an experiment, rather than as a true act of love. (It is a bit strange, but in other galaxies and star systems, the sexual energy is seen as something one can use and experience, without having to get physical.) In most galaxies there are male and female forms, but they know how to combine the physical and sexual energies in such a way, as to experience a transcendental **union** that is sacred and profound. Thus they truly experience the Divine in far higher and more evolved ways than humans ever can in the 3rd dimensional forms, although they will remember when they can raise their consciousness levels to the 5th and higher, and return to the cosmic fold.

Of course, this does not mean that you will not enjoy having a mate, or mating with them, it is just to make you aware that sometimes this could feel surreal as your soul tends to experience human life through the lens of the galaxy of origin, as this is your first incarnation on Earth."

SOUL GROUP: The Spiralling Ones

"This soul is an old soul, with many lifetimes on Earth. In the beginning she came in as one working with the Goddess spiralling or serpent energy, sometimes referred to as the kundalini energy. So, we find her as a dancing priestess in the temples of Hathor in Egypt, when Egypt was still a colony of Atlantis. She was an initiate, training to be further initiated into the full use of the *Kundalini energies* and the *Goddess secrets*. As a temple dancer, she trained to do the spiralling dance, performed during certain times of the month, according to the sun and moon phases related to menstruation cycles, when you always offered your first blood to Mother Earth and the Goddess, in gratitude for its creative flow.

As you were still a young, beautiful, nubile acolyte, not yet initiated into the priesthood, thus not yet ordained, you caught the eye of the High Priest of the Temples of Amun, the dark priesthood. He set out to have you, as he wanted to perform certain sexual rites forbidden by the Temples of Hathor and Isis, as they violated the Divine Laws, and often were used in Black Magic rites.

The minute your eyes met his, it was like looking straight into the eyes of a black viper. Indeed, just that one glance, felt like you were being pierced by a dagger, bringing fear to the fore, which developed into a full skin rash. When you reported this to the Priestess, whom you served and who had initiated you, you described him and she knew he was up to no good. She warned you that even with extra protection in and around yourself, never ever to succumb to him, in any form. She said she would help you as much as she could, and reported this matter to the High Priestesses, warning you further never to get involved with the Dark Ones, especially not in their rites, for that would result in you being hooked and enslaved for life.

He then haunted the temples, especially where you were, so to counter this danger, you were withdrawn as a dancing girl, and moved to serve in a different section, to protect and shield you. One day however, you were lured outside into a hidden courtyard you never knew existed, by a message from a servant. To your utter horror he appeared there. Now he was almost 50 years older, but immensely powerful, with hypnotic eyes, which held you prisoner. Before you knew what had happened you were in his power, and somehow, he managed to move you out of the temples into his own abode, totally in a hypnotic trance state. He raped you, fed you drugs, holding you there day and night, performing dark magic with you, through his abusive sexual powers.

By now, all of the Hathor temple were searching for you, and the High Priestess found you, through her clairvoyant powers. She appeared to you, shook you awake from this bondage, and through her powers, you escaped and with the help of the temple sisters, you were taken far away into a desert to an underground temple, to heal. During this time, you had extensive skin rashes with stomach problems, indeed your whole body needed to be cleared out and completely purged. You had trouble finding yourself again, it was like he somehow had taken possession of you through your mind, as he still controlled you remotely.

As much as the priestesses tried to help you, there was a part of you still fascinated by him, and you refused to let go, so he found you again, teleported himself into your bedroom, and had sex with you again. This time though there was such a passion between you, that you lost all resistance, and returned with him. For the rest of that lifetime, you were his sex slave, abusing the kundalini energies, which your soul holds. With that you developed a disease in your sexual area, which consumed you from within, and you died in horrible pain.

In other lifetimes you often wanted to return to what you were in the beginning of the lifetime as a Hathor priestess. Then, at some stage in your life, he would appear again, and start using you in whatever way he wanted. He can have sexual intercourse with you in the astral planes, such that you might not even be aware that he is doing so. It comes from the dark powers he used in those lifetimes, so in this lifetime, it might be subconscious, but it is still there.

In two lifetimes you were happily married to the man you are married to now, who is your *twin flame*, and therefore loves you dearly, but you always seemed to leave him, the minute this other man came into your life. You shove everyone else away, become obsessed with him, and then he controls you anyway he likes, abusing the sexual energy, through the hooks, cords and ties he keeps in place. In that, you now have the same old obsessions coming to the fore, and with the fantasies, you are playing directly into his hands. You might not be aware of this consciously, but this is what is happening. The same old things repeat, as if you are in one sense wanting to fully surrender, although something is warning you, and alarm bells are ringing everywhere. **He is not your twin flame**, but rather a puppet master, and therefore is playing you again, and you are allowing it.

Your husband is your true partner, and has been with you throughout these lifetimes when you were so much under the control of this man. He senses your withdrawal, and that it is happening again, and is trying to get you to understand that this is unhealthy, but you push him away, thinking that he does not love or understand you, although in reality his love for you is true and steady, and you are the one who is obsessed with this other controlling man. *Now, he moves in the astral realms where he can literally have sex with as many women as he wants, without having to be there physically with them. This* mostly happens when you are asleep, when he has sex with your lower astral body. So indeed, he is abusing his powers again, and of course, you cannot accuse him of this, for you have no evidence that this is really happening. **And he knows this.**

This is a *puppet master* par excellence. He is not innocent at all. He knows exactly what he is doing, and has had quite a few other physical affairs with his subordinates, but always carefully hides them, as he controls his victims, so that they cannot accuse him of anything. He uses the sexual energy to feed off women, so that he can rise in power, in its many forms and expressions, as he chooses. He has done this for many lifetimes, and is doing it again. Your body manifested all those symptoms to warn you, there is nothing spiritual about this at all! What you remember deep down are the *dark rites*, which used sexual energy for black magic, and something here still sucks you in, as you did not resist, but allowed it. It is time to educate yourself in *kundalini energy*, to understand its good purpose. Not black magic, but the white and pure uses for it. Learn about *White Tantra*, the chakras, energy centres and the opening up of the *pingala* and *kundalini* channels. You will find that your soul remembers, for this is indeed what your soul does, or is created with and for.

Now, in its purest form, it can be opened without a sexual partner. It is the Divine creative force energy, and in its highest forms can be used co-creatively by those truly seeking to work together, as a creative energy source. It is also a way of bonding together with a life partner in a deeper and profound way, once you recognize the Divine Masculine within him, and he the Divine Feminine within you. *Yet this has to be with a pure partner who reflects and treasures and loves you, and whom you trust.*

As with all energy, there is a dark side to its powers, used to destroy, to put black magic spells on people and things, to control minds and others through sex. He has always followed the latter path in all his incarnations, including the present one. Your soul is now at the crossroads, where with his appearance, you can finally break free from his stranglehold. You can finally claim your own powers back, and then all the physical ailments will go away, and never return. You will have to protect yourself while you sleep, otherwise he will continue to have *astral sexual intercourse* with you and you will not remember. You need to call in *Archangel Metatron*, and ask him to put his coat of armour around you, to totally cover you from head to toe, with only holes for your eyes and glasses in front of your eyes, so that you can see out, but nobody sees into your eyes. Then ask for angels to guard you day and night, and not allow him near you.

You must also cut all ties with him, even if this mean looking for work elsewhere. Stop obsessing about him. He is playing you, as he has played you before. Cut all negative hooks, cords, ties, incantations, (like spells), from your sexual area, even if done by the help of a powerful healer. You can call in *Archangel Michael* to help cut negative cords, hooks and ties, but when incantations and spells are involved, it is much like voodoo. Someone must help you release them.

In your case, don't feel shame or blame, but rather understand that you finally have the chance to free yourself from his control, once and for all. Also take comfort in the fact that he cannot do anything to you, unless you allow it for some pay off on some or other level.

Perhaps it is the excitement, the hidden that you are subconsciously seeking, the fireworks (even if negative), that passion, which is lacking in your own relationship with your man. However, you can ignite the kundalini within yourself. Learn to ignite your own sexuality, to enjoy sex with him, and teach him to pleasure you, and you will both have fun, and grow closer. If you do not voice what you want from your relationship, then how can he know? He cannot read your mind, and is devoted to you (your husband). So there again, the partnership is what you wish to make of it and if the spark has gone, then you can always work to ignite it within yourself, and then it will ignite in him again.

For you in truth carry a wonderful gift of the *Divine Feminine* within your soul. It is a beautiful energy source, and creative force. If you learn to ignite this within yourself first (without a man), then you will be rejuvenated, and full of *joie de vivre,* which comes when a woman is in love with herself. It is a wonderful way to attract to you the right kind of love, the true love, you so seek. But remember, to seek the **wholesome**, the **purity**, which is always filled with love and light."

———

SOUL GROUP: The Spiraling Energetic Ones

"Soul name: She expresses and lives the Spiraling Energy of the Divine Feminine, is the keeper of energy and is one who works with the spiralling energy cosmically within the laws of Alchemy and transformation, the Transformative, powers, transmutation.

The galaxy of origin is Lyra with Sirius B, and the wormhole galaxies between Orion and Sirius, and the Milky Way Galaxy. The tonal chord is high D and the soul colours are beautiful dark navy blue with gold, with red, with violet and magenta, orange with gold-green and turquoise, with soft green and pinks, with lilac and orange-gold, and then beautiful platinum, gold and magenta with soft white and pinks, and golds.

It is important to know and understand that those who work with the *spiralling energy*, will always be called to the highest service work, with regards to this. So, this lifetime is more about doing this work, than any relationship, no matter how much this lures you, for indeed, if the inner work is not done, and the soul mission and purpose not fulfilled, then there is the lingering essence of not having completed your mission. Thus, for you, perhaps the question should not be so much, *"Will he return, or will I see him again?"* But rather *"Will I fulfil my soul mission and purpose, by working with and using the spiralling energy, and become a master of this, as my soul contract sets out?"*

When you were around twelve years old, you were placed in an *Initiates School* for girls and women, and he went to one for boys and men, so the training was mainly separate, but did overlap. For one first had to learn to let the Kundalini arise within oneself, and to work with it, as co-creator, before you could have sacred union to work with the self-same energy, thus multiplied. One had to be a master of the first, before moving onto the second, and all the 33 subsequent octaves of the knowledge, regarding the higher uses of the spiraling energy. It took 33 initiations in the senior ranks, to finally attain a degree of mastery.

In those years until the age of about 17, you were totally dedicated to this task, and you shone. You were one of the star pupils, with a great love of learning and an innate knowing of how to utilize the energy within you, and to use it wisely in co-creatorship.

At the age of 17 to 21, the women could choose between two different paths – to remain single, learning to use this energy in co-creative and enlightened ways, which took immense self-discipline, and often led to immaculate conception (without a man being physically involved), or with a male partner, whom the High Priests and High Priestesses would carefully select, as they needed to be the perfect match in frequency and vibration, but also a soul match. Indeed, body, mind, spirit and soul.

You sought the latter path, believing you would then be able to reunite with him, to have sacred sexual union, according to the strict laws, as set out in the attainment of soul mastery. You had met him occasionally at combined ceremonies and classes which you shared, but he kept his distance which you never understood, for it seemed as you now grew into your womanhood, he seemed more distant. You often secretly wondered, if you were not beautiful or smart enough, or intelligent enough for him, as he did notice the other women.

When the time came for you to meet your perfect match, it was not him, rather someone 7 years older, who was your true match, and a *twin flame*. He was tall with beautiful eyes, and a regal bearing, trained in the mystery schools elsewhere and had now been sent to meet you, because this is how things were done in ancient days.

You looked into his eyes, and felt a jolt of recognition, a deep soul reconnection and yes, there was love. And as much as your sacred union, and the marriage brought ecstasy, bliss and a deep bonding, you never could quite give your all, for the other man, seemed to come into your mind's eye, when experiencing the deepest and most sacred sex with him. You felt guilty, for he often asked you why you withdrew at soul level, not being fully present. Those rites needed to work with the Kundalini energy in co-creatorship, not in creating children as such, but in other work.

For a while you needed to be separated, to complete your training, while he needed to return to his original school, for higher learning for six months. During this period, you met again the one you were infatuated with, and as you were married off, as was he, he was suddenly interested in you again. At first you kept your distance, out of a deep respect for your husband, but then succumbed and broke the most pertinent and important of all the rules in the school, by having sexual intercourse with him secretly. In the middle of this, your husband appeared in etheric form (as you all had been trained to do, for one could have sexual intercourse with your spouse even though he was not physically present), and you felt immense shame and guilt, and stopped things right there. But he would not budge, and grew angry, forcing you to have sex with him. It proved too painful, and far from what you had anticipated, for he was rough.

To your utter horror, you later discovered you were pregnant. Within the school, there were certain laws and taboos, pertaining to higher service which you promised to adhere to, which you had now broken. This basically meant that your training would be put on hold, and you would have to repeat certain initiations, as you had failed the higher degrees. Your husband returned, and to his credit, did not condemn you for having had sex, which led to more guilt and shame, as you felt you had betrayed his trust in you."

***

SOUL GROUP: The Loving Ones

"This was at the time of the Lion Kingdom, and the complex was filled with rose gardens, and the sweetest smelling flowers, trees and shrubs, and crystal fountains. It was one of the most beautiful places on Earth.

You worked in the temples of the loving heart and womb, which are connected. When the heart closes so do the sexual areas. When it is fully open, they also open up. This allows a union of great tenderness, if her partner also has an open heart. In men it opens up the prostate and coccyx area, so his penis becomes an instrument of the loving heart, to enter and fill her with more love, thus gifting her with the deepest aspect of his heart and soul. They are both filled with each other, their love for each other grows and expands to bless all they encounter.

Here you would work with the heart opening, sensing and feeling to detect blockages in the heart energy field, and the *Heart-rose*. The heart-rose has 33 petals, you would scan it through your third eye area, to locate pain, hurt, anger, fear, resentment, any emotional baggage, unforgiveness etc. You opened them up, to cleanse and clear each in turn. Emotional pain, and unforgiveness closes the heart. You exposed the wound, the root problem, helping them to dissolve the emotional charges. They would see the truth, as the Divine sees it, understanding just how the soul in question, or the situation, actually *served* them, and exactly how this contributed towards their own soul growth and good. When this happened, the person shed tears of gratitude and was able to thank the other, as their heart and soul overflowed. In this way they would heal.

Sometimes when they just could not open their heart, you worked with the *Rose of the Yoni*, the sexual energy centres, and soul memory banks. Usually they were closed from pain, or trauma associated with the act of physical union, so again you had to open the wound, to facilitate the dissolving of the memory bank leaving only love and gratitude. This area now opened up its 33 rose petals fully, and the happy person assumed vibrant, radiant health and vitality, and was rejuvenated, being capable of love in much higher and more profound ways than ever before.

You loved this work. Indeed, to you it was not work at all. You loved helping people, and you loved seeing how lives changed completely because of the healing that occurred. That was a reward in itself."

SOUL GROUP: The Illumined Ones

"Soul name: The Illumined One who anchors in the Christed Consciousness and thus is a conduit for the three-fold flame of love, power and Wisdom and is a teacher, a guide, and thus a way shower soul.

The soul in question, needs to trust in his own intuitive inner knowing and guidance, and not seek so much counsel outside of himself, the more he does this, the more confused he will get. For all the greatest knowing is within the soul, and no matter how much information is given, it is his own free will and choice in living his life on Planet Earth, as the soul contract will outline the path the soul has chosen to walk during an incarnation here, yet he will determine the outcome.

Often souls tend to veer off the path, and then struggle to return again and again, or they allow others to lead them astray. Thus, it is imperative that the outside voices and noise are stemmed, and not allow to intervene with the inner soul knowing, and Higher Guidance given. Otherwise, the soul will tend to be shown six-hundred paths, by other incarnated souls, when in fact there is *only one single path*, the soul chose before incarnating. Remember this!

In truth, if you choose to be with a given soul, and choose to walk a path with her, then that is your own free will and choice. If you recognize her, as you did, and then intuitively pick up information, then that is good. The question should not be who you were in a past life with her, but rather what is your **intent** with the relationship? If you are only willing to enter a relationship with her, for an interim period, while your marriage is being dissolved, and already knowing there will not be a future with her, then why you do you date her?

Is it fair to the soul in question? Is this fair to yourself? For being energetically involved with a soul, is already creating karma, and energetic bonds, and thus one is not free. *One is already binding a soul to one, even if just for two years, and in this process, negative cords, hooks and ties are created, especially if sex takes place.*

Men tend to forget this. A woman's sexual centres are connected directly to her feeling centre, and is a sacred temple (as much as a man's). Anyone who enters there, is thus entering the most sacred sanctuary. If this is not done in pure love and pure intent, then this will lead to karmic repercussions, hooks, cords, ties binding souls together, until these have been severed and removed, and thus rescinded.

It is better to walk the path alone, if need be, and to first heal from the previous relationship completely, do the inner work, work on the path of mastery of the soul, than to engage in a relationship, which you know in your heart-of-hearts is but fleeting, passing, and of no substance.

Rather ask yourself: why are you engaging? Is it not better then, to make crystal clear to yourself and the other soul, that you do not seek physical intercourse, but rather just friendship? This would be far better than engaging sexually, for what most human beings do not understand, is that the sexual energy bonds, for the man in discharging his semen is imprinting his own DNA into and onto her. He is imprinting his physical family history and all it entails, onto her, like putting a stamp onto her, or imprinting a tattoo! If one is not consciously getting to the point, where one totally takes responsibility for one's actions, and intent, one cannot grow in mastery! If an act is not so steeped in love and responsibility, and in the utmost knowing that one wishes to walk a certain path with this soul, and wishes to walk it responsibly and with full commitment, to grow love and respect in the deepest and profoundest sense, then it is best not to engage!

This relationship has a negative karmic pattern, yes, and in a lifetime in Avalon, when she was a Druidic Priestess and you were a Priest. In this order, no partners were allowed, for they were viewed as a distraction from mission and purpose, pulling energies in all directions. One needed to be fully engaged in the work, and totally so. One would assume the highest state of marriage within oneself of masculine and feminine, and thus one did not miss what one did not have. In those days, in the 7th dimensional state, one only engaged in physical sex, even in partnership when one wished to create offspring (and this was the common man, not the Druidic priesthood.)

You however were infatuated with her, from the moment you first set eyes on her, and it was lust not love. For you saw something attractive in her, that you lacked, namely her purity and innocence. She just loved sharing her experiences with you, because she felt your empathy, and understood, and saw you as a good friend and companion. For she had vowed to stay pure, and loved her work so much.

Then you seduced her, and she fell pregnant and you refused to acknowledge the child. You were afraid to lose your status, and being expelled from your current training so requested to be posted elsewhere – this was before she finally had the guts to tell the High Priestess Druid what had happened to her. You told her directly that you would not take responsibility for the child.

This hurt her deeply. You had taken her innocence, and now were forcing her to lose her position, as a consequence of engaging in sex with you. She felt such remorse, even though met with kindness and compassion by the High Druidic Priesthood, that she committed suicide. It was too much for her, your betrayal and abuse of her innocence, and leaving her to face the music.

So, there needs to be a deep forgiveness here – within her and within you. You never felt love for her, only infatuation – you knew exactly what you were doing, and still did not honour her soul, nor her loving service to a much broader and wider circle of souls. Indeed, you did not honour anything about her. You just selfishly took.

The lesson here for your soul, is your **intent!** Again, are you just infatuated with her, and just taking from her, because you wish to gratify yourself and your ego? Get honest with yourself! There is this attraction to you from deep within herself, but again, it is karmic, as you owe her a great karmic debt, and must ask for forgiveness. More than this, you need to forgive yourself too, and to master the lesson in this lifetime, to not selfishly take, because you want self-gratification, even if disguised in some other form.

It is not so much what she needs to forgive, as well as the shame and blame, she had to go through, and felt for herself. It is the shame and blame your projected onto her, as you told her straight, that she had succumbed to your advances, and that you had merely been testing her, like in an initiation, which was an untruth!

In this case, it would be better to do the inner healing and forgiving, and then set this soul free to walk her path with love and through love, so that she can find a man who will truly love her for who and what she is, and walk the path of pure intent, truth, respect and trust with her.

Rather choose to walk your path alone until you love yourself so much, inside and out, that you will master yourself in this regard, and love yourself into wholeness. For if a man is not whole within himself, and does not master himself totally, especially as regards sex, he cannot step fully into soul mastery. For in truth, the sexual energy is not even attached to the physical form. It is an energy force on its own, and only those who truly seek to understand this in the deepest spiritual sense, will be given the insight and understanding, the loving essence, of how to utilize this energy correctly, and thus to use it for the highest good, even for self-gratification, or in whatever other form.

Thus, this has been a lesson in soul mastery, so rather give this beautiful soul, the freedom to be. She deserves to be treated with respect, and not to have false expectations with regards to yourself, so she is able to truly be with a man who will want to be with her, and respect her and love her just the way she is.

As far as your Twin Flame is concerned – she has not incarnated. She has already passed her lessons in mastery, and ascended and thus did not need to return here, and indeed had no desire to do so. She is always with you, and you meet with her in the inner planes when you are asleep. Souls can never be separated, and indeed all is One.

This is not to say that you cannot have a loving relationship, but know that with the immense shift into the 5th and higher dimensional state, relationships are shifting too. Gone are the days, where one just had sex for the sake of it, or casually engaged in a relationship. As one's own vibrational frequency rises, one needs to have a perfect match in frequency, otherwise someone who is of a lower frequency, brings distortion in one's own energy fields.

This time is all about self-mastery! It is about finding the deepest truths, and walking the path as a master. Do not allow yourself to be distracted just because you feel it necessary to have a companion in your life, even if your intent is now pure.

Rather work on the inner marriage, the inner you, and then become a master. Master yourself. Find an ever-deepening love inside yourself, for yourself and more than this the **Divine**. Become so **at one** with the **Divine**, that you are totally fulfilled, just like the Ancient Druids knew. (Marriages were only allowed much later when Humanity fell into the seas of forgetfulness, and could not master their own appetites anymore).

Long before the Druids, the High Priest and High Priesshood already knew this.

There was sacred marriage, but then only in very high vibrational frequency matches, with equal partners needing to merge into **One**, to co-create together in a sacred manner for the higher good of all. It was done abiding by the strict laws pertaining to this, only merging for the highest good of a cause greater than the sum of themselves.

Moreover, one knew that art of sacred energetic union, which is the highest of all forms of union, and then only in purity, with pure intent, with sacred agreements between the two souls, and only in that form. Not physically. The master controls himself physically, emotionally, mentally, spiritually and at all levels. When standing in one's highest mastery, there is nothing lacking. One is all and everything! Nothing is missing!

One embraces the Omni-Verse within oneself, and thus one is Omni-Verse!

It is only when the highest states are reached, and one energetically transforms one's physical embodiment (resurrection into the highest dimensional forms) that one can totally merge at soul level, in wholeness (each one whole and complete with only the middle part overlapping – thus in the space of infinity).

You still have a long way to reach this state, and it will only be attained if you are willing to walk the path alone, until such time that you are ready to merge with your twin flame (who then will appear to you in the highest vibrational essence) when you have ascended into highest frequency bands and dimensional forms, while on Planet Earth.

Your soul chose this path of mastery.

You have free will and choice.

You can choose to follow the lowest paths, or you can choose to follow the highest.

The choice is yours.

All paths first start with self-love. With loving oneself totally, wholly, and completely. Inside and out and the Divine. Only then can one love another soul to the same extent. Such is Divine Law. Love and all loving relationships first start at home – within you!"

———

Sexual Energy, Purity and Sacred Sexuality
(Part 2)

Extracts from Soul Readings

SOUL GROUP: The Intricate Ones

"Soul name: The Exquisite Intricate One who brings in the insight and understanding of how Universal Life and Life forms are interwoven, and all exist in one single universal Divine Energy field, and thus she works with energies and energy fields and the programming and interaction, expansion of them cosmically.

The man you are currently involved with is a star seed soul like you, and you are soul mates as you belong to a complimentary cluster Soul Group. You know each other from the soul work done on galactic levels, where you worked and played together. In other galaxies there is no partnership or marriage like people have here. A couple simply decides to walk the path together for as long as wished, some mate for life, others not. It is a pure soul choice. There is no attachment, for the minute you fasten to another, issues around ownership emerge, with the pull to and fro, with the energetic soul strings being attached. Remaining autonomous gives each other the freedom to be, though there are still some flexible agreements in place, so they are each able to evolve into something different over time, depending on the free will and choices of the two souls involved.

In truth one can never fall *out* of love, for love is eternally present. One merely would love to love someone for shared experiences as souls agree upon, often moving on to other experiences, so a soul can, through free will and choice then choose to be with another soul, or not. That is entirely up to them. This does mean that some choose to remain together because of their own free will and choice, and because they wish to serve in this way.

If you start understanding this, then you will know that there are no hard and fast rules. If you now choose to walk your path with this soul, then there is nothing stopping you. You may well find that, at the given moment when destined to meet your twin flame, you will. And what happens thereafter, again is both of your choice, for the *twin flame relationship* is the most difficult and challenging of all.

Now, we are not allowed to read his soul records without his permission. We can only give details pertaining to your own soul and how it interlinks with him.

You have had quite a few interludes galactically with him, both were working and living on the same Mothership, deciding to be with another for a while. You were wont to work in different fields and came from different home galaxies, so this often meant you went off to work elsewhere in the Cosmos and met again at some point. You never really walked the path together, merely a relaxed kind of relationship where you loved deeply yes, without any implications of ownership involved.

When entering higher soul mastery, there is an understanding that all attachments form energetic strings, and the consequent push/pull, chase/flee eventually causes more pain than it is worth. It is possible to love someone deeply, walk the path together, but not attach in any way. It involved simply giving each other freedom to be themselves, and thus gain this freedom yourself, knowing sexual energy is not attached to any physical form.

On Galactic levels you merge *energetically* more so than physically, only using physical intercourse to beget offspring, which can also be achieved through a completely non-sexual act – with just a merging of seed which is placed in an incubator, where the baby is formed. In ancient times in Lemuria the same methods were used, but Humanity sunk into the 3D, and then it became necessary to have sex in order to procreate. Understand this and you will free yourself from any false expectations.

Now, the times when you were together, you truly loved being together, and it was a lovely free-flowing expansive love. Free from any false expectations and not projecting things onto the other, it was easier to simply enhance each other beautifully, and dance in tune and in step. You managed this beautifully and when you needed to part, there was the deep knowing that you could still energetically connect and merge in union, even though galaxies apart. One can either do this through teleportation, or simply energetically.

Read up about tantra and you will start to understand that indeed, one does not even need to physically touch someone to merge sexually. This can be done purely and energetically. But people have forgotten this. Yes, you are compatible. And yes, you can walk together, if that is what you both truly wish to do. The outcome is not set in stone, as nothing truly is. It is free will and soul choices made which creates the outcome. All are but soul lessons in mastery.

With all relationships one needs to take leaps of faith. The question then is if you want to take that leap of faith or not. That is entirely up to you.

At galactic core you have sometimes worked together on projects, and you loved this for you gently enhance each other (In your highest soul bodies, as in this one it may be different for the human ego does tend to get in the way).

Again, it is entirely up to both of you.

Why not just allow things to develop at their own pace? Simply allow. Without pushing, or expecting, but simply allowing it to unfold naturally. Remember that all lasting relationships require trust and respect. Thus, one can only grow over time, and it does not just come. Loyalty cannot be demanded nor bought. Trust and respect are the same. It takes time to truly get to know someone and it takes time to explore the different soul expressions and life with someone.

Love merely changes expression.

It is eternally present.

So beautiful and precious soul, why not make the most of this time, as it is presented to you. Go and follow your heart. Your own inner knowing will be truthful. Listen to it and then follow your own inner guidance, and know it is good!

Keep the heart open no matter what.

And know that in every relationship there will be both support, and challenge. It is through the challenges that one grows ever closer together, as much as the support. Just love."

————

SOUL GROUP: Those who Balance and Harmonize

"Soul name: She brings to the fore the greater wholeness and balance between the physical and non-physical, the yin and yang, and is one who is a balancing force, yet within herself as much as outside herself and thus brings all into harmony through the balancing within and without.

Let this soul know that the true sacred marriage and partnership first needs to be found within oneself, before this can be extended outward into a whole and complete relationship, and sacred union with another.

Note that you are an **energetic** being, for in truth the physical body is **energetic**, and therefore when one is energetically involved with someone who is not in the highest alignment with themselves, and not whole and complete within himself, the resulting imbalance will cause pain.

People tend to forget this. They have this deep longing for wholeness from a loving relationship, but often find separation and pain. It is here that the greatest shift in consciousness must happen, in the midst of the immeasurably powerful dimensional shifts. For indeed, the new 5th to 7th dimensional partnerships strives first for androgyny *within* with its wholeness, before trying to attract a partner who will reflect this. One has transcended the old and worn ideals of the 3D, as far as partnership and union are concerned. One is now seeking a more advanced relationship, but this union, this sacredness, this wholeness first needs to come from deep within oneself!

There is so much hype about needing physical sex, and thus with kundalini awaking, there is a greater understand that this is not absolutely necessary, you can raise the kundalini alone, and find that sacredness of union with oneself. This is the most enlightened path now, for then you will radiate forth the right frequency to attract the man we indicated to you in the last reading.

There is no need to go and advertise yourself, and display your wares on the Internet. Dating sites fail, because ideally it is better to meet a soul in person, to truly know if you are a vibrational match while many just seek a sexual thrill, which is in truth damaging. Women should understand that every time they have sexual intercourse, her partner leaves his DNA imprint implanted into her. Thus, she carries parts of him within her for the rest of her life, unless this is consciously cleared. Remember this!

It is better to walk the path alone for a while, and allow the Divine to work within you, and then, at exactly the right moment the soul destined to meet with you, will be there, finding you, without you needing to do anything. For souls who are destined to meet, will meet, and always in perfect *Divine Timing*!

See this time of incubation, as a time when huge shifts in consciousness press the reset buttons for the whole of Humanity. With it comes a whole new and higher way of life and living. The old ways of loving relationships won't work anymore. What is now being orchestrated, and being born and is taking shape is a much higher vibrational frequency matching, where one first bonds at **soul** level and energetically, before one mates physically. It makes for wholeness, not neediness, for the days of self-gratification and self-service within relationships are done with.

Instead of yearning for the old form of the relationship story, why not use this time wisely to truly go deep within yourself, and to marry your masculine and feminine, so your right and left side, inner yin and yang are perfectly balanced.

Use this time to work through all the emotional baggage within you, from all past encounters and relationships, allowing the Timelines to close, for new Timelines are opening. You do not wish to carry the old ones, the old programming, the old you into a new relationship. You need to be reborn, reinvented and then your whole concept of what you wish for in a relationship will shift. You will find that what attracted you to a man before, is no longer valid. You now seek a much deeper, more profound **soul** connection, which is so much more than just the physical. Look deep inside of yourself, and you will know this is true.

Why short-sell yourself, when you can have the very best?

Your soul is a very special and unique soul, and you have this immense powerful work you are called to do with the bears, and with being up there in the north. Now, look how that is serving Humanity, the Divine and yourself.

There is so much inner exploring you can do at this time, when you have the freedom to simply be yourself. Connect deeply with your own soul, and then tap into the soul knowledge, and truly look at how you can navigate the dimensional shifts by doing the inner preparation work.

Instead of resenting this alone time, see the hidden blessing contained within it. See how this is serving you. For in truth one can be alone, and never be lonely! For indeed one is always surrounded by so many invisible helpers and forces and immensely powerful Beings, who are there with you day and night, 24 hours, and through every living and breathing moment. Look at the immensely powerful gifts Mother Nature is gifting you with. Look at the blessings the people around you bring. The more your inner eyes open, the more you start seeing beyond the obvious, and find that indeed love is everywhere!

For the Beloved, in truth is within you!

Not outside of you – within!

It is when you finally realize that you are the Beloved and the Beloved is you, you will cease to desperately long or seek for the Beloved's face everywhere. You will find that indeed, there is no lack of love. For love can be dispersed in the One, or the Many! Yet love, is never absent. See and feel the love of many, and you will feel and see the love of the Beloved One. For they are one and the same!

The Beloved is not **outside** of you, but deep **within** you!

When you finally find the Beloved within, you will be ready to attract the Beloved outside of you, and he may well come in a form you never expected him to manifest himself in!

When you start loving and seeing with the eyes of the **soul**, you will finally experience and see a different world and in being that new world you have just discovered, you will find him where you never looked for him before, indeed, there he is, waiting for you, ready to embrace you, whole and complete, as you embrace him – whole and complete. Such is the New Union. The new Marriage in the new World, which is already here, in the now. For in truth this is a time of great dismantling of the old way of life, the 3D. You are shifting even as you are reading this, beautiful soul. You are not the same person you were before the lock-down. You have changed. The world has changed

You are such a beautiful being. You have such amazing soul gifts and talents which you need share with the world. There is the immensely powerful bond you have with the bears – nurture it and bring it forth.

You have a deep connection with Mother Earth – she is calling you. Are you listening?

You have a deep soul connection to that land, which comes from the time you were there before there was a North Pole. It was the time when that land was still tropical, and when there were forests and rivers and lakes and when there were elephants and mammals roaming there, mountains, trees, and beautiful lush vegetation.

It was here that you roamed as a caretaker soul of Mother Earth, and all upon her. You walked in harmony with all creatures, and with all within Mother Earth and upon her. You loved being able to serve from the heart and soul, and you did so with all your Being.

In that lifetime he, your Twin Flame, the man you are still to meet, and you were very much in harmony working together, and you tended the creatures great and small. You both came from the Bear Constellation and you brought the Bears with you and helped them to settle here on Planet Earth. You were their guardians; their keepers and they were like your own family. In that lifetime you fell in love with Mother Earth and asked if you could settle here with the first volunteers, and this was in the time of Elysium. Such unity, such oneness, is what your soul remembers and what you so often look for.

Yet, this is possible in this lifetime, indeed, it is coming, but first realize that you need to find the harmony and oneness and wholeness within yourself!

———

SOUL GROUP: Those who balance and harmonize

"Soul name: She brings to the fore the greater wholeness and balance between the physical and non-physical, the yin and yang and is a balancing force, yet within as much as outside herself and thus brings all into harmony through the balancing within and without.

You bring to the fore greater **wholeness** and **balance** between the physical and non-physical, the yin and yang, and are a balancing force. You bring harmony through the balancing **within** yourself – then it manifests outward.

There lies the key: you are being prepared for his coming. Yet you first need to bring that balance within you to the fore, and the innate harmony within, before this will manifest outside, in the outer physical reality, by meeting him at the destined time, as divinely orchestrated!

Isn't that amazing! You do not need do anything to attract the Twin. You just need to do the inner work and be simply your own beautiful soul self, and allow the Divine to bring him to you, in the perfect timing, and perfect moment!"

SOUL GROUP: The Harbinger Souls

"In the ensuing years, as the Black Magi took control over Atlantis, the temples were under attack as they wanted to destroy the priesthood and all which pertained to the Law of One. They planned to infiltrate it, and when thwarted, they launched atomic lasers on the temples. In the case of your island, invisible and invincible shields were put up to deflect them, and the security systems were revamped. Additionally, the initiations were stricter, to ensure only those pure enough to withstand such attacks, and not succumb to the lies of the Black Magi offered, were chosen.

Even with stricter security measures in place, a certain faction of the priesthood was infiltrated and brain washed, and when detected, it was too late. Whereas before the island was devoid of conflict, or any attempts to undermine the authorities, now suddenly there was unrest and dissent amongst the junior ranks. You spoke at a gathering of young initiates, reminding them of the purity of the law of One, when something strange happened. A youth, suddenly transformed himself, and there was the young man you had been so hopelessly in love with years before. He was a Black Magi who used his powers and the knowledge of the island and priesthood to gain access. You were struck dumb and were paralyzed, literally, unable to speak, nor move, nor think.

He held a crystal wand which he directed at your third eye. You felt a stabbing pain and, in that moment, had no control over yourself or your faculties. Fear set in, for the man now addressed the crowd – which was unheard of. As if in a trance state you saw the alarm being raised, as the invisible shields were positioned, enclosing both of you and the students in a bubble, as your knees gave way and you fainted. When you came to you were in a completely different place in a room on the main island of

Atlantis. Your ex-boyfriend, had teleported you and all the other students to the main island, and now held you prisoner.

You feared him now, like you never had before, as he used you sexually, which came as a shocking loss of your innocence, and he also implanted a control box, and had you totally under his control. You did what he wanted you to, as you had no choice.

In that lifetime he eventually turned against you so much, that every time you dared defy him, he abused you sexually, locking you up without food or water for days, as punishment. You lost your will to live and died during one such imprisonment. Indeed, fear led you to forget your own powers, you had all the training to counteract him, but never used it.

Interestingly in two other lifetimes, you tended to incarnate within certain religious groupings, where the women were severely suppressed. In two lifetimes this led to you being abused sexually, and you were often used in certain sexual rites which were not kosher. (There is the darker side to this too.) These were fanatical secret society groups, in the Middle East, one in Jerusalem and the other in Lebanon. They went under the mantle of Christianity. The outside world never knew of the inner and hidden rites, and once you were ensnared into such a community, you could never get out.

In one such lifetime you were born with immense psychic gifts, and then were used for prophesying. But when you dared tell the truth, you were severely punished for doing so, mostly sexual abuse. That forced you to often ignore your psychic truth and tell the leader of a group, a ruthless man, what you thought he wanted to hear. This brought great inner conflict, and then self-hatred, as you felt ashamed of abusing your own gifts in this way, and then deliberately shut down your third eye, as you felt you would be safeguarding yourself from being attacked by this man and others. Most women there were kept as sex slaves, and thus had no rights and you often would gather them around you, to try and give them hope and show them love. To your credit you gave much of yourself there, to try and help them, but never could help yourself. You died of venereal diseases in that lifetime, with cancer in your sexual parts which spread into your anus. Thus, the discomfort in that area in this lifetime."

———

SOUL GROUP: The Loving Ones

"Soul name: The Loving One who opens the hearts and souls of all she encounters, and who is a love-bringer, love-healer, love-igniter, love-spreader, loving blessing to all whom she encounters, and is there to ignite the Flame of Love everywhere!

The tonal chord is E and the soul colours are beautiful pink with silvery blue, soft violet and lavender, with beautiful hues of blue, green, magenta and pinkish red with pink-orange and then shades of beautiful gold silver and platinum with pink.

This soul is one who had had lifetimes here before, and works with the Codes of Love. These are held in the Divine Feminine, the Mother God and she works with the heart-opening, and loving essence of all Creation. This is pure, unconditional love, the all-encompassing love which surpasses all understanding. It is the love without judgement, without fear, without criticism, without labels, without boundaries. It is the infinite love of the Divine Feminine – something she has for **All** that she ever created from deep within her own womb and gave birth to. It is true love.

With you, it is essential to work from the depths of your heart and soul, to love what you do, and to do what you love, and to bring this loving essence, like the fragrance of the beautiful Rose, and the all-radiant sun, to all whom you encounter. It is to open the heart fully, and to let the deepest prayer of your heart be: *"That Divine Love expresses itself through me, joyously, beautifully, exaltedly, delightfully, tenderly, compassionately, miraculously and powerfully – so that my whole life becomes a beautiful song of Love, the songs of songs."*

It is when you close your heart-centre, when you fear being hurt, when you close yourself off, that you will suffer pain. For you, it is essential to keep that heart open, no matter what, truly asking that your heart and soul are opened up to ever greater and more profound ways of loving and being loved, and to lovingly serve in all circumstances, and every way that you can.

We find you in your first lifetime on Earth, in the Temples of Love, in what is now Brazil and what has sunk just offshore of it. There once stood huge Temples of Love, created from pink rose quartz, shining with this pinkish light which could be seen from afar. It was a beautiful and magnificent palace, and in the middle, there stood three rose quartz Crystal

Pyramids, which held the Divine Feminine energy on Earth. This was at the time of the Lion Kingdom, and it was a complex filled with rose gardens, and the sweetest smelling flowers, trees and shrubs, and crystal fountains. It was one of the most beautiful places on Earth.

You worked in the *Temples of the Loving Heart and Womb*. For the Heart and womb are connected. When the heart is closed, the womb and sexual areas are closed. When it is fully open, they open up. That is when one has union with great tenderness, if the partner has that open heart too, for with men it opens up the prostate and the coccyx area and thus then the penis becomes an instrument for the loving heart to enter the woman, and fill her with more love. He gifts the deepest of his heart and soul by giving of himself to her. They are both filled with each other, and their love for each other grows and expands to bless all they encounter.

You worked with the heart opening – in that you would sense or feel or detect the blockages in the heart energy field and the Heart-rose which has 33 petals you scanned via your third eye area, detecting any pain, hurt, anger, fear, resentment, or any emotional baggage, unforgiveness etc. You worked with the opening up, the cleansing and clearing of each in turn, for these issues close the heart. You opened the wound – the root problem, and helped the person to dissolve the emotional charges so that the heart centre opened up. Instead, they would start seeing the truth, as the Divine sees the truth, and they would see how the soul in question, or the situation actually **served** them, and how this contributed towards their own soul growth and good. When this happened – the person would have tears of gratitude and be able to thank the other, as their heart and soul would overflow with gratitude. In this way they would heal.

Sometimes when they could not open the heart, you would work with the *Rose of the Yoni* and sexual energy centres, working with the soul memory banks there. These are usually closed from pain, or trauma associated with physical union so you expose the wound to allow the memory bank to be dissolved, until there is only love and gratitude. This area would then open up its 33 heart rose petals, and when open fully the person would assume vibrant, radiant health and vitality, rejuvenated, and able to love in much higher and more profound ways than ever before."

———

SOUL GROUP: The Illumined Ones

"The *Illumined Ones*, were as guilty of this as were the twins from the other soul groups, but for the Illumined Ones, this proved to be the most painful episode in their collective history.

It is vital to understand this, for as the male began withholding his seed, and separated his mind from his heart, the female began closing her womb energies, and withdrew from him. Consequently, the whole tragedy started to play itself out, so that many of these twin flames have had to find a way to reunite again, to restore the beautiful balance of their first time on this planet. For elsewhere in the Cosmos, they knew how to use this immense Divine Gifting in the correct way, and that is how they sustained their karmic links and ties here. They now wish to heal this breach, and these immense karmic wounds and debts, more so perhaps than any other soul group, for they, knew what a supreme gifting the sexual energy was from the Divine, as well as the sacred Divine union and fire."

––––––––

SOUL GROUP: The Loving Ones

"However, in subsequent lifetimes, the two of them engaged in liaisons with other sexual partners, as by then their integrity and yearning to keep themselves as pure channels of the **Divine** had abated somewhat, so they introduced others into the union. This is where problems started – when this sacred act became one of lust. What should have been a beautiful and profound symphony of union, and experience of the eternal burning of the sacred flame, was depleted through this misuse of sexual energies. This occurred especially during the lifetime in Babylon, when this entity worked as a *prostitute Priestess in the Temples of Ishtar,* which was later repeated in the land of Turkey, and also later in that lifetime when she wanted to become a yogi. She landed up in a harem solely to pleasure the Maharaja, who bought her services as his concubine, enticed by her sexual knowledge. In that lifetime the sexual energies were too strong so she left her training to focus solely on the pleasures of the flesh.

In this lifetime, she has made the decision to rather not get involved on that level again – if the love is impure, and there is no intent to share a sacred union, which in itself will be a blessing, if she decides to follow her own inner promptings for Higher Service, and starts seriously training to become a yogi once again. In this she is helped profoundly by *Ascended Master Hilarion, Quan Yin, Lakshmi,* and by *Kali,* who, in spite of the darker side, is actually the harbinger of *Rebirthing* on all levels, bringing in a choice between the lighter and darker side of life itself, and the use of the sexual energies in an uplifting and profound manner.

Her *twin flame* has reincarnated, but is not on the African continent at this moment in time, after been born here as he decided to go to America. However, this has been his journey in reconciling himself with the higher forces of love and loving service, and in the last few years there has been a profound inner shift of striving for spiritual knowledge to empower his own soul. He will have to endure more training, before his soul is willing to reconnect with the soul of the *African continent,* so that once again, so he can bring his own knowledge back to teach others. Once they meet, the old potent sexual energies will return, at first sight, and this time round they need to understand the sacredness of their union and flame, and not allow any third or other parties into it, or else the same mistakes will haunt them.

A learning process will still be necessary to use her instinctive knowledge with crystals, incense, music and perfumes, to open up the heart center, and to teach people how to connect with the loving energies, in loving service to others. Here one could open up a practice, or Center, where this is practised, combining **White** Tantra teachings, and other methods of opening the heart to sacred union. A partner is not needed, as there is plenty of work to do on your own, in order to understand the immensely powerful beauty of the sexual energies, learning to use them again in the correct manner, to bring the powerful life force back to the planet, in higher loving service.

While meditating, it is beneficial to honestly ask for guidance on how to reconnect with the heart, and to use your own latent memory banks, for you have all the training from that lifetime in Egypt. The temples where this was practiced have been destroyed by the priesthood of Anum, but they still exist in the ethereal. You may invoke *Serapis Bey, the Ascended Master* whose ascension seat is in Giza, to assist you with remembering these ancient rites, and then to write down whatever comes. For the people of this time now need to remember the correct and loving use of the sexual energies, as all life is sacred – it is but a worship of the **Love** of the **Divine** and an expression thereof."

SOUL GROUP: The Harbingers

"In a much later lifetime you were part of a family, which had a long tradition of being active in the *Mystery Schools of Alchemy* in that area, so you trained as an acolyte from the age of five. Indeed, you attended school here with *Mary Magdalene,* and many other girls from these families. There, you immediately found yourself drawn to sound energy work, singing, chanting and playing instruments and gongs. Mary Magdalene later left for Egypt for higher training, but you stayed on. Your name in that lifetime was *Mary Salome* (the Mary being a title of High Initiate and High Priestess). You married at sixteen, and the man chosen for you was likewise a high Initiate, who also went to Egypt, for the Mystery schools were all linked. You were later shipped off to Egypt to join them, where you married.

You were moreover highly trained in *sacred Sexual Union*, he was your *twin flame* and you achieved a sexual alchemy, which entailed you both going through death, just to be resurrected through the very strict, disciplined rites, always for highest service.

Interestingly, once again in that lifetime, you proved to be the stronger one, less inclined to be misled. Unfortunately, your twin has always been disposed to be a hot-headed rebel, fascinated by a certain branch of the *Mystery School in Haran*, which worked with certain elements, creating different effects and reactions, but which were not practiced in the highest alignment. You warned him, but he refused to listen and slipped away in the night, leaving you behind. You were unable to abandon your work, and also had two children from him.

So, you decided to return to France and indeed did so with Mary Magdalene, who by now was fending for herself as well, as Jesus had endured his death and resurrection phase, and was now making his way to France, via a different channel. You were accompanied by a High Priestess and landed in France, went to your birthplace, and entered higher training on sound energy work. News arrived that your twin had distanced himself from the Mystery School, and so divorced himself from you. You were obviously heart broken, but continued the work which had become dangerous, with men turning against women so violently that you were murdered along with Mary Magdalene, after they burnt the entire Mystery School to the ground."

———

SOUL GROUP: The Infinite Star Beings of Light

"Soul name: She bursts forth with Light and Radiance and brings that star of hope, glory, and inspiration to the fore, within and without, and in all whom she encounters.

The Tonal chords is High G and the soul colours are bright blue with yellow and then silver and magenta, with violet, and blue, and sea green, deeper emerald green, indigo, and then navy blue, with pure platinum, soft pink red, and soft light orange.

This soul is an *Indigo Child,* born like a burst of starlight, working with her soul group as star children, star people, who actually appear like a burst of light in their soul forms, although they have light body forms, they often arrive on the scene and just like stars twinkle, shine, sparkle. They add that light, radiance and cosmic beauty to everything and everyone, igniting hope and glory, and inspiring others to shine their light so much brighter.

This part of your soul has not incarnated before, although two other parts did. You incarnated mainly to just experience life here, as you could not possibly understand how the other two parts could have got lost. So, this is like an experiment for you, wanting to demonstrate you would stay focused, and could not be shut down, but there you are, experiencing just the opposite of your intentions! Free yourself, to go forth and shine!

Your *twin flame* has not incarnated, he did not want or need to, as he had found his last incarnation here too dense and violent, and decided it was not for him.

However, you do have **Soul mates**, although very few of you are here on this planet. Do not despair. This does not mean that you have to walk your path alone, no you will naturally draw those souls to you who will love you, indeed adore you, appreciating all the sparkle and fireworks. You are very fiery at times, being in essence of the fire element, so sometimes you "fire up" all right! You can't help it. Just remember that fire can singe and burn, so when feeling fiery, do not use words like fire, and then certainly never fire them at someone deliberately, with the intent to hurt and harm them! Sparks that you shoot out are meant to enhance life.

When in an intimate relationship, you have a tendency to shrink from conflict, but when you do, your fire singes your partner, as there seldom is a middle ground, it is either/or. This confuses those who live with you, for they never quite know which one they will encounter. Sometimes it is good to count to ten before using magic wands, and releasing those fiery arrows. Also remember that being able to laugh at oneself is the greatest thing one can do, and not to take oneself so seriously.

Yes, sparks fly, but as you are a spark of light, fireworks can sometimes be good to get the air cleared, even lightning and thunder! Although you must learn not to hold grudges, or unforgiveness for yourself and others, especially your partner, for he loves you in his own way, and he is often a little bewildered about how to get this across to you. He is more introverted than you are, and he often expresses himself through doing things for you, wanting to make life easier for you, or even quietly going to fix things. Often this gets up your nose, instead of you being grateful for them. So, remember, that gratitude brings more to be grateful for, and sometimes those we love the most, need our **Thank you**, and appreciation more than anyone else, including ourselves!

There is the potential here for deep and abiding love.

––––––––––

SOUL GROUP: The Precious Ones

"Soul name: The Precious One who brings Divine Love to the fore in precious ways, like that of a most treasured, heart-felt gift, and thus is one who through her own purity, pure intent, and pure crystal-clear soul clarity, brings the gift of inner sight to all those whom she meets and thus gently, beautifully and purely guides them to express their own highest soul selves with great love.

The tonal chord is high E and the soul colours are beautiful blues, with soft pinks and soft greens, with touches of pure orange, pinks, and rose reds and bright sunshine yellows, framed with pure white gold with pure violet.

This soul was created to express the *preciousness of life* in all its forms and expressions, and like a precious gemstone, or pure diamond, the Divine thus created her flawlessly, of high carat, so she may reflect the purity, the preciousness, the crystal clear clarity of such an exquisite gem, exposing anything not of the purest God force light, intent and Love. With this comes crystal clarity, and often inner sight, which lovingly helps others to see where they have veered off the path, gently guiding them back to their highest soul selves and path, with truth and integrity.

You have incarnated before and there is a very strong twin flame bond with your husband, which stretches to the beginning of time, when your soul was created. You are thus part and of one soul, as all **souls do have 12 soul fires**, and equally divided between the masculine and feminine, in perfect balance and harmony.

You first arrived here with a contingent of souls from Orion, in the wake of the *Wars of the Heavens*, when the people from Lyra settled on this planet, as their own home galaxy had been destroyed. Those from Orion brought with them the Wisdom Keepers of the Galaxies, the infinite wisdom and application of the Divine. You both therefore worked in a type of university.

Interestingly your soul has a significant connection to the Goddess Sophia, who embodies Wisdom, and holds the Keys and Codes of Wisdom. She indeed, is your *over lighting Ascended Master*.

Now in that lifetime you came in as *Twin Flames*, wishing to co-create together through *sacred sexual union*. You first went through intense training separately, to develop the highest soul growth and inner soul fires, before being allowed to have *sexual intercourse, as sexual energy is not attached to the physical form*. In those days you had 7th dimensional light bodies, which were not as dense, so you did not need sexual intercourse to procreate. *You knew how to raise the kundalini without a partner, activating your chakras to the fullest extent, all 12 and 72 of them (there were 72 functional then), merging the soul fires, without needing to become physica*l.

This is the highest form of sacred union there is, and one can experience the Divine in immensely powerful ways, which are even accessible on one's own. Thus, this is a sacred path that only *Twin Flames* could walk, needing an outward vision and quest, greater than the sum of both. Ego was not permitted to get in the way, and it required years of dedicated training to reach such a state of purity. Indeed, one can merge sexually in the highest and most profound ways, without physical bodies getting in the way. This was the purest and noblest of all unions, as love between the two deepened, when they both dedicated it as a sacred gift to the Divine, experiencing the Divine in beautiful, profound and transcendental ways, becoming the Divine Masculine and the Divine Feminine. That was the original state of innocence, which Humankind totally lost when they misused the sexual energy, and subsequently misused it, not only for procreation, but for lust and abuse.

Through this there was deep unconditional love, trust and respect, and a deep cherishing of each other. The more profound the union, the deeper the merging, the more one grew in the likeness of the Divine, not aging, as the physical body constantly renewed itself, through correctly utilizing the sacred energies, and through a total dedication to serve the Divine in the highest ways, in co-creation. One did not create offspring together, but new forms of creative expressions, which benefitted the greater whole! Such was the purity of love and union in the 7th dimensional state – the highest state of purity!

The **intent** and the heart were still pure, and filled with pure, unconditional love.

There lies the crux of all sacred knowledge, for those who finally are able to understand!

For the greatest tragedy of Humankind, was the minute they forgot all of this, and became ego-driven, then used or abused one another, even selling others into slavery. After a thousand years of highest service on Planet Earth, in that lifetime you eventually returned to Orion, and resumed life there."

SOUL GROUP: The Illumined Ones

"In other lifetimes you tended to be severely challenged in keeping your soul pure and truly following the highest calling. You were incarnated millions of years later in Atlantis, and this time served in the *Temples of Isis*, and were dedicated to her, where the High Priestess often took on that title, but as a representative on Earth. You were however born when the *Golden Age of Atlantis* was already tottering and falling to the *Black Magi*, (the same old faction that destroyed the Lion Kingdom), and thus the temples were already under siege. You were trained in higher healing techniques, using the *White Flame* to disintegrate the blocks and fear within the person you were dealing with. *It involved working with the White Flame Fire, the fires of Purification, and the Fires of Illumination from the 7th Central Sun, both of which the Goddess Isis holds cosmically.*

The priestesshood was infiltrated, and although the High Priestess and Priest did their best to keep the teachings and practices pure, there was a rebel element who did their utmost to sow dissent, and undermine the authorities.

In that lifetime, your twin did incarnate, and you were lovers. You had sacred sex together, as these rites were performed under very strict rules, requiring strong discipline and focus. It took years of training for it was alchemy in its highest form. One did not live together, but apart, only sharing sexual intercourse at certain times of the year, when particular planetary and galactic events occurred, and specific energies were released to amplify them. *The rest was an **energetic** not a **physical** union.* This is so often misunderstood in terms of *Twin Flame* union on Planet Earth. The sexual energy has nothing to do with the physical form, but rather with a certain energy force needing to be awakened, not to be confused with so-called *kundalini*, which one can awaken in and around the physical body, yes, but there is a much higher and hidden aspect which was removed from Humanity, because they abused its power during the time of Atlantis."

———

"Soul name: The Intricate Energetic Dancing one, who works with and anchors in the Spiralling energy of the Divine, and the cleansing, clearing, balancing of Divine Creation, and the Feminine Divine.

This soul is one who has just been through a type of merging process, where another part of her soul fused with the fraction of her *incarnated* soul. It was done mainly to activate the *true soul path* and mission to a much higher degree, as you were meandering somewhat off the path, and had agreed prior to incarnation on Earth, that this would happen during this present time, when the Earth was reborn and Humanity had to evolve into the 5th–7th dimensional state. In this regard the man is the *Twin Flame*, yes, and acted as a catalyst, while also holding the third soul flame steady, so that the two others could merge within you.

Sometimes when one meets a twin, especially in the case of two high calibre souls, then the energy can become too much to handle. It is intense, it is immense and usually will act as a catalyst for change. *In your case, you are the one it will impact more, as you now have two parts of your soul incarnated, so you literally have two flames merged within you, and he carries one flame. There are 12 flames in all.*

In the beginning, when not familiar with such energy (and you both work with the spiralling energy of the *Divine Feminine*, which spins up and down, clockwise and anti-clockwise and is a twirling, swirling energy), you will literally be spun into a higher dimensional state, and the truth of your soul. As you had not yet had the time to fully anchor in the other soul flame, you had to go through a type of rebirth, or even *near-death experience.*

So, your soul left your body, as you sat naked, ready to go through a process of alchemical fusion of the soul flames, you had to be and remain in a greatly altered state. It was as much a moment of being born again for you, as it was an actual rebirth. It happens for instance, in the case of a *walk-in*, however yours was not that, but rather a *merger* with another soul part. This took place on a much higher dimensional frequency, and if you had then stepped right back into your physical form, it would have disintegrated. You would not have been able to hold the physical form. The higher guides who work with you, put your physical body into a type of light bubble, so that it could maintain bodily functions (like being in an incubator), to allow you to step back into the body, once the merger was complete.

What triggered this was a lifetime with your *Twin Flame* in Avalon, when you were both highly trained *Druidic Priests,* and practiced alchemy and magic. Now Avalon existed millions of years before Atlantis, and is not to be confused with King Arthur. That Arthur story is a fairy tale.

In that lifetime you both could shape-shift into any form you wanted, and merged energetically. In truth, the sexual energy is not attached to the physical form. One can merge energetically, and the Serpent (kundalini) energy force is activated to the highest degree. Note this is not the lower kundalini, attached to the bodily form, but the higher soul kundalini. It was harnessed to manifest and to work magic and alchemy. Therefore, one partook in *a sacred sexual union*, according to strict rules and rites, merging at soul energy levels, and not so much physically. The physical part was done in a sacred ritualistic manner (almost like white tantra but a bit different), and through the merging of the sacred soul flames, *one could co-create in immensely powerful ways, and literally manifest anything into form.* It was not used to create children, but to create matter and form, and even transform or create new forms.

When you were together, something triggered between you, as planned before incarnating. You merged at a different and higher level, and since you both are inexperienced at this (in this lifetime) and literally shifted through dimensional states, you did not ground yourself properly. If ungrounded you tend to float.

All this then amplified the whole, as you were still ungrounded, as the higher soul part of you took over (the part that was in Avalon), and you lifted off into the higher realms. Your higher guides had to step in to ensure your physical body would not deteriorate or die, for it was not yet time for you to completely leave the planet. You still have a lot of work to do. You will have to learn to put grounding roots into Planet Earth, and to open your *Antahkarana Bridge,* to be firmly rooted in Mother Earth. This all transpired, because when you were together, the kundalini between you was activated, and this is the spiralling energy of the Divine Feminine. When activated too quickly and in such accelerated energetic form, you could have died. It was only because your higher guides stepped in, that no harm came to your physical body.

In that time when you vacated your body, you were shown your next steps or pathway, to leave your husband, as the old negative karmic patterns which drew you together, had been cleared. You were married in another lifetime in England, through a dowry contract, and a political alliance which has been worked through now.

The fact that you resolved and cleared the energies in the mental hospital, comes naturally to your soul, as it is the soul work you are destined to be doing in this lifetime. You just had never done it before, because you chose to rather follow where others directed you, instead of truly listening to your soul. Following the merging with your other soul part, your whole life will change, as the work your soul now needs to do concerns *energy clearing of the old stuck energies and the old abusive patriarchal systems, of those sites in and around where you will be led.* You may choose to continue the corporate work, but know that you will be increasingly drawn to energy clearing, symbolized by the tearing open of the base chakra. The base chakra for so long reflected fears concerning survival, and the lack consciousness of Humanity, that of being imprisoned and enslaved. Your task is to free

Humanity of all that programming, to clear its base chakra and that of the Earth.

Your twin will be a catalyst in this, and the more you merge the more this will happen. Yes, you will have a son together, but that will come later. This is a special *Platinum Sun child*, and this will manifest into form around 2021.

You will often find your body shakes from head to toe, when the spiralling energy is activated, when required to do cleansing and clearing work. Your third eye will open, and you will see what was there before, as you did in the hospital. So, all these happenings served to wake up your soul to the highest degree.

Your husband will be fine. This is not saying you cannot stay friends, or that you cannot work out something, which will suit both of you.

With regards to the twin, remember that you both have free will and choice, and the ultimate solution for both of you may not be marriage at all. Perhaps a merging, and partnership? That will happen as and when the time is right. The energy between you is too potent now, and may cause ups and downs. Allow this to happen. He needs to first clear baggage from his marriage, and some issues concerning his own manhood. So, let healing come for both of you, indeed all of you.

Whatever needs to happen will happen in perfect Divine Timing. Not before. Not too late."

———

SOUL GROUP: The Unifying Gatherers

"In her own Star System, one mates for life. The soul records of a new born child are read just after birth to establish the inherent genius, the intrinsic soul purpose and mission, using highly advanced methods to determine whether the *Twin Flame* has incarnated. In the growing up period, one parent, if not both, will be constantly with the child, through its learning process as an anchor of pure unconditional love. From the word go, such a child is immediately guided to express its genius, so that it can fully step into its highest soul purpose and calling. Only when a certain degree of maturity is reached as a soul, does it desire to mate.

At this time the soul records are referred to, and thus the soul in question will put her intent out like a prayer to the Divine, to attract her *Twin Flame* or *Soul Mate*. Note, that she is fully prepared. She has understood and loved her own womanhood in the highest degree, and has not partnered with anyone else, for all sexuality begins within **self**. This includes a full knowledge of the Divine Laws, and how to apply them as co-creator. Thus, in putting the intent out to meet her Divine Other, he is already there. Not elsewhere. He would not have partnered with anyone else either, for he, too, would have remained single until the time he is ready for union. When they meet, there is an instant recognition, and a period of three years in which they can get to know each other on **all** levels, and establish a deep rapport, true love, and only then, does sacred union occur.

For if the bonding is not done at **soul** and all other levels, the deepest sacred sexuality cannot be expressed. It is something few humans understand, for they lost their innocence and have forgotten the sacredness of the gift of sexual energy itself. It is used too cheaply, and what is not understood, nor cherished, causes pain and dis-ease, especially if brutalized, or misused in any form.

Deep down your soul remembers this, and it is searching for the ultimate union, as you know this so intimately in your star home, but alas on Planet Earth with all the distortion, this often brings a premature engagement with sexual energy, when the soul is not ready to engage soul to soul. Instead of waiting to gain understanding and degree of inner soul-filled readiness for true union and deepest soul intimacy, before embarking on physical intimacy, they leap in unprepared. Consequently, pain ensues, and the sexual area will close off, for if trust and respect are absent, something deep inside closes, even if unconsciously.

The man in question is a **Star Seed** like you, and a *soul mate*. However, it was not destined that you would be together in this lifetime, as his mission differs from yours in many ways. It was just at that time, a way to meet someone of your own ilk, to remind you of home, and the truth. Your *Twin Flame*, or Divine Other has not incarnated, for you have three children at home in your Star System, who he now looks after while you are busy here. You visit them in your sleep state regularly, and have the deep sacred sexual union with him energetically, in your **soul state** – for the soul is pure energy. It might boggle your mind, but there is a deep remembering and resonance inside of you, as you read this.

Now, on this planet you will find that you are looking for a perfect match for yourself like you have with your Divine Other, in your home system.

Alas! No earthly man can compare, and you will always find that whatever you do, there will be something lacking in them somehow. Especially that sacred sexual union you so crave. One can only truly reach this state, with someone on the same wavelength and frequency band *energetically*. By no means does this mean that you will not find love, nor that you cannot love an earthly man – it just means that you need to love yourself so much, that you will not settle for less than you are worth. Even if it means walking the path alone for a while, and truly doing much of the inner work.

One can awaken the *Kundalini energy* and the sacred union within oneself, it is one of the paths of *Sacred Sexuality*. However, it requires huge self-discipline, and the understanding that there are many centres in a woman's body she can activate herself. Essentially the *Kundalini energy*, stands separate, on its own, and can be awakened without sexual intercourse, or engagement. Opening up all the transmitter channels, energy systems and vortexes in the physical, mental, emotional, and spiritual, and all 12 bodies, makes the Kundalini rise on its own. Indeed, it does not need sexuality to awaken, nor to express itself, which is once again a false human conception.

If you truly wish to walk the path of awakening, then first start within yourself. The *womb is the most sacred area* and therefore then also a sacred temple. Who you allow in there is essentially what will keep it sacred or not. It is a matter of free will and choice."

SOUL GROUP: The Ones who Know and Unravel

"That lifetime you were so vibrantly alive with loving expression, so much so that you felt you would find that bridge between Heaven and Earth, and give that heavenly ecstasy and bliss to whomever it was you served in that way. For these priestesses served by giving men a real *reconnection to the Divine Feminine,* and thus also holy bliss as a result, through expressing their offering in highest service. They were trained in very secret ways to serve, and this is largely misunderstood, and often cheapened through the misuse of sexual energy, when in reality *it is one of the greatest gifts of God and the Goddess, in order to experience an ultimate state of transcendence, that altered state of bliss, and a way to experience the Divine in higher service and to step into co-creatorship.*

In this lifetime that longing for a man to fill you up, really is a longing to fall in love with yourself and to explore the total expression of womanhood.

Think of your body as a canvas, and you exploring what makes it come alive, vibrant, radiant, fully turned on and tuned up. If you are not doing this, then you are missing out on three quarters of the greatest elixir of life there is.

So, then why not go and train yourself in the Tao arts of the Ancient Chinese knowing, discovering everything about the wonderful energy centers of your physical form, breaking out from any earlier restrictions to move into full blown, activated vibrant womanhood, with full stimulation of the yoni, and there you go. You will be so in love with yourself, and all that makes you a woman, that the memory of that wonderfully free, blissful lifetime will return.

As you wake up, so will your partner, for you will inspire him to rouse the Divine Masculine within himself, and suddenly your level of intimacy will shift, for you will both be fully present with each other, in ways never felt before.

The heart center is there to open up fully, plus the womb and upper transmitter channels, for there are three major energy centers in the body which must be fully aroused to experience the full spectrum of Enlightenment. The kundalini and sexual energy when fully vibrant, expand *the fires of Enlightenment*, so you can access higher expressions of life and living, and expand your conscious awareness to new and advanced levels, knowing how to channel the sexual energy the correct way.

You are a very beautiful and deep soul, and perhaps here it needs to be understood that there are many paths of mysticism. There is a high tantric path which the Ancient Mystery Schools taught, which truly speaks of the highest path of sacred sexuality. It is one of the most advanced means to enlightenment, understanding the full use of sexual energies as an elixir of life and the path requires dedication, but when two embark on it, it will bring the most blessings."

SOUL GROUP: The Harbinger Souls

"This soul has had quite a few incarnations on Earth and was disposed to join religious groups, ashrams, spending most lifetimes as a monk. He was especially drawn to the Himalayas, often living as a hermit, or a Tibetan monk, or joining the ashram of a guru, but mostly we find him as a monk within the Buddhist community. Thus, he took vows of poverty, obedience, chastity, the begging bowl, prayer and chanting. These vows will have to be revoked, or else he will never be able to have a loving relationship with a woman, for they will dominate and prevent it.

Call in *Archangel Michael,* and all the souls who ever witnessed you making a vow, signing a contract, taking an oath, even a blood vow, especially those pertaining to lifetimes as a monk, and ask that the angels holding you to these vows be dismissed, along with the souls who witnessed you signing the contracts, making vows, or oaths, or whatever else, to sign your *Soul Book of Life,* releasing you from them. Remember to also hand over all outward symbols, such as monk's robes, prayer beads, begging bowls, rings, or any other external signs, or tattoos, or whatever else, from those times.

You will not be able to find the intimate relationship with a woman that you so wish for, because in the previously mentioned lives, you often substituted other monks and boys to assuage your sexual need for a woman, a practice that has always taken place within such monasteries. *One cannot suppress the Divine Feminine, without it emerging in some other form, especially when dealing with sex. One of the greatest lessons in mastery that Humanity and religious orders have to reconcile, is that both the masculine and feminine in equal measure, are necessary to truly find God.* God does not need a religious order – The Divine Masculine and the Divine Feminine unite in the Godhead, and the Godhead embraces **both**. One can also have a deep and intimate relationship with the Godhead, embracing both masculine and feminine, without needing to belong to a religious grouping on Planet Earth. In the rest of the Cosmos, there are no religious organizations, for they understand this principle.

Interestingly enough, your soul on the other hand, will be drawn to work with groups, for it is a harbinger soul. *A harbinger soul* is one who gathers souls around him, for common causes, which can be anything. Of course, there is nothing wrong with ashrams, or gathering people for worship, or prayer, it is just that once structures, rules, laws, etc. are formulated, the **soul** tends to be suppressed, if the leadership is not geared towards equality. A *harbinger soul* such as yours, tends to work best within groups and communities, for common causes. These can be anything, from conservation, to music, to whatever stirs your soul, but do gather souls together, to direct them towards the Divine in some amazing way.

In those lifetimes as a monk, you most often ended up there, because it was a guaranteed means of shelter and food all your life, and because parents nudged you from a very young age to do so, as they could not provide for you. It was also a status symbol in the community to have a family member in a monastery, as this often guaranteed assistance in times of famine and hardship. The family had access to an insider within the religious groups, which was considered desirable.

In one lifetime you were totally bent on serving in that way, and spent so much solitary time in a cave high up in the Himalayas, in meditation and prayer, hardly ever seeing another human.

As most lifetimes were spent in religious orders, if you release those vows, you will have to learn to love and appreciate yourself. If you feel an obligation to get married, just for the sake of marriage, to beget children and conform to society, you will not find the happiness you wish for. For there is a void inside, that insists you are not whole and complete without a wife. That is nonsense. For every soul is whole and complete within itself. The Divine never creates imperfections. First of all, learn to love and validate yourself. You will only be able to love a woman, to the extent that you love yourself. If you cannot even love yourself, how can you love another?

You do have your *twin flame* incarnated in this lifetime. Interestingly in three lifetimes when you chose to become a monk, she was born in the same villages as you, and you shared your childhood. As you were definitely unavailable, later in life she was married off to someone else, so when you finally met and fell deeply in love, you could never be together, because of your restrictive vows. In two lives you had secret love affairs, and even children, but you never could look after or acknowledge them, for this was forbidden.

Do the inner work to release those vows and agreements, which otherwise will keep you monk-like. You may not even have been aware of this, in this lifetime, with a healthy interest in sex, but that monk in you will feel so guilty at some stage, if you actually engage in sexual intercourse. Here the need exists as well to let go of all the blame, shame and guilt you felt in other lifetimes, when you interacted sexually with this woman, as well as boys and men. Again, in monasteries this is a way of life, never publicly acknowledged, and a great deal of time and effort is made to try and keep it secret, behind closed doors.

Even in this lifetime, you will experience that monk-like shame and guilt, at breaking the rules of the order. In the monasteries and religious orders, even if everyone participated in breaking these rules, there were repercussions and you paid, for example, beating yourself up, doing extra meditation, doing hard labor or unpleasant chores. So, release these remnants of self-punishment, shame, guilt and blame, and forgive those who did the same to you. Indeed, in three lifetimes, you were raped as a little boy by much older monks, and that deep scar or wound never healed, and so you perpetuated the wrong, and did the same to others. Forgive and let go. All of that needs be released. Love yourself enough to do the inner work – set yourself free to finally have a deep and loving relationship with the woman whom you are about to meet – your *twin flame*.

In those lifetimes as monks, you often felt a deep inner longing for a "normal" life, as a husband, with a home and family. Working in the villages, you often gazed longingly at the women and children, asking the Divine that you be released from your restricted life to finally experience the joy within a family.

Now this lifetime gives you that opportunity."

———

SOUL GROUP: The Loving Ones

"This soul has had many incarnations on Earth, sometimes in the role of a disciple, acolyte and even a temple priestess. Yet in the last incarnations, she allowed herself to be dominated by the male aspects of the religious movements, so lost her way somewhat, tending to suppress the natural feminine features of her own soul, which is essentially attached to the Divine Feminine, like her entire soul group, which serves her in opening up the thousand petals of the heart, and spreading the soul perfumes and pearls of love everywhere.

When this soul first incarnated here, there was balance between the feminine and masculine. The female aspect served lovingly and powerfully in her own right, but then things were displaced, and men began to fear the feminine power of love and sexual energy, which created the imbalance which has haunted Humanity for thousands of years.

In that incarnation you worked with soul perfume – each soul has its own perfume, or essence, and you worked with fragrances and incense, to bring this feminine aspect of the Divine into the meditative state. You worked with young expectant mothers, showing them the way of Divine love and loving communication with their unborn children, and how to surround themselves with immense love, like a bubble. The practice of bathing in these perfumes with rose petals plus chanting, brought babies into the world, who were calm, did not cry, and were conceived, carried and born with huge love. You served women of all ages using perfume like a loving ritual, to allow all to feel the touch of the Divine Mother, as you literally became Her by transmitting Her. People felt such vast love coming through you, and what you worked with, that they felt themselves totally surrounded and held in the arms of love.

She is one of those souls, with her soul group, who embody the *Divine Feminine in the heart of love*, so she embodies this within herself, and a love that issues forth from deep inside. It is still there now, but very repressed, so hence she feels a tingling in her heart area, as it is there that the heart energies connect with the sexual energies, moving out of the others. When the outer chakras, or all chakra wheels are functioning, and the higher chakras open, then she will work and heal from an open heart, where love will be infused in all that she is and does. It will bring about a profound shift from deep within, which she will radiate.

All in all, this is a time for transformation, and deep and profound healing.

This is a very special and evolved soul, who has come in for her final incarnation here, having taken on the challenge to heal herself, and women as a whole, from deep within, and in the sexual area in particular This is to free them from thousands of years of abuse and misuse of their bodies by men, bringing in the profound and new understanding of the sacredness of union, and the correct use of the sexual energies in higher service to the Divine."

THE SOUL Group: The Singing Ones

"This soul belongs to a soul group who give voice to the sound of the Divine Feminine, thus the Goddess energies and these sounds, colours and energies flow into one stream. The *Kundalini* is the serpent energy and belongs to the Divine, the Goddess herself. This is often confused with some false teachings that kundalini is the sexual energy – that is not so, it is but half of the truth, and it is not the truth of the Ages. *In fact, the serpent energy is the vortex energy of the Goddess herself, pure energy in the highest form, reflected in the spiralling patterns and designs in nature, in the frequencies and spirals, and it is indeed the foundation of all of Creation.*

When you had that experience, it was to reawaken your soul, which you had forgotten. You reconnected to a part of you that had incarnated as a *Druidic High Priestess* and holder of the *serpent energies*, who worked with the Earth and the *Cosmic serpent energies*, and embodied this within themselves. The Priestesses also were the keepers of the Grail, through sound, using it to activate the Earth and *Cosmic kundalini energies*, by channelling their vortex energies within and without, tuning into the Earth serpent energies, to amplify them through their singing. In this way, in a higher sense, they healed the Earth and the people, and helped her to sustain the 7th dimensional frequencies.

At that time Glastonbury was in the 7th dimensional state, and therefore in perfect balance and harmony. These priestesses embodied these Goddess and serpent energies within and out, and were often asked to go into the rural areas where there were faults in the Earth energies, or where weather patterns, or any other energies were unbalanced. They also partook in the healing of individuals, transmitting serpent energies through a staff which looked like the *Caduceus*, which is the medical emblem, with the intertwined serpents around the staff. They could literally ignite this staff, touch the person and heal them instantly. This was accompanied by singing and toning.

It is similar to Reiki, but in a far more potent form, for the serpent energy is far superior, greater than Reiki energies, and considered sacred. Subsequently sacred sexual rites could only be performed by those priestesses with male partners, consecrated by these energies. It was considered so sacred and sanctified that the act of love became an act of honoring the Goddess in the union, igniting the serpent energies with the beautiful interflowing of the male and female flames. This was a beautiful and balanced way of truly experiencing the Garden of Eden itself.

However, during this time, there arose discord and strife within this community and land. Foreigners arrived, and the *High Priestess of the Serpent Temples* had a vision of great darkness accompanying them, as they had no respect for the serpent energies, and did not honour the Goddess. She warned the tribes in a huge gathering, not to allow them to put a foot on this land, for they were the servants of darkness, who had fled from the *Wars of the Heavens,* from Marduk, and in fact were the Princes of Darkness themselves.

Skirmishes between the people and the Dark Ones ensued. As they were peaceful, lacking skills in war and destruction, great calamities struck and the *Sons of Darkness* wrought havoc, and destroyed the sanctity of the land. The Priestesses had their hands full singing, and trying to repair the damage, but the dark ones burnt and killed everyone and everything.

The High Priests and Priestesses knew they had to recall the serpent energies, for they could not have them fall into the hands of the enemies, who would misuse this power to blow up the whole Earth – in fact they were in the process of doing exactly that to their own planet. They then asked the Goddess for guidance. She ordered them to shut down the energies, to close down the sacred sites, and make them invisible to the darkness. They moved all of this into the ethers, and the fairies, gnomes, the devas of nature and all the angels, Archangels, the Seraphim assisted in this process. Thus, all was removed from the inner earth, into the etheric realms.

As the people really needed guidance and help, and as some High Priestesses and Priests could not return to their own galaxies, because they were feeling the great pain and bewilderment of their own people, some volunteered to stay on. This soul was one of them, for she was brave and fearless. However, the dark Ones destroyed the sacred shrines and sites, and she was cornered by the Dark leader, and all of his ilk. She stood there bravely and berated them for destroying their planet, wanting Earth's demise, and plotting to wipe out all life.

In sheer anger The Dark Lord and his men raped the priestesses, and killed the priests, and as their cries for help were heard, the Earth split open, and immense fire poured down from the heavens, destroying everything. A deluge fell, and land masses sank under the sea. In that very moment Marduk blew up, and in the chaos that reigned, Earth was thrown out of orbit, and all life upon the Earth was destroyed, with only the inner earth surviving.

Many of the pure ones had retreated into the inner earth before this all happened, helped by the High Priestesses and High Priests."

––––––––––

SOUL GROUP: The Loving Ones

"Soul name: The Loving One who learns the art of Love.

She is here mainly to learn the art of love and loving, despite the illusions which life on this planet presents – the illusion that love can be held onto, bound or put within the confines Humanity presents as law. This soul is here to teach Humanity the art of limitless love, and how to return to the state of true love, by first learning to completely love and accept the self, before being able to truly love and embrace another.

She has had past incarnations here, working as a High Priestess in the Temples of Isis, Aphrodite and Venus. She was dedicated to the art of love, bringing its unique special gifts, the opening of the womb, also thus embracing male energies into the same, gifting men with *Divine Feminine Love*, during sacred sexual rites.

These rites, were in themselves considered to be holy, and not a form of prostitution, but a far higher meaning of the use of sexual love – by *becoming the Divine Feminine in all its beautiful and loving forms and then gifting those who came to the Temples with the experience of a true union with the Divine in the sexual act. It was thus used in the art of opening up* the feminine embodiment, and embracing manhood totally, to allow that beautiful balancing of male and female.

This involved stringent rites, and only men who truly deserved to be gifted in this way, experienced this gift (they first went through initiation rites themselves, to establish purity of intent). The Priestesses themselves went through tremendous and stringent purification rites, to be chosen for this role, trained in the proper use of this power for higher service. Very few ever made the grade.

In this lifetime now, the remembrance of this is very dominant. *For she has served, this role, in Egypt, Greece, and in Rome, in the capacity of becoming the essence of the Divine Feminine, to gift others with this act of immense open -hearted giving and receiving of the Divine – the merging as **one** of the masculine and feminine, in order to experience the ultimate blissful transcendental union, the first union of Divine Masculine and Divine Feminine.*

Understand first and foremost, that certain souls are pure in essence, and that in a deep and profound way, the purity and the immense higher healing use of sacred sexual acts, is in essence a powerful gift to give to others – but the purity of intent has to shine through. This is why there always has been the rigorous training, and the teaching of the open-heart energies, so that these beautiful and open-heart energies, can overflow in the sexual union.

In this way, then the men who engage with these priestesses in sacred union, then had their masculine and feminine parts balanced, and the priestess herself was gifted with the male energy, helping her to open up to become a transmitter channel for the Divine, For *sexual energy is essentially the consciousness energy*, acting as a tremendous force to open up the channels to the Divine, to transmit powerful messages to the planet, and energy into the ley lines and planetary portals, as it links up to the planetary and cosmic web of light. It took long years of apprenticeship and training, before the energies could be used appropriately.

In this lifetime there will be very few men able to actually link up, and have this type of relationship with this soul, there lies the challenge. This is mainly to teach her first and foremost the love, the immense love and acceptance of self, and not to resist the current initiation rites she is experiencing at the moment, at her own request."

SOUL GROUP: The Loving Ones

"In the beginning of time, you worked with the Shakti energies and also in the temples of love in Ancient India. Back then women were equally empowered, and there were far more advanced priestesses, yoginis and gurus, than men. You taught in those temples the full activation of the Divine Feminine within, working with the sacred womb, and working energetically with the full opening up of the heart and soul, the chakras, and the kundalini energies.

The *High Tantra* was taught, with a primary emphasis on Goddess energies, for during a trance-like state the women were able to tap into the immense Sacred Fires, and to transmit messages or prophecies to those who were pure and truthful to their very core. They then became *highly trained oracles for the Goddess*. It is only when reaching a type of higher consciousness which spans all dimensions, and dissolves into form-less-ness that this type of state and transmissions can be achieved. Women can do this through their total higher alignment with body and soul, so therefore they are far more powerful in this regard. The male then ignites these higher powers, as he comes in love with the intent to bring his beautiful Divine Masculine energies into her, with pure love, and in that they become **as one,** she expands into his energy fields, and he holds her energies together.

When this is in progress, he enters a trance state too, but in a different way. He can only experience the fullness of his own male-hood, or the Divine Masculine, through her being in that trance state, so indeed they gift each other with transcendental experiences that are impossible to experience on their own. In this case, both were highly trained to move **ego** (the negative ego) out of the way, totally dissolving into each other and becoming **as one.** There were those outside the temples who never understood this, so attacked and raped the women, castrated the men, shutting them down. Indeed, you were beheaded."

———

SOUL GROUP: The Loving Ones

"In that time women ruled those Polynesian lands, and chose their partners, according to their capacity to love and honour them, and to help care for the household. A woman only mated with someone equal in body, mind, spirit and soul. As you were a highly trained shaman of the tribe, you only chose a man who would enhance your healing work, for anyone less would block the energy flow, for during the sexual act, when especially the kundalini awakened, it could actually **burn** the partner, resulting in intense inner pain, if they were closed at soul level, and not on the same soul level frequency band. People have forgotten all of this, as the information went underground, as a protective measure for the practitioners who would face persecution, for the patriarchy wanted to control and abuse sexual energy, and feared the power of women.

The woman is the transmitter as she holds the energy, and if the male is on a different frequency band, he won't stand the heat so to speak, as he has to come in absolute love, without ego, trust, respect with a deep honoring, and appreciation of her. Of course, the same applies to her as this works both ways, but she naturally will come from an open heart, because a woman **feels** and a man **thinks.** There lies the key difference.

This particular soul has lived many lifetimes, attracted to you, and was your lover, but due to his lack of truth and integrity, often failed in endurance to withstand that "fire" as a consequence. For you hold the codes, and even in the sexual act, they will be transmitted through your energy systems. That scares the hell out of those who are not ready for this, for they are not advanced enough to understand.

It would assist you greatly to learn about sacred sexuality, and also the *white tantric path* in the ancient mystery school traditions, to better understand more about these sexual energies, and how in this regard, the woman is the transmitter of them, igniting the man. That is how the men attained the Christedness, as a man called **Jesus**, could never have been activated, without his soul partner **Mary Magdalene** igniting him.

Thus, you have in the past, opened up to men not worthy of sharing this fire and flame with you. You are following the correct path, by doing the work, but it would also assist you to ask how you can channel those energies in a more profound and correct manner, truly in total love. The advanced paths of the Mystery schools had two paths – one involved a partner, and the other was a solitary path, in which you could reach that enlightened state by yourself. The practices are the same, for the sexual energy is not attached to the body. That is an illusion. It is an energy on its own."

SOUL GROUP: The Loving Ones

"Soul name: The Loving One who opens the hearts and souls of all she encounters, as a love-bringer, love-healer, love-igniter, love-spreader and loving blessing to all whom she encounters, and is there to ignite the Flame of Love everywhere!

This soul is one who has had lifetimes here before, and works with the **Codes of Love.** These are held in the Divine Feminine, the Mother God and she works with the heart-opening, and loving essence of all Creation. This is pure, unconditional love, the all-encompassing love which surpasses all understanding. It is the love without judgement, without fear, without criticism, without labels, without boundaries. It is the infinite love of the Divine Feminine, something that she has for **all** that she ever created, from *deep within her own womb, and gave birth to.* It is **true love.**

With you, it is essential to work from the depths of your heart and soul, to love what you do, and to do what you love, and to bring this loving essence, like the fragrance of the beautiful rose, and the all-radiant sun, to all whom you encounter. It is to open the heart fully, and to let the deepest prayer of your heart be: "That Divine Love expresses itself through me, joyously, beautifully, exaltedly, delightfully, tenderly, compassionately, miraculously and powerfully – so that my whole life becomes a beautiful song of Love, the songs of songs."

It is when you close your heart-centre, when you fear being hurt, when you close yourself off, that you will suffer pain. For you, it is essential to keep that heart open, no matter what, truly asking that your heart and soul are opened up to ever greater and more profound ways of loving and being loved, and to lovingly serve in every way that you can."

———

CHAPTER 3

Different Forms of Sexual Expression

Extracts from Soul Readings

"Soul name: He is one who brings in the understanding of love-in-action and being, to experience love and loving, and to be the force of love-in-action cosmically.

This soul is an old soul, returned to work through his karma, as his soul group wishes to move on to higher evolutionary states, and not to lag behind. Yet, this soul has a tendency to do just that, often in entanglements from which he cannot extricate himself, and this has haunted him over many lifetimes. It is almost like he wants to, ought to, wishes to, but then falls back into the same old negative patterns and strays. In the beginning there was no such struggle, for in truth this is a beautiful soul, and when fully empowered at soul level, shines with the brightness of his wide-open heart, allowing his inner most being to overrule his mind, to truly work at being love-in-action. This is a great blessing to those whose lives he touches, with his innate kindness and deep caring and love for the Divine, when fully present, aware, and in the highest service to the Divine.

Cosmically he works as a counsellor who travels the galaxies and universes and works with souls who have experienced some kind of trauma, helping them to heal and get into the highest soul alignment with the Divine, in pure unconditional love.

We find him first incarnated in what was the *Lion Kingdom*, and he came in from Lyra. He was a beautiful, giant of a man with reddish hair, and a big heart of pure gold. He worked in the inner Temples of Love, doing energy work with the heart energies, often clearing the energy centers of those visiting. He was like a huge bear, giving bear hugs, and showing all the highest pathways of love.

During this lifetime he was involved with the one soul he mentions as a possible love interest, in that she worked as a temple priestess, and he shared sacred sexual union with her, according to the highest standards and regimens, in the understanding that unconditional love starts at home. Thus, this was done with utmost sincerity, respect, caring, and love, trust and a beautiful and very special bond existed between them, truly a great blessing to them and others.

However, during that lifetime, like so many men, he fell under the spell of a certain man who arrived from nowhere, with a very magnetic personally, who seemed to feed his ego especially through the adoration of men and young boys. He was not from Lyra, but came in as part of a contingent of emissaries from Mars, and found the planet to his liking, mostly for those he saw as potential prey. Lyra was already falling apart at the seams, with two brothers fighting for the throne. This man had turned the weaker of the two against his brother, by deliberately having a sexual relationship with him, which violated Divine laws, for he wished to have the power of the planet for himself.

He also fed on the energies of those now ensnared in his web, by doing so-called favours for them, then wanting sexual favours in exchange. He was very generous with material gifts, but very demanding in what he wanted in return, often biding his time, and then suddenly springing demands on the person, when most vulnerable.

For you in that lifetime it started very innocently, as he came on the pretext of wanting a heart opening, and then played on your innocence and wide-open heart. He lured you into his lair without you even noticing, although you were aware of vague feelings of disquiet, and the woman with you felt the same and warned you repeatedly. She had visions of him causing your death, but you refused to listen. He forced you into a sexual relationship, using you like a pawn in his own power games. In the end he committed murder, and had you appear on the scene, (you were totally innocent) and you were arrested, tried for murder and put to death.

Yes, you did do things you often regretted, which were not kosher. Yes, you were repeatedly involved with the same man and all his games, and every time you promised yourself you would let go, but fell repeatedly. It is time to cut the negative cords, hooks and ties he has established in your sexual area, especially in your groin, or you will develop dis-ease there as you age. He cannot play games with you unless you allow it. It is time to get back to your truth and integrity, and your core heart and soul. Deep down in your soul there is hate, resentment and pent- up anger towards this man. So let go of all of that.

You know you do not love him, in the sense of wanting to be in a relationship with him. You have in truth never been gay – you are very much a man who loves women, and cosmically you are very masculine, living happily with one life partner. It is just on this planet that you have become entangled, and paid the price.

Know that it is self-love, which frees you, and self-worth which will ultimately give you the strength to stand up for yourself."

SOUL GROUP: The Eternal Counselling Ones

"The souls she is referring to, were sister souls, who in past lives were with her in institutions which she always seemed drawn to. In about 6 lifetimes she chose to be a nun within a convent, and her inclination to love women stems from that time, so she would naturally be drawn to sister souls who feel familiar, after living and working together in such close proximity.

As one can imagine in a closed community of women, who took oaths and vows never to marry, it was like living in a prison of the church's making, so they had love affairs, as sexual energy cannot be suppressed, and will always surface in one form or another. Both women were lovers from those times, and sometimes both simultaneously. So that is why this soul is confused.

The soul records are not there to pronounce something right or wrong, or to pinpoint anything, it is just that these sister souls shared lifetimes with you as a nun. Before this, you were married off to suit dowry agreements in three lives (in France, Germany and Belgium), then dumped at the convent, when the men wanted to conveniently get you out of the way.

It was also a political issue at that time – when a wife gave too much trouble and had produced children, then she would be pensioned off to a convent. So, in those lifetimes meeting these two who were in the same boat as you – dumped there not because of a religious vocation, but for political and social reasons, drew the three of you even closer.

You were in a Dominican order, so carried out good deeds in the community, mostly feeding the poor, nursing and counselling. In between all of this you lived in a strict religious regime, so at night you slipped into each other's cells to share love making. The three of you formed an intimate trio in all these lifetimes, sharing this sisterhood, viewing this close sister love and bond you shared as being a special favor from God.

You even secretly made an oath that your souls would always find each other in future incarnations to love each other, be there for one another, while maintaining the sexual bond. This oath is as valid as a vow, and needs to be released and the angels keeping you to this oath, must be released too.

The same applies with all other vows such as chastity, poverty, obedience, begging bowls, service and chastisement (self-flogging as chastisement for sins), for they are still valid, and so nothing will change until these are released, along with the administering angels being dismissed.

Therefore, here in particular, you will have to release a blood vow the three of you took in that lifetime, by cutting your wrists and mingling blood. These vows are the most binding, and will perhaps need a longer time to release, or else this will keep you bound to each other over many more lifetimes. The astral sex was real enough, and was one of the ways that you had sex with the one in the USA, in times spent apart, or often when the Mother Superior had punished you, and locked you in your cells for a few days, even weeks, because she wanted you to stop being lovers. In that way you had sex with each other anyway.

Again, sexual energy is not bound to the physical, and one does not need to be with another in physical form to have sex. There is no right nor wrong, merely soul choices which were made."

SOUL GROUP: The Compassionate and Loving Ones.

"There is this sisterhood the soul belongs to at a soul level. Naturally during lifetimes on Earth, she would be drawn to sister souls of this order, forming close bonds, which is the love between sisters for each other. They were never meant to become sexual bonds – unfortunately life here does not go according to Cosmic Law, but rather to human laws, which cause pain. In this regard the sisterhood in its true form serves what is pure and simple, in compassionate and loving ways.

Hence it does not engage in sexual intercourse, or sexual energy exchange in any form. However sometimes living together as nuns in such close proximity as these two souls did in previous lifetimes, led to sexual energies being expressed as a love bond, which in its true higher form, does not exist. So, let us get this crystal clear. This is an old karmic link and bond, from a specific lifetime, in what is now France, when you both were in a convent, ordained as nuns of the Dominican Order. Your lover was much older, and used her powers to manipulate her junior, touching her body and engaging in sexual pleasures with her, controlling her so she did her bidding, thus misusing her seniority, and also so-called love for her own ends. In the meantime, she had an ongoing affair with a priest, and also had sex with some other nuns. So, she had men and women as sexual partners, while professing to be pure.

Now, those oaths that she had you make, those vows of obedience and eternal love still bind you to her. She does not honor them herself – so it is time *little one* to cut all the negative sexual cords and attachments, she placed in your sexual parts, and to release all oaths and vows you ever took, even those of chastity, obedience, and in her case, love – meaning sexually manipulative love. She made your life a misery, but you bought into all of this because you felt that you loved her, even though she abused you, and you knew of the priest, for she bore him three children. Through it all you helped her, you covered up for her, you even smuggled babies out of the convent for her. So, thus this is not balanced love, as much as you would desire for it to be so. Sometimes when these bonds have formed over many lifetimes, and in this form, one perceives them as more than that – when in reality it was love between sister souls, which should have been **Agape love**, and never have turned into **Eros**, as it did. So old bonds are holding you prisoner, along with the old manipulation, vows and oaths that hold all in place.

This has come up now in your life, after having done so much cleansing and clearing, but remember that it works on multiple levels and forms. Just like the skin has many layers, so does the soul memory bank.

She came into your life as contracted, to remind you of all the karmic debt the two of you had to clear up in this moment in time. You needed to awaken to this again, and this time round she served you, by openly choosing the same priest to go off with again! So, she alerted you to the inner releasing and clearing work needed to release both of you from old negative karmic patterns, to be free to love with your soul free at last. Then it can truly shine in truth and in its highest purity, which is that of a compassionate and loving Being.

Love and compassion first of all needs to be for oneself, and to embrace and love yourself totally, unconditionally and completely as a **whole**. She has finally shown her true colors and the truth of her own soul, which is quite naturally to be drawn to a male counterpart, as she has been created for this. It is just that you often were in environments where she manipulated you into believing the contrary, because she could have you doing what she wanted you to do, and be. You allowed that to happen.

So, let go of all of this. It is no longer serving your own highest soul growth and good. You are now in an immense initiation in the inner planes where all that no longer serves your highest soul growth and good, will fall by the wayside, and you will be cleansed and purified inside and out, for there is great work your soul needs to do, and it needs to travel the path alone for a while."

SOUL GROUP: The Creative Sounding Ones

"In this lifetime there is a bit of a struggle of orientation, for in essence this soul is androgynous and was part of the Lemurian civilization, who shared in creating the beginning of Atlantis and that civilization. He never forfeited his androgynous state as did many Lemurians later in life, and served as the sound healer artist and priest at the *Temples of Sound and Colour*. There were crystal pyramid temples for healing with sound and colour, and creative paintings which people hung in their sleeping quarters, as they enhanced the energy flow, helping with realignment and healing of their auric energy fields.

In the present lifetime this work is coming through in his androgynous form, which is both male and female and not to be confused with being gay. Where both genders are present there is balance and harmony – one does not contradict the other, but they flow as one into a single body and form. You must have the higher understanding of this as the state where perfection of form reigns, in order to make peace with this from very deep within. It is a state of higher being, for it is the state where perfection of form reigns. Therefore, use both the male and female aspects, and understand that in the greater Creation there are myriads of these lifeforms, and it is not unusual.

At a later stage in life, you will meet someone who is also androgynous and it will be like meeting someone you have not seen for a long time – like a long-lost friend. A deep and profound loving friendship will be there, and you will feel yourself reflected in this man in many ways – since both of you are androgynous, this will take on a different form – more so than can be explained here."

SOUL GROUP: The Purifying Ones

"So, the question here concerns the relationship to the "Helens", and it seems as if the soul is referring to two or more Helens. There is not much clarity in questions, as there is a tendency to be diverted from the truth. What is it the soul is really wishing to know? *For in essence all soul encounters, and especially with this soul, are in truth a journey back to herself, for other souls will always reflect in detail, like a crystal-clear mirror, everything impure within herself, every veering off-course, all the lies, all that she is not loving about herself, and not letting go of, in emotional baggage and charges, and what she is not living as **Truth**.*

Now, one can lie to others, and to oneself, but you cannot lie to your own Maker!

The essence of this situation began when all three of you, for there were three in the beginning, worked together in the *Temple of the White Flame in Atlantis*. You served as acolytes, and were taught and taken through initiations, before being ordained as priestesses serving in these temples of Pure Light, as the White Flame Temple was the highest, and therefore the initiations were the most stringent. Only the purest-of-the-pure even made it to the rank of priestess, after intense purification and initiations.

In these temples, the essence of all teachings was to **know thyself**, and be true to yourself and then to **know the Divine** within you, and be true to your highest soul calling and purpose, to be pure in body, mind, spirit and soul, and to understand that the highest path of purity, demands this. Nobility is not something one can just buy – one has to first become pure of soul and spirit and body, before true nobility can rise to the fore. With it come dignity, honor, and highest service.

Now interestingly your name in that lifetime was *Helen* and they were called Helen too! There were 3 of you who came to the temples in a single year. Now, the relationship between you is something which began even before Atlantis, in the time of Avalon.

So, here we had 3 souls who were already entangled in a type of triangle, who were not being true to themselves, as in Avalon they had broken vows to stay on the highest path of the White Flame. In essence in Atlantis, you were meant to return to the highest truth within to serve, each in her own unique way, not necessarily in tandem. Meaning not in any partnership, but purely as a soul serving the Divine. One did not partner in that lifetime in the temples, for it was considered to be a distraction from the highest service, as partners tend to pull your energies all over the place and deplete them, and children even more so. Now, if one did have a certain sexual partner, it was supposed to be with the male complement.

You were happily training and truly excelling in the early initiations, when your paths crossed with both of them. They too had passed the first initiations, and now went into the second phase with you. Now from the minute you saw them something deep triggered within you, and you had a sense of foreboding. Your inner alarm bells went off, which was appropriate. These two souls were in a secret sexual forbidden relationship, but at that time, a certain element had infiltrated the temples (which later led to the destruction of Atlantis) as some had been deliberately placed there by those who wished to break or undermine the power of the priesthood in Atlantis.

The one Helen had fiery red hair and green eyes and was stunningly beautiful and had not only secretly engaged sexually with the other Helen, but with another man, **not** from the temples. He, in fact was the one chosen to infiltrate them, to abuse the sexual energy, and of course to break rules as one way to undermine things.

He was manipulating this Helen, and she was so sexually entranced by him that she was given the task of seducing the women. In her eyes, (being misled by the man) she thought she was to awaken women to the pleasures within themselves, but in truth she was an instrument used by him (and those whom he served) to undermine and to infiltrate the Temple. So, one could almost describe this as a deliberate act – a virus-like rebellion to corrupt the priesthood, so as to break their power.

Now this Helen, had seduced the other Helen, who was more pliable, mouse-like and quiet, and then set her sights on you. At first you wanted nothing to do with it, for you so wanted to rise in rank, called to work with the White Flame as a priestess. You were born with the Sign of the Goddess under your left breast and were immediately taken to the temple and indeed, your soul shone as one dedicated to serve, and also willing to go the extra mile.

This Helen was a pro however, and you were as innocent, as a baby, even though your training incorporated knowledge of how to stimulate the vagina and clitoris, and to pleasure yourself, as this opened up special zones and, in the beginning you were trained for a very specific purpose. You knew how to correctly **channel** this into **energy** to serve in an ever-higher purpose. Helen however would have none of it, and brainwashed you with lies. She told you that the High Priestess was purposefully suppressing what should come naturally, which was the desire to have a sexual partner and even **more** than one. In the end the three of you became partners in secret, and subsequently ganged up against the others.

Your mentor and teacher loved you dearly, and saw how something within you had changed. You became inattentive, surly, unhappy, arrogant and moody, which you had never been before. When she confronted you directly, knowing the truth for she was psychic, she tried to get you back onto the highest path, and the truth within yourself, but Helen was more powerful and she held both of you (and also the mousy one) in an iron grip. She even gave you potions to drink to open up your sexual juices, and the orgies included other students. As this now became an intolerable situation, the Temple Council had no other choice but to ask all of you to leave. Indeed, it closed its doors on you forever.

Before you left, your teacher tried her very best to make you see the folly of your choices, but you refused to listen, even though deep down you knew she was speaking the truth, your pride would not allow you to admit it.

However, once away from the temple premises, you found life in Atlantis as it had become, very difficult to adjust to. The Power had shifted to the *Black Magi,* who caused the demise of Atlantis, controlling the masses though implants and control boxes. *You were literally forced to have one implanted, and then coerced into the role of teacher, teaching what you were ordered to.* The situation with the Helens turned into a complete quagmire as you started to question them. For the first time seeing and acknowledging how you had been lied to, and how your sexual entanglements with them had not brought you inner peace, nor the deep harmony within, that you had experienced in the temple, when in the highest service, *before* meeting them.

One night you felt a huge Presence in your bedroom, as you cried to the Divine in despair. *Archangel Gabriel* appeared to you, as he works with the *White Flame* and said that you would have to break with all of them to return to the path of Purity, and that his angels would assist you, but you had to truly be willing to serve from the heart and soul, and allow yourself to be purified, for your soul cried out for this. Something within you changed and you resumed being true to yourself and slowly but surely, all your teachings came back to you, but now with the understanding why you had been taught these truths! It was like you had to first sink into the depths of darkness and despair, before you could grasp the greatest truths and understand the highest pathways and why purity, and nobility, dignity and honour were demanded.

However, what you did not bargain for was how the red-haired Helen would react. She actually attacked you physically, demanding you have sex, whipping out a dagger, and stabbing you in your heart, killing you.

So, understand that there are old negative karmic patterns, which need to be cleared up between all of you. In subsequent lifetimes your soul has truly tried its best to return to the path of purity, but every time you met these two, something pushed you way off track again, allowing them at crucial times to manipulate you into believing them, when they were in truth enticing you away from the deepest soul truth within. That is the role they played out time and again. Now, remember these two souls in their own way, also need to wake up to their own souls and soul truths. Each one has free will and choice. They can choose to get back to the truth within or not, just like you.

There is a hidden blessing here, which you now need to see – you now have the opportunity to finally break through and return to the highest truth within your own soul, and to **live** it. *Archangel Gabriel* is there with you, and on call, day and night and he will help you, with his counterpart the *Archangel Hope*. You work with *Lady Nada* in the inner planes and she will help you, with *Mother Mary.*

All of this is a wakeup call. Now, this does not mean that you cannot love the souls in question. In truth there is only love. Perhaps the greatest of all love, would be to gently lead them and yourself back to the highest truth within.

Your soul is really seeking that deeper connection to itself, to the truth within and then to love yourself so much, that you first of all seek to love and nurture yourself, to forgive and let go, and then to also release all the shame and guilt you felt so intensely in Atlantis when you finally realized what had gone wrong. In other lifetimes you almost tended to punish yourself again, by buying into the old negative patterns, and succumbing to them, instead of mastering the soul lesson here.

You are now all coming full circle. In truth these souls are serving you – they are reminding you to take your own soul power back, and to stand in your highest truth and mastery. It means loving yourself so much that you will first seek to heal deep within you, to forgive yourself and them, for what happened, and then to get back to the highest soul path of purity."

————————

SOUL GROUP: The Way Shower Souls

"We find you incarnating together in ancient lands, where the Americas are now. In those days, giants lived there, and that continent was part of Africa, and looked very different, having a more temperate climate. You were part of a tribal community, who held the *Pueblo tribes* as the centre of wisdom tribes, with the *Hopi*. They were part of the original 12 Tribes which roamed the Earth, and thus were of the copper-skinned race. You were a Wise Teacher, and a *way shower soul*, teaching life skills, the wisdom of the Ages, and counselling. Within the tribal communities there were high initiates, who went through stringent initiations and tests, before being allowed to assume the status of a Wise Woman or Man, in a teaching role. You all trained together until you reached puberty, and afterwards shared only certain teachings together.

Before answering such a calling to train, the Astrologer Priests did a soul and astrology reading, to determine what training each individual should be taken through to direct him/her to walk the correct path, from the moment of birth.

In your case, your birth charts correlated in many ways, and you were identified as being of the same soul, yet he was more scientifically orientated than you, and you were more orientated towards people and teaching, in a social sense. He was more introverted, and you more outgoing and sociable.

In the early years a deep bond developed, as you watched each other's backs, and assisted one other. Yet, when he reached young adulthood, he became rather rebellious, and was often sent on vision quests, so as to temper his ego and sense of self-importance, and arrogance, with his show of bravado, which did not sit well with his soul. You often mentioned this, which he resented, and you knew that he brought this onto himself, refusing to listen or follow the strict teaching and supervision of his teachers.

At sixteen he rebelled against his teacher, and was asked to leave, as he was too disruptive and untrainable, and he refused to listen which not only put his own life in extreme danger, but others too. For he did not realize that initiates were often put into potentially life-threatening initiations, where they needed to let go of all fear and follow their inner guidance and the teachings to the letter. Once they did that they survived. The minute they did not, they began to struggle, as fear beset them.

For years after he left, you pined for him. You often encountered him in your dream work or vision quests, and while sleeping, you were energetically involved with him – for he could astral travel, or project himself in astral form. You never shared this with anyone, as you were confused and did not know what to make of it all. So, you kept quiet about it.

You later engaged in a partnership (one did not marry) with an apprentice, a soul mate and you were a good match. He was stable, kind and caring, and strong within himself.

At around forty, the Twin suddenly appeared out of the blue, having shifted within himself, and learnt self discipline through training in another tribal school with an extremely strict, disciplinarian teacher. When he reappeared in your life, you were torn in two. On one hand, you had this contented and fulfilled relationship with your current partner working alongside you, and then this twin arrived, who ignited you sexually in ways your partner could not, and with whom you were still very much energetically involved. You had three children by that time, and loved them dearly. Eventually you succumbed to his sexual advances, while loving both men. This continued for some time, because your partner travelled and taught for a few years, and in his absence, there were plenty of clandestine meetings. Yet you always had feelings of immense shame and guilt for cheating on your partner, who trusted you.

He surprised you in bed with the twin, so things erupted. He was understandably extremely hurt and betrayed, while your twin gave you an ultimatum, wanting you to leave with him, as he was now forced to return to the tribe to face the consequences of adultery (as per the initiate laws). You could not leave the children or your husband, as deep down you knew that he brought a steadiness to you the twin lacked. He was too volatile, and sometimes just too rebellious and headstrong. He left, and it took years for you and your partner to restore the original trust and respect you had shared.

Yet you were still energetically involved with, and tied to your twin for the rest of that lifetime, sometimes becoming unbearable to live with, as both men demanded your attention – one in the physical, and the other in astral form. It led to inner conflict, feelings of shame and guilt, as you felt that you were still cheating on your partner after promising to never engage with the twin again, so you beat yourself up about it. This eventually led to disease in your sexual parts, making sex too painful to endure. Yet the energetic merging with your twin continued, leading to more guilt.

In this lifetime you have not met your soul mate as yet, but now the twin has returned as contracted. As your question is about him, note that the twin will be very much alike, as much as he is also a total opposite. You will find that once the initial infatuation wears off, you will often be challenged by him in ways no other man has ever tested you. In addition, he will have a tendency to push buttons you never even knew existed. In this lifetime you will both be forced to be truthful, real and authentic.

In this regard there are no hard and fast rules. Nor are there any pat answers as to whether you will finally be together or not. There is plenty of negative karma between you to clear up, for in other lifetimes he often just deserted you and left you to face the music, with the children he created, as a lover, while you were married to other men. In this lifetime it is all about responsibility – taking responsibility for what you both co-create together, and him being more accountable for his actions. Sexual energy will be intensely present, as it was in other lifetimes, and it needs to be tempered with action steps, with the will to walk the extra mile with you, to take responsibility for actions or non-action, no matter what."

<hr>

SOUL GROUP: The Blissful Ones

"Regarding this man – if he is not willing to engage with you in physical union in this world, then he is not living his own higher soul truth. If there is still physical intercourse with his wife, then this is not living his truth. So, even if one dilly dallies in the spirit world or other dimensions, there is already a breach of truth, and integrity in various aspects. However, this is free will and choice, but know that even if ethereal bodies merge, that is as much a union, as if in the physical, for all is part and parcel of the same. One is not separate from other bodies, rather part of a single whole. So, then whether you like this or not, it will have an impact, for there are three in the union, not just two. Thus, there is now an element of division, in some form. So, there is a merging, yes, but still in the presence of the third party. Is that a true union? Only you yourself can answer that.

Again, trying to divorce the physical from the spirit and soul is impossible, for it is all one and the same. It is one single entity and form. It is a way of life expression that your soul chose in this lifetime, and therefore is just part of your own soul, as much as everything else is a part of you. So, then, as far as this is concerned, ask yourself, how can you anchor your soul work into physical form?

Then ask yourself, "How is this union in higher levels serving the physical manifestation into form?" Be honest. If he prefers to stay with his wife and family with his love for them, he is busy enjoying the best of both worlds. How is this serving you? See, this is an old pattern repeating itself.

Let us return to Atlantis. You worked in the *Temples of Higher Healing*, as did he. As priests you knew that if you chose to marry, then you could only serve in the lower ranking temples, for it was a well-accepted fact that those with families and husbands were constantly pulled in all directions at once. So, if you aimed to become a high priestess for instance, you had to remain single and utterly dedicated to higher service. In that lifetime you were very happy and content, training for the *High Priestesshood*, when you met this man, and all your higher intentions fell apart. You had a secret love affair with him again, first in the ethereal, but later in the physical. Soon you could no longer totally focus on healing work, and made mistakes. You were called before the Council, everything was revealed, and you were demoted to the lesser priesthood, as was he. You blamed each other for not being able to rise in rank, and had children. He left the priesthood and went off with the woman he is now married to. For the rest of your life, you were intensely bitter, unable to forgive him for letting you make a mistake in judgment. In that lifetime he later committed suicide after joining the *Black Magi*, and being forced to do awful things.

So, in essence then he is bringing you the choice again, to either stay with the status quo, like he is, and never have a physical union, for he likes having more than one wife, so to speak, or you can then decide to totally devote yourself to anchoring in *your life's mission,* and let go of him. It is then his free will and choice which path he chooses.

If you opt for the higher soul path this time, then you will raise your vibrations and frequencies sufficiently to exclude him, so he cannot share that vibration, without some serious work. In doing this, and by not engaging with him, you will attract more and more souls who do the same work, and find you are so fulfilled from deep within and loving yourself so much, that you no longer need a man to fill you up or validate you. That will be the greatest gift you have ever given yourself, to stand in your own power, on your own two feet. You will then anchor in the Divine frequencies and vibrations, healing thousands of souls – that is how powerful a healer you truly are.

When you do that, you will find that something deep inside of yourself has changed. You start to be the love which is there inside of you, and **live** it. It is then that a man will walk into your life who is a soul mate, living his purpose and mission with all his heart and soul, and he is single and free. He will just be like an enchantment in your life, a beautiful and precious soul, who heals people with sounds and colors, and was trained in Tibet. He is a gentle and precious one, and you will feel from the moment you meet him, that he is huggable and lovable. You will make beautiful and heavenly music together – in physical and soul union, which will be sublime. However, it is now your own free will and choice which way you go. Put your soul mission first, anchor it in, and live this with all you are, and blessing upon blessing will flow. Put another first, and patterns will repeat themselves. It is your free will and choice."

SOUL GROUP: Those who Know

"Worthiness and self-love appear to have nothing to do with sexuality, yet they are connected. For if there is any trauma or fear regarding sexuality, and the expression thereof, at some level the body will close down with the person withdrawing, stemming from a deep fear of being used and unloved. Yet, interestingly, abuse is always attracted by this soul, coming from her own low self-worth and self-esteem.

In order to finally break this circle, there first needs to be forgiveness for self at the deepest levels, to release all shame, blame and guilt, as in truth there is nothing to be ashamed of, or to feel guilty about. At some level your soul took such lessons upon itself, in order to grow and they will repeat themselves through many lifetimes, as they have done, if not finally mastered.

Often within a family, the mother withdraws sexually from her partner, and then the child assumes her role. Few realize this, but it does play out in the family dynamic. It is not necessarily that the child wilfully seeks it out, as there are so many factors at play here. The abuser may not be the father, but a relative like an uncle, or a grandfather. Usually, past life issues come into play, where there were old marriages, or affairs or links between these souls. Now every soul has a different story, and with yours the person who abused you has a long history with your soul, and you were sold into slavery and marriage with him. As happened his wife or the person in his life, withdrew sexually from him, and it is this old ownership bond which needs to be dissolved in this lifetime.

These negative cords and attachments in the sexual area can be broken, and old marriage and slavery contracts released with the help of *Archangel Michael*. You may even petition the Lords of Karma, for final clearing and discharging of all old past life sexual abuse, if this serves your highest soul growth and good.

Remember though, that children often enjoy sexual attention, especially from their father, as with all abuse, there is the other side. If it is not bringing any pleasure, often those seemingly being abused, will simply leave their body and become a witness from above, in the company of angels and archangels, garnering immense loving support from the heavenly realms. Nothing is just one-sided, as the Divine strives for balance.

You are a daughter of The Divine – the Divine does not create imperfections, only perfection. There is nothing wrong with you – there is so much **right** with you!

Sexual energy was created by the Divine to become an energy of loving expression to ignite the sacred fires and the kundalini energy, which, in the most sacred moments, lights up and creates the *Fires of Co-creation*. In such mergers one becomes so much **One**, in a transcendental state, that if forged together, there are moments of accessing the 7th Heaven – literally experiencing the God and Goddess. One becomes **one** with **GOD** and all of Creation, in such moments. It is something to cultivate. So, connect with the deepest power and sacred temple of your own womanhood, and allow the Divine sexuality to flow and express itself through you in Divine love, and you will experience a totally different type of union, so healing and empowering for both of you. A Heavenly blessing.

Then forgive the men – all the men, for in truth they did not know what they were doing. It happened when they closed their hearts and went into their minds, fearing female intuition and powers. It is a legacy from patriarchal societies with the constant wars, where men raped, plundered and enslaved others. So often they tried to cut out their hearts, when in truth they sought and craved for love in the deepest sense. One cannot judge. One can only find a deep forgiveness, and then thank them for the soul lessons mastered, and set them and yourself free. Forgiveness, true forgiveness allows us access to the highest states of pure, unconditional love. It sees only love with tears of gratitude, for in truth nothing is ever in vain – everything has a hidden blessing and brings immense soul lessons in soul mastery."

***

SOUL GROUP: The Manifesting Ones

"You came in with a whole contingent of these souls from *Orion* at the invitation of the *Lyrans,* who were primarily the creators of that civilization, wishing to create a massive temple for the *Goddess Olympia*, as a huge beacon of Love, Wisdom and Light, which would literally light up the world.

With this impetus, the first temples arose on a massive island complex, within a lake, and the Mediterranean Sea did not yet exist. It was a spectacular beauty, for the Lyrans were master architects and engineers, and constructed the buildings, and your group manifested the gardens, fountains, and whatever else you felt would enhance the energy, beauty, serenity and power of this place. Sadly, this later became an arena for the dispute between two brothers fighting over their dead father's Kingdom.

Your priesthood was also infiltrated by *Black magicians* or Wizards using the black arts. Initially you were not at all interested, but unfortunately grew infatuated with a much younger practitioner. You were very beautiful, with long dark auburn hair, stunning blue eyes, young, as no one aged back then, knowing the secrets of eternal youth, and being so well versed in the sexual arts, so you set out to seduce this young man.

He played the game, for he in turn knew that you had amazing powers he wanted for self-service and gain. You were blinded by his beauty and arrogance, which you found intriguing, for he was unlike any other man you had worked with. More than this, he was in his flower of youth, and the sex which followed was more exciting than ever experienced before.

What you however did not know, is that he practised black magic, and was feeding you a black substance to shut down your spinal column (which in your case was vital to be open and fully functioning, in order for you to do your work).

The black force came through your sexual centers, implanted there by his seed, and "tricks" in keeping your spellbound and tightly bonded to him, through implanted sexual cords, hooks and ties. They went up your spine into your throat area, where he completely blocked off your transmitter channels, closing them down. When you finally woke up to what he had done, it was too late, as you were completely shut down, and powerless to put your intentions into manifestations. This knocked you over, and you finally saw him for who and what he was, but by then you were so hooked up and into him, that you literally became a puppet on a string.

In addition, he was with those of his ilk, on the side of the destructive brother, as a massive war broke out, and now used his control over you to seduce other men, controlling them through you. Black magic at its peak, and it was very hard to understand now, but the men you had sex with, who were not bound by the dark, became so. It was like the energy binding you to him would infiltrate their energy centres, spreading like a virus in them, closing them down.

In the end, with all his abusive powers, he blew up a huge chunk of the Temple complex, which then sunk under the sea. This resulted in full-scale wars, with three quarters of the original land masses sinking under the sea.

You both died in a horrific fire which he unleashed with his bombardments hitting an invisible shield around the main temple, which boomeranged back to your home, and completely destroying it with intense fire."

———

SOUL GROUP: The Glorious Ones

"In your real soul state, you are not only a glorious Being, but you sing praises to God, with immense love in your heart. Your praises resound through the Heavens and your love flows like a might ocean – wave upon wave of love pouring into the Cosmos and filling the whole with praise songs and love! How glorious a calling is that? And how wonderful and joyous a Being you are in truth!

See, this all stems from Atlantis where you worked the in temples of the Most High, dedicated to the singing of praise songs, and making of beautiful music, chanting and worship, all in a beautiful place between mountains, with crystal clear waterfalls running into the canals below, stunning natural forests and unsurpassed tranquillity, serenity and peace that goes beyond human understanding. You stood in your magnificence, with your beautiful and strong voice, soaring over the others as you led them in chanting and song. You were the nightingale of yore, with a glorious presence that inspired others to lift their hearts and souls in loving devotion and awe to the Divine.

Then one day, he came into your life. A tall man with dark auburn hair, and in that day, you sang like never before, and your life was never the same. You were obsessed with him, and in subsequent days searched for his face in the crowds – and yes, he came back. However, there was something about him, although he tickled your fancy that also had cold shivers running down your spine, and alarm bells going off everywhere. Nevertheless, you chose to ignore that. He arranged to meet and your forbidden love affair began, as he was not there to worship at all, but rather to steal your joy, your glory and your powers – for that was his briefing. You in your innocence, believed him, went all out, *and lost your voice.*

Thus, you could no longer sing. Your love affair was exposed, for the High Priestess was shown a vision of events during an attempt to heal you. You were expelled from the temples, sent for rehabilitation and higher healing, but instead you sneaked away with him. Subsequently he totally dominated you, and made life miserable, but you would not have anyone say a word against him, even though he abused you till the very end."

____

SOUL GROUP: The Rose-ray Loving Ones

"In those lifetimes, you often yearned for true love, and usually found that men desired your body, more than being interested in loving you. It has led to soul wounds, for you have felt that void through many lifetimes. Although you were serving in your own way, you often suffered abuse from those to whom you sold your body, but you allowed this to happen, fearing loss of income. You experienced mental instability, stemming from old emotional baggage.

In this lifetime, you came in to try not to fall into that habit, but to keep your path clear and experience true love at last. Therefore, you also feel that intense call to serve the Goddess, as you have always done, albeit in a way that was practiced in the *Temples of Love of the Goddess*, as a highly trained acolyte and priestess. The difference was that then you went through initiations which prepared you for the role, so you did not attach. You knew how to serve by becoming the Goddess through meditations, and certain rituals, and were in a type of altered state when the act took place. *You acted as a transmitter channel of the Divine Feminine, through the sexual act. It was considered to be a blessing of the Goddess for a man to receive this – no abusive behaviour was permitted and the men were put through rituals to shift them into a transformed state. They truly believed that they were experiencing intercourse with the Goddess herself. In that pure state then this was a type of higher service, done with love and devotion, with no shame, just loving service.*

Notwithstanding, in later lifetimes this memory bank got in the way of your relationships with men, and in that you have to learn in this lifetime to see your physical body as a temple, sacred and worthy of love and devotion. See just how union between a man and woman has something sacred and beautiful and profound about it. That is the most important lesson you have come in to master.

This soul returned to Planet Earth to pave the way for the *Divine Feminine* and therefore has strong connections with the *Planet Venus* and Lady Venus, who is the other half of Sanat Kumara. She served in the temples of Venus in Roman times, as a prostitute who worked in their temples. They differed from those in Egypt, and those wanting sacred sexual intercourse, would have to pledge themselves to some kind of higher service temple work, and payment often came in the way of offerings, rituals, and ceremonies.

They were highly skilled in the sexual arts and in pleasing men, who literally felt that they were having sex with the Goddess herself. In light of this, you often had sex with generals, and political leaders, and in the interim were involved with politics and underground movements, against your own better judgement, and the High Priestess of the Temple. You were involved with those fighting amongst themselves to become Caesar, and then were assassinated because of your relationship with a general.

In other lifetimes this proclivity continued, leading you to become a high-ranking prostitute for Kings and noblemen as a courtesan, for somehow you were drawn to the higher ranks of society, where you were well paid. In one lifetime, you were one of the French King's mistresses, and then in another, that of a leading general. In all those lives, you suffered rather sudden and violent deaths, which has led to mental instability in your life, when soul memory banks are triggered. The most painful trigger which needs to be released is that of the *French Revolution*, when you were the mistress of the King himself, and guillotined alongside him. You were stripped naked and shamed, before being executed in front of the crowd. *This tendency to serve in the way of the sexual arts has been with you for many lifetimes, as somehow some part of you always felt that you became the Goddess in the sexual act."*

SOUL GROUP: The Leading Lights

"In that lifetime she was a Priestess working in Lemuria and Atlantis, serving as a transmitter channel for the Divine energies. Indeed, she was like a radio transmitter, in the same way as it transmits airwaves, so she transmitted the energies of Light and Love from the Divine or God. She thus was called then the *Transmitter of Light* in higher alignment with her own soul.

She meditated in the inner sacred sanctuaries of the Temple of Light, dedicated to Helios and Vesta and their Sun energies. Hence, she sat in a certain chair with her own encoded crystal key in her hands, transmitting the light energies. This process of decoding has since been forgotten, for the language of light exists on very high frequencies, and only the purest souls can transmit it, for it is indeed the light language of the Cosmos, and comes in a high frequency and vibration. She would transmit this encoded light into crystal clear quartz wands, later decoded by her, and these light knowledge contents were spread throughout the temples and Atlantis. This temple was known as the Lighthouse, as it acted as such, guiding ships navigating the coast.

In that lifetime, she came under the influence of a temple priest, who had under his jurisdiction, a school of light encodements. Thus, he not only taught the techniques of decoding, but also how to open up to become a cosmic transmitter. So, the same teacher has appeared in this lifetime again. In that life he was highly ranked, just below a High Priest with all lesser priests and priestesses under his tutelage.

However, he knew that to maintain this rank, there could be no sexual relationships with any priestesses, as it was known any such liaisons derailed them, as the sexual energies were considered sacred and a gift from God, only to be used in certain rites, with assigned priests. You were not one of these however, and fell in love with him, haunted him, spied on him and stalked him to ask him questions, under the pretence of being his most avid pupil. Nevertheless, he told you straight that you were just infatuated, and under no circumstances would he risk sabotaging his high position, so it was best for you to cool down.

This only made you even more ardent, he reported you to the High Priest, who in an effort to calm you, sent you to a less important temple in the outposts of Atlantis, to create some distance between you two. You were excellent at your job, but with this infatuation, mistakes crept in, and it was his concern that your attention was divided.

At this smaller temple, you were under the tutelage of a very beautiful High Priestess who tried to get you to understand that infatuation violated the rules, stressing it was impossible to do your transmission work, if these sexual energies and desires intervened with your transmissions, for the sensual energies were used in a different way according to strict laws. In this event you regained your composure, and over time came to love being at this temple near the sea.

However, you met another man, who was totally infatuated with you, and once again you were very aroused, meeting him in secret and enjoying sex, which soon affected your work, as instead of being fully present during the transmissions, you were present with him. Your work degenerated even further with mistakes, one of which was fatal.

Indeed, it cost the priesthood of Atlantis very dearly, for they lost ground against the Black Magi, and in this event, the first war broke out and the first landmass sank.

You then confessed and were pardoned, but it left a rift between you and the other priests, as your own guilt over events, and the manner in which you simply could not forgive yourself, grew into a feeling of alienation, or separateness, and of course, being disconnected from the Divine Source. Consequently, you committed suicide although you had been fully forgiven and pardoned by the High Priestess and others."

SOUL GROUP: The Spirit Workers

"In those three lifetimes as a man, you often felt the need to discriminate against women, especially those drawn to religious orders. Indeed, women were originally part of the order, but they were later sabotaged by men, who threw the female lamas out, and closed their gates to them. Many lamas used women for sex, having children through them, for an all-male colony could obviously not reproduce. So, they were used to create the vessel (physical forms) for the male lamas to incarnate in. That is why monks went from village to village having sex with women, to guarantee the next generation of acolytes for their religious order. In one of these instances, you raped a girl, and used your powers to force her to stay bound to you, and to produce three children. Later this boomeranged as she rebelled, questioning the morals of this order, with their abuse of women, and their unacceptable methods of creating offspring for their next generation of lamas. For this she was publicly shamed and stoned to death, while you watched. However, something very deep within you snapped, and you vowed that in your next incarnation you would come in as a woman, to experience just how that felt.

In the next three incarnations you did just that, assuming a female form, and interestingly always felt yourself attracted to religious orders, and especially to those of gurus, yogis and lamas. In the latter times, you were once again in Tibet, and then in more recent incarnations, you fled with the lamas to India. You worked in the ashrams, cooking and cleaning, and ended up as a prostitute for the monks (who were not supposed to have intercourse with women, but did anyway.) It always felt somehow right for you to be used in this way, because on some level you felt you served the Buddha by having sex with them. In this lifetime, many of these previous lifetimes have come to the fore, as you have battled with your own sexuality, not wanting to be specifically either a man or woman, then choosing to be with both a man and a woman, and then kind of hovering between the two. Again, not being that comfortable in your physical form."

CHAPTER 4

Karma and the Choice of Partners

Extracts from Soul Readings

SOUL GROUP: The Light Bearers

"The soul who wished to be born to you and your wife, was also a light bearer soul, but internally there was something untoward between you at the time, in that your wife was over anxious, fearing the consequences of motherhood at some deep level, and also the prospect of dying in childbirth. Interestingly, this has happened in more than one lifetime, so she really feared death if she went through with the pregnancy. This might have been subconscious, as she has many unexpressed fears within.

Therefore, losing the child was not really losing it at all, but rather the fact that she only came in for a very short period of time, and then decided to abort her mission, for it was too sensitive, and so hard to adjust to the very dense physical form. Thus, it was nothing to do with either parent in the end, but rather the soul being a very highly evolved one from the Light Bearer Soul Group, who just could not adjust to the density of the 3D human form, this was particularly true since the last time it incarnated was during the time of *Krishna*, when the planet was in the 5th to 7th dimensional form, in a much lighter body.

So, the soul is hovering around both of you, asking that you not mourn its passing any longer, but know it is very happy to be back in the home galaxy, and that it was grateful for having experienced the density on the planet. It will come back into form, when the planet has shifted completely into the 5th and 7th dimension again, when it will be able to hold form in a physical embodiment. It loves you both, is always sending love to you, and is working non-stop elsewhere in the Cosmos to bring light to needy souls – work it truly loves. So please do not make yourself ill for nothing.

In many ways the physical maladies of your wife have to do with suppressed emotions, and not living life according to her highest soul calling and truth, but we cannot read her records without her permission, and therefore this is all which can be said now.

As for a child – if all is finally healed inside and out, there is no reason why one will not appear for both of you, if you truly choose this, perhaps through adoption or other means, if that is what you truly wish. First the healing must happen at soul level for both of you, before the rest can happen."

SOUL GROUP: The Divinely Shining Ones

"In other lifetimes the fatal attraction to the man who beat her up then ensued – always like an intense infatuation and recognition. In this lifetime the added protection which she had asked for was there, as he married someone else. She now must do a ceremony of releasing all old marriage vows with him, and check herself for any remaining negative hooks, cords and attachments left in her sexual area. The pain is a reminder of that time in Egypt when she was paralyzed on her right side, and the memory bank triggered from the encounter, subconsciously is also to caution her against continuing the old destructive pattern with him. She needs to do plenty of cleansing and clearing in her pelvic area to help with menstruation cycles, for in his abuse of her, he placed a knife in her solar plexus area, which caused paralysis.

She is called upon to become that radiance of the Divine again, and to do as much as possible the inner clearing work, and to relearn to use her hands in Reiki or any energy work, also with crystals, healing herbs and plants. Whatever she blesses and radiates from her hands, with the love of her heart, will be received by the recipient. So, *if she does not give healings, she is short-selling herself on many levels, for in essence this soul group radiates the Divine Higher Healing Powers and Love, and everything they touch is healed via this Divine energy flow.*"

SOUL GROUP: The Co-Creative Ones Who Ignite/Inspire

"The man you were with was a soul with past life karma to clear. You incarnated a few times onto the planet before, in order to gain life experiences, as said elsewhere. Well, you were together in about 7 lifetimes, and interestingly they tended to be in the areas of *Egypt, Greece, Turkey, Israel, Italy, the rest of Europe and England*. In four of them you were forced to marry him for your dowry. Indeed, in three lives you were sold off to the highest bidder, as your family were in financial trouble, and needed to save the estates and lands, so married you off to this wealthy man.

You resented him from the start for you felt that he had no manners, you turned up your nose at him because he was lower class, and you flaunted your liaisons with other noblemen, after giving birth to the heirs. He drifted away and had other women who loved him for who he was. It made for a stormy marriage, but somehow as you grew older, there was a truce, where you tolerated each other for appearance's sake, while actually growing quite fond of each other, when all was said and done, although neither one wanted to admit it. Thus, there are marriage contracts and dowry vows to release here, otherwise there will always be a sense of ownership of each other, and deep-seated anger within at being married off like cattle, sold to the highest bidder. You resented your parents and blamed them for your unhappy marriage and state of being, and never really reconciled with them afterwards. The same applies to your husband.

If you do not release the marriage contracts and vows, you will be bound by them – for the angels administering them will keep you to them, until the contracts are released and dissolved, the *Book of Life* signed, and the vows and contracts dismissed. You may wish to call in **Archangel Michael** for help to release them, and will have to call in everyone who witnessed you making those vows and signing those contracts. They will have to sign your *Golden Book of Life* and the release, with your ex. It would be best for you to do the inner releasing and cleansing work, especially concerning self-love, self-acceptance and worthiness. Again let go of your proclivity for perfectionism. If you beat yourself up, you do not need enemies – you do it to yourself! Remember that much of this might be subconscious. In acting as a higher guide to other souls, you often have to help them to realize the same, and therefore in helping yourself to release and heal, you will become a much better teacher and guide."

SOUL GROUP: The Shining Ones

"First of all, you chose your mother, since you had a karmic link to Egypt, where she often took care of your children, while you were working, or going off on long spells with your lover. You had five children with this man, and she raised them all. She was your sister, and often went without food, in order to feed and clothe them, because you went on wild sprees, and left everyone behind.

So, there was a karmic link to the mother. However, during her pregnancy with you, she went through a traumatic time, which she never shared. At one stage she wanted to abort you, and had secretly gone to someone who performed them illegally, because your father had deserted her for another woman. She felt she could not kill you and returned to her parents – her pregnancy caused some upheavals there too.

She reconciled with your father, and you were born, but much of your mother's resentment towards him lingered as a memory bank for you. Many of your feelings of being unwanted stem from this, and must be released. The relationship between your parents was very strained at times, and as a child you felt that you were guilty of causing the rift between them, for you loved both. So, then the deep feelings of not being wanted, or being in the way emerged. It is best to just let this go. Both parents loved you very much in their own way, but they were going through war and trauma before and during this time, often never expressing the pain which was there, as they had been brought up to do. So let go and forgive. In truth the problem was that they did not love themselves very much, and therefore had a hard time expressing love to others."

SOUL GROUP: The Shining Ones

"This soul is a very old soul, with many lifetimes spent on Earth, and in the process became entangled with numerous souls and therefore in her soul contract, she will attract all the men that she has had as husband, lovers, or even masters, in other lifetimes. Consequently, it is nothing new for her to have more than one man in her life, and she is now meeting up with all who had contracts with her through marriage vows, dowry agreements and in the latter one, a blood vow.

Unless all of these are released, she will be bound to these men at some level, and therefore not free to truly do her own thing, or align with her true *Twin Flame*, who has not yet appeared in her life, because he is also working off karmic ties and links elsewhere.

This all began many lifetimes ago in *Egypt,* when she was a very beautiful *princess of the Royal House.* Originally, she was married to her half-brother, her current husband in this lifetime. As was the custom of the time, there were certain rituals and rites performed between them, and they had three children, before he was assassinated.

She then had to flee the court, but could not safeguard her children, was betrayed, and ended up being a concubine to the Vizier of the new Pharaoh, used as a type of sex slave by her current lover. He requested she flaunt her sexual prowess (which she had learnt in the rituals and rites with her brother husband) and to display it to his male guests, he wished to entertain to win political favors. She hated this, and made plans to escape, with the help of a much younger man she was forced to please sexually, who then fell in love with her, and smuggled her out of the palace.

They fled Egypt together to Nubia, but there he soon found other younger women to entertain him, and she was left destitute and aging, dumped there doing manual labor to feed herself, as a Royal Household slave. That lifetime ended with great bitterness and despair, waving her fists towards heaven, believing that fate or destiny had dealt her a bad hand.

In other lifetimes this triangle repeated itself in many forms, and in some the male interest was her son, who she did not like to share with his wife, and spoilt him. So, there is a strange type of lover/son bond between them, which they will have to resolve in some way. The lesson has repeated itself here, with the need to work through the karmic ties and negative patterns created in those lifetimes, but also to come back to unconditional love of self and others, to give each other the freedom to be and become.

With regards to your husband – there is a great brother/sister/husband bond there carried over in many lifetimes, sometime incestuously, and sometimes when you were not even physically related, but related within families, ending up having affairs, or even marrying as in the case of close cousins. This was exacerbated in certain lifetimes, with dowry agreements made between families for property reasons. The last one was in Germany, Austria and Hungary, where the noble families held large tracts of land.

Often this was a type of loveless marriage where both agreed to have children together, with lovers on the side, as was the custom then. There are not only marriage contracts and vows to be released, but also dowry agreements and other contracts pertaining to land, money, and prestige. For instance, in one lifetime, she had to sign away all her dowry rights to him, to keep her children. This is one of the reasons she never had children with him this lifetime, because of a deep-seated fear that she will have to forfeit them again in the future.

The lover (in the middle, who wants her back) often used her in a sexual manner in a display of ownership, (a sex slave situation) and in one instance was a brothel owner in Paris, where she worked for him, and was his lover, while he acted as a pimp. On three occasions when married, he was inclined to neglect her, and always had other women, as she had other men. So here too the contracts and vows have to be released, especially when her body was sold. There are immense sexual hooks, ties and clogging up of the sexual area, which need cleansing here and now, before she can have children. For in meeting all these men again at this time, her soul chose to be reminded of this, to totally cleanse and clear all karmic patterns and ties and vows etc. to be freed to find her true love in this lifetime, without encumbrances.

In those lifetimes this soul felt used, and that her *freedom of being* had been stripped away. Sometimes she felt strong anger and hatred towards these men who had the power to do with her what they liked, while she still had to serve them sexually, tied to them, *and* then often dumped when she was older. There was despair and bitterness, and feelings of depression and a void.

So, in this lifetime all of these cords, hooks, ties and feelings or emotions carried over from those lifetimes, have to be released. The fact that she is involved with them all at this time, is not an accident, but rather by design. She must truly learn to love and honor herself, to appreciate and honor the sacredness of her own body, and then most of all, to understand that unless she loves herself totally, finds her own worth, not seeking to be completed by a man, no matter who, but to be whole and complete in herself, she will not be able to find true love."

SOUL GROUP: The Vibrational Ones

"He has karmic links with the soul or entity asking these questions, and in this case they have known each other as souls in many incarnations. Sometimes souls become involved in love or loving relationships, due to created circumstances, tending to link up again and again, by choosing to have incarnations on the same planets, wanting to experience life together there, in order to work out karmic links. There has always been an intense attraction between them, in fact the one is fascinated by the other, but this always tends to unravel somewhere along the line, as they do not belong to the same soul group.

In this instance yes, the attraction has come over lifetimes, as lovers, and sometimes simply companions. In other systems, and not on Planet Earth as such, they had an intense love relationship, which later became destructive, as both went too far with their talents and abilities, *experimenting with the effects of sound on the life of certain species – how the vibrational frequencies actually worked, and affected the greater whole.* In the end this led to their own fatal destruction, with this karmic tie thus needing to be worked though in subsequent lifetimes. Thus, the karmic links go beyond just this planet, and therefore there is feeling of familiarity, and knowing each other deeply. In that lifetime too the passion on the physical level was very intense, which added to their woes.

The entity concerned as said, tended to self-destruct, because he sought the limelight. This obsession haunted him in ways that impacted other lives, along with his ego, and his continued search for something to fill the void, and his oversensitivity and deep unhappiness, never left him. He passed away in a traumatized state, and is now being debriefed, in the sense of being prepared to resume his life in the Bear Constellation. During such debriefings, in the case of traumatized souls, they are held in intense love and in his case, with his soul group, this involves healing through the vibrational frequency of sound."

––––––

SOUL GROUP: The Creative Ones

"Soul name: She is the Creative expression of the Divine – that which loves to create beauty, in all and every form, with great love and beautifying the Cosmos. You are very creative in this lifetime, and at times spoilt for choice, wanting to do it all immediately and perfectly, and of course everything takes practice, commitment and endurance, in order to see projects through. You tend to dabble here, there and everywhere, never committing yourself to truly creating something extraordinary and amazing – you see this all the time in others, yet somehow do not perceive the same tendency reflected in yourself.

The underlying reason here lies in *Atlantis*, when your soul wandered onto the planet – literally. You were on a *cosmic cruise ship* (just like those on Earth, but a spacecraft) and felt like staying here for a while longer. You were a soul who was creative with colours and paint, and who consulted and read auric energy fields around the body. Atlantis was 5th dimensional, thus the auric fields were much larger and brighter. You discerned what would uplift people, add energy to their fields, inspire them and bring more balance, beauty and harmony into their lives.

Your canvasses were amazing, as you used a type of *crystal concoction* with paint, in more colours than are currently available because we have lost most of them. Due to your cosmic journeys, you often painted ethereal colours and hues, as seen from the star systems and galaxies. You literally brought immense beauty and spectacular moments into the lives and homes of others, through your created works of art. They immediately felt uplifted, inspired, and just vibrantly alive and well, when they had one of these incredibly beautiful pictures/creations in their homes.

You thrived in Atlantis, and *fell in love with a man from Earth*, married and had children, while continuing your artwork. But Atlantis was hijacked by the Black Magi, who started to control the populace's minds by implanting them with control boxes. In your case, this first happened to your husband, who on returning from a trip away, suddenly became angry for no reason – he was shouting, fighting and abusing the family, something unprecedented. You just could not understand this behavior, and neither could he in his lucid moments, when he was himself again.

You requested he accompany you to the healing temples, where they discovered a control box had indeed been embedded in him, without his consent or knowledge. You suggested that he go to another temple, where they could energetically remove this. You returned home, and without any warning he reverted into a monster. He tore the furniture, and all your creations into shreds, and when you tried to save them, he turned on you in such rage, that he literally throttled you to death.

Your soul was in severe trauma, as you finally realized this was the end of your sojourn there, so allowed your soul to leave with the angels of transition, to go for healing in the inner planes, before resuming life in your home galaxy (reuniting with your other soul parts).

You then incarnated again in what is now Jerusalem, to try and resolve the negative karma with this soul. He was a fabric merchant, which you loved, for you sewed beautiful garments with the apprentices, and also decorated the homes of your wealthy and royal clients. (This was during the time of *King Solomon*).

Your husband often went away, and you basically ran the business with your two sons in his absence. Your designs were more and more in demand, and your son hung them in clients' homes, as you were not allowed into certain quarters. It worked well enough for he was on the same wavelength as you, sensitive and creative.

Your husband again returned a changed man. He grew quiet and withdrawn, and sometimes had fits of anger, so you all tried to avoid him and keep him away from customers, for at times he struck out at them, wishing them bodily harm. This was so unlike the gentle creature you had married, and you encouraged him to share just what had happened to him on his journeys, but he just left the house, ignoring you for days afterwards. One day, a regular client who loved your creative work, a good friend, with whom you shared long conversations as he was very deep with plenty in common, came into the shop.

That day, he was bending over your immensely beautiful work, moved to tears, when in stormed your husband. The next thing he drew out a dagger and cut your work to shreds. The young man at first froze, then tried to help you safeguard the work (for it had taken hours and hours to make). Then your husband killed him, and turned on you. Your sons tried to intervene, but he stabbed you in the heart, and you died.

After this episode you avoided the planet and this soul. It has taken you a very long time to return, and only because you wished to finally work through this negative karma.

Interestingly, you returned as his daughter in another lifetime in Europe, and managed to break free from the family, married the young admirer previously mentioned, and happily settled into married life, working together in a textile business again. In that lifetime your father worked off much of his karma with you and your husband because as Jews you were persecuted, and he helped you to escape, although he later died in a concentration camp."

———

SOUL GROUP: The Beautiful Ones

"Soul name: The Beautiful One who brings that touch of loveliness, of beauty, of higher healing and incredible love into the lives of all, with a gentle touch. Nature always triggers the creative force deep within her. It will inspire her to create something beautiful or unusual and to share her own talent to beautify, and create beauty which delights others. Whatever form beauty expresses itself in – that is what her soul loves. Whether this is music, or art, or painting, or creative needlework, or design, or even just baking cakes, or cuisine – whatever she loves doing from the depths of her heart and soul, will be a delight to others and enhance their lives.

This soul has quite an interesting soul pathway, and has had many lifetimes on Planet Earth. Interestingly she has always been involved in enhancing the beauty of women, in some form. In the case of her parents, the connection goes back to a lifetime in what is now the Balkans, near the Black Sea, where she worked as a masseuse at a bath house. She also beautified clients with henna and oils, and although she was a slave, she was very well received and loved by everyone, due to her loving energy, and the way she brought out the beauty of form in those whom she treated.

However, she was owned by her current parents, as they owned the bath house. They had bought her as a little girl, captured from a galley and sold on the market. They trained her in this work, and at a certain age, taught her the fine art of sexually serving men and women alike. She hated this, for she resented the fact that her own beauty was sold, and she was often abused or misused, and being a slave, treated as though she had no feelings or soul. There came a time when the owner and his wife were both very ill. As the most senior slave, she assumed the running of the spa in their absence, which helped her, as she could delegate the sex work to others. This freed her up to do what she loved doing – beautifying others. There was another beautiful slave very much in demand, but who had a deep jealousy lurking deep inside, and she was spiteful. Often the clients sensed this, refusing to be treated by her, and demanded to have you instead.

There was a very powerful and influential man who made use of your services time and again, for he was infatuated, and often gave you things secretly for he was a good man at heart and treated you gently. So, you were quite fond of him. However, since you were no longer doing that type of work, she took over, but he did not like her, and demanded your services. Then the owners insisted that you resume your duties with him, which you did. When you were absent from the main building, this other woman spread untruths and rumours about you, which then reached the ears of the owners, who called her in. She told horrendous lies, as she wanted to be the boss.

You were summoned and then asked to redeem yourself. However as much as you stood in your innocence and truth, they believed the worst, and locked you up for punishment. Then the client heard about this, and offered to buy you at a price they could not resist. So, they sold you, but not before nearly starving you to death.

In this lifetime they are your parents, and you chose them so that you could forgive them, and reclaim your freedom to be the best you can possibly be. You are thus born free, not a slave to anyone, and if you sometimes feel that they are making your life a misery or are too demanding or anything else, it is because the sense of ownership is still programmed into them. It is best for you to release the contract where you were sold, release them from ownership, the contract, and the angels keeping it in place.

It is advisable you walk your own path in this lifetime, and if you have to walk it free from your family you may do so, for truly you have worked this karma off now and your soul has been freed. So, claim your freedom to be, and just allow them their freedom to be.

You are worthy of loving yourself unconditionally, and deserve of love. So, love yourself totally. *You are not a slave anymore.* You are a beautiful soul, serving in your own way and for the highest good, and therefore treat yourself as though you are worthy and lovable, and love yourself all the more, and then others will love, and treat you with respect. For you are love. You are beautiful. You are one who beautifies life, and you truly deserve to stand in your own light and shine, and radiate forth, not in the shadow of anyone, whether it be your parents, husband or anyone else."

————

SOUL GROUP: The Divinely Sounding Ones

"Soul name: Beautiful sounding One who vibrates at pure Love of the Divine.

This soul is a *volunteer* soul, who came from her galaxy for the first time, although she has been involved with this planet via her incarnations in the *Pleiades and* on *Arcturus*, she has not been in physical form for long. In an attempt to get to know what life was like here, she assumed a body, (as a *walk-in*) after the Second World War, but found that she had trouble adjusting to life, so aborted her mission.

When in the Pleiades, she was briefed on life on this planet by her guides, and warned that it would be very different, not the peaceful and tranquil state of her home galaxy. She works with sound and vortex energies in healing, *in creating with colors and geometrical patterns, so she is here to return this knowledge.*

When she chose her parents, she chose her mother as she had been her sister in that short time when she took over a body, sharing a very close bond to this soul, her elder sister in that lifetime. That sister missed her so much when she left, by committing suicide. So, in this lifetime she chose her as mother, although before birth she had already been warned of complications. Her mother carried her deeply-held low self-worth over to this lifetime, having a tendency to attract men who honed into this. However, this soul still incarnated, wanting to experience life in this extremely difficult situation, to better heal this propensity in others.

It is very difficult for those from other galaxies to understand the violent and the self-destructive tendencies of humans. When you have only known peace, and no hatred, or strife, you cannot heal those who are suffering, as you inherently lack an understanding of this pain, as well as the ways in which this affects not only the physical body, but the emotional, mental and spiritual bodies. In your home galaxies and all your incarnations, you were a very evolved and advanced healer.

You work as said, essentially with Sound Healing using the vortex energy and combining this very high frequency with ethereal and very high energy colours. Even using crystal bowls, or playing a violin for instance, would naturally, if you allowed yourself to go into deep meditative state, *bring about high frequency sounds in a spiraling form.* This would help spin the energy wheels in the body faster, which combined with colour, would dislodge blocked energy to transform it into pure light energy.

You incarnated into such a difficult home situation, so you need to apply this healing first to yourself. You have all the tools, but because pain is so foreign to you, you tend to hold onto and nurse it deep inside, instead of letting it out. You also have built up resentment, albeit unconsciously, to certain aspects of human nature, which won't assist you in healing. Mostly because unconditional love for oneself and others means precisely that. When a healer is resentful deep inside, or has unhealed areas, then she cannot be fully present in the state of sacred healing love, and transmits her own inner pain and resentment onto the patient. It is only in healing from deep within, that your own powerful healing abilities will truly blossom and come to the fore.

Your soul chose this path, as explained before. So it is truly not what others have done or not done to you – it what you are doing to yourself which counts. It is how you choose to release what is there, moving into forgiveness, dissolving emotional charges within, that will affect your outer life, and how you relate and heal. This is ancient knowledge, and what your soul has to experience to heal on this planet. All the higher healing abilities cannot be transmitted through you, until you learn this basic healing principle. Thus, your soul only had ties with your sister, and those of the family she took on when she was a walk-in. But this was for such a short period of time, that there are no karmic bonds as such, except with the sister. In essence then all are new ties.

You must be very careful whom you let into your energy fields, as coming from a galaxy which never had much interaction with this planet, makes you extremely sensitive to other people's energies, the energies of homes, of work places, and even outside. You often feel strange, or drained, or even disorientated and fatigued. *This happens when you are not shielding yourself sufficiently and absorb these energies like a sponge. You are not normal – you are different.*"

SOUL GROUP: The Ones who Serve through Joy

"This soul inherently chose to incarnate at this time to bring in the greater meaning of life in *this higher state of joy*. This extends to the state of being, where one is the *source of joy* to others, and transmits it in all you touch or do. *Joy is a vibration and it affects everything around it*, thus when this soul does not find that state of joy within, it will have the opposite effect, transmitting the lower energies such as anger and resentment. He chose his mother who was a joyful happy being, and just content with being that. He chose her because of the old soul ties between them, and because she served in many lifetimes on Planet Earth with joy. As they already shared this bond, he knew she could provide him with a background of joy from which to serve.

She fell in love with a young soldier returning home, with his easy-going manner, his pleasant treatment of her, so different from other soldiers. She evoked family disapproval, for they felt that he was not good enough, and tried to make him leave town. Their liaison resulted in a pregnancy yet her father forced him to leave, using underhand tactics, so he disappeared from her life. She was required to look for alternatives, which caused a further family rift in her family, as she insisted on keeping the child, for whom she felt this immensely strong and profound connection. She was later forced to abandon him, as she could not provide for him and was very much at the family's mercy.

This created more despair in this poor soul, and she became mentally unstable and was removed by the family. The ties with her are still very much there, and this deep seeking of that love, that unconditional love from women, became a quest for him. Later in his childhood there was an accident, causing severe trauma, with the choice to abort his mission, which was linked to his mother's, or whether to allow another entity to take over his form. There were negotiations, and he decided to rather incarnate at another time with the correct mother, as he felt that he could not relate in the same way to the mother who had assumed that role, and he suffered from a profound sense of abandonment. Thus, this soul aborted mission.

The other reading done for this soul, was for the *one who assumed this body at that time, and who has returned and become entangled with the wrong people. But all is not lost, as this is the time when he will have to wake up to his own true mission.* Therefore, he will have no recollection of his early childhood, and working with energies as said, for he did not incarnate as a baby, but later on, because of the urgency of his mission. As a teenager he always felt that he was not really interested in what school had to offer, and thus sought excitement, as young men are wont to do, taking a different path, meant to become a diversion from schooling, to progress into what he thought would lead him into his mission.

The soul has to combine both readings, and understand that much of his inner soul self has been severely repressed, with due knowledge of those who trained him so that he would not use his inherent talents and abilities, and follow orders. It is not that the genius does not lie there, but rather choices he has made have caused whatever he had in his soul memory banks to be severely repressed, with plenty of denial. The women he has been drawn to, are all from another lifetime, when he was the leader of a vast army, with a great taste for plenty of women. He served in the *Roman army* as a general, and became politically entangled. In this lifetime, with the shock of assuming a physical form he wished to regain that power at a subconscious level, and hence his choice of career.

Circumstances squashed his own interests, as he was ridiculed at school for something he said regarding science, and for exposing the teacher's inadequacies. In that moment of ridicule, and thinking he was stupid (rather than the teacher, who truly was), he thus decided not to venture in that direction. *As he allowed the system to take over his life, he gave his own freedom of choice as a soul away, and so needs to open himself once more to rediscover his immense abilities.* The woman he is currently with, was his wife in that lifetime as a general, and he never really liked her, because it was a forced alignment. In this lifetime the lesson was to love her unconditionally, and thus wholeheartedly as she is, and vice versa, thus they came together again.

The second woman was a concubine who he captured and forced to have sex, and she became his slave for his enjoyment. In this lifetime, the lesson is to set her free with love, and let her be herself.

In the third instance the same applies, in that this one did not wish to be conquered, and resisted him, so he fell very deeply in love with her. However, she was not going to let him do this, and used him to get secrets which she in turn delivered to her people, and later managed to escape. Thus, again there is a type of passion and attraction, but not really that deep, although there is a soul connection, and they are more or less of the same soul group."

———

SOUL GROUP: The Highest Serving Ones

"Yes, you chose both parents, wishing to incarnate in this milieu. In past lives you had a close bond with your father, and this time you also wished him to be your father. As he was involved with your mother at the time of conception, you hovered around them both. You also had connections with her, and had been sisters, but that turned sour when your father married both of you in *Israel. It was legal* as per community laws, if a woman was left widowed by a brother, the other brother had to marry, and give her children in his place. He was already married to your elder sister, and then had to marry you. Your older, very plain sister, was jealous, especially as you produced a male heir, and she only daughters. So the atmosphere was very competitive, with both of you as rivals trying to outdo each other, to curry favor with your shared husband.

In this lifetime, the father has again united with this soul (your mother) and you chose to be born to them. So, in this life, this strange rivalry for want of better word, was added into the mix. Not that your mother did not love or want you, it was just that from the day you were born, she always felt that you were your father's daughter, more so than hers. This karma needs to be just let go of, for in a sense you both have worked through it.

Due to this father/lover bond between you and your father, you always subconsciously sought that same bond with a lover or spouse, with this inner need to have someone there for you like a father/lover, and of course a husband cannot be that. With your first husband, you took on an old soul who had been your husband in past lives, all those marriages taking place only based on your dowries, and never from true love. Clearing that karma will return you to unconditional love for yourself. Release pain and anger from that marriage, unworthiness as well stemming from emotional abuse in some form, carried over from other lifetimes.

Due to the karmic bond, your soul was contracted to meet up with this soul again this time, but also, remember your soul is here to hold that Sisterhood of Rose's attunement – that of unconditional Love, so that in Being that unconditional Love you Raise the vibration of the planet – You literally teach the Art of Unconditional Love through loving unconditionally. *Just like the Rose can only be in a state of self- expansion, giving love with her whole being, exuding perfume – so it is with your soul.* It is in loving unconditionally – yourself and others, that the splendour and beauty of your soul reveals itself, in and through unconditional love. You also had karmic bonds with your second husband, your soul took this upon herself, because of the higher healing which has to come to all women on the planet, that healing of past abuse and slavery, to find pure unconditional love and forgiveness deep within oneself, and live it.

He was a Roman general, who conquered your people, a Germanic tribe on the border of what is now Hungary and Austria. Owing to your great beauty, he kept you as a sex slave, and forced you to entertain his guests as well. As you were the daughter of a nobleman, this made you a prize, and were taller than the Romans. He forced you to have abortions, and to do other kinds of hateful things. Indeed, you hated him with all your soul. In this lifetime that brings you back to unconditional love, to finally let go of the anger, hatred and pain, and everything, to return to the state of pure love. This is again what your soul undertook for its journey here, and in a sense, this is another huge lesson in love. *For it teaches you more than anything to love yourself unconditionally, and in this way, he taught you many lessons in love – for self, for your child, and self-respect.*

This is not about right or wrong – merely lessons in love your soul took upon itself, and he was but an instrument who agreed to come into your life and teach you all of this.

Because you truly desired to have a child at one stage, you attracted the most beautiful and intelligent being from one of the outer galaxies who wished to incarnate here; to teach unconditional love and acceptance, bringing the gift of *intuitive knowing* with him. He is a very highly evolved soul, and because of some medicine taken during pregnancy, he developed the inability to express the high intelligence of his soul.

Most autism is caused by general ignorance about the ill effects of the environment, medication and other stress factors. But that is not your concern. The concern here is that you truly bonded with this soul on many levels, even before he incarnated, and he was drawn to you because of the immense love, beauty and high calibre of your soul.

He communicates telepathically, and most importantly he is so highly evolved that human communication systems do not allow him to share his highest values and soul intelligence. There is nothing wrong with him – but rather that he is so intelligent that he does not know how to express this, and they in turn do not know how to respond. Instead of feeding him drugs or anything artificial, rather tune into his soul telepathically, and he will share with you what he already knows. These souls have immense genius to give, but are often viewed as second class citizens and not as *fully embodied Divine Cosmic Beings*, which in truth they are. Again, he teaches you unconditional love and acceptance, and to listen to your own heart and soul.

As for your husband – that was karmic debt, and in him leaving you, you have resolved your karmic link, and in that he gifted you with this beautiful and amazing soul. Both you and this soul have been given the freedom to explore greater love, for the greater good of Humanity – something which would not have happened had he stayed with you. Again, see the gift and appreciate, and the rest will happen exactly as it should.

The disease has come about because of an inability to be grateful for what life has offered you. In that sometimes there is that deep resentment concerning what you think others and life should offer you, and not understanding sometimes, that they offered you immense gifts in unconditionally loving yourself and others, and more than this, the gift of true Grace – the Grace that comes when one becomes grateful for the lessons in soul mastery. For each soul brings a specific gift and gifts of expanding the heart, and bringing in more love. It is when one closes the heart that disease starts coming – for inherently disease is the result of feeling separated from the Divine, and separated from Love – when in reality Love is never absent but always present in all and every form. It is just people sometimes do not understand or see this – *The Soul knows*.

The man you are referring to, was drawn to you because you both have this lesson to master – that of truly loving yourself, and most of all, not cutting love off, including the body, and every living cell.

As your soul is truly a *Sister of the Rose*, lessons always have to do with **love**, in all its forms and expressions, and with the heart chakra wide open, plus all the physical, emotional, mental, spiritual bodies, then you will understand what amazing lessons in love these all were. It is teaching you to go back to the core heart of love to discover that love never ever is absent – it is there in and around you all the time. Divine Love holds you in its deepest most precious Heart. How can you then not be loved? How can love not be inside you, around you, within you – **You are Love. You were created as the Rose of Love. You are Love.**

Here lies the deepest truth of your soul and being.

Instead of always looking for love outside yourself – look at how love is there *inside* of yourself, and has never not been there.

First of all **Love Thyself**.

That is the first Cosmic Law.

If you do not love yourself, how can you expect other people to love you?

If you do not think yourself worthy of love and acceptance, then how can you love and accept other people? For what is within will manifest without. Cosmic Law!

Love is at the core of your soul. Open yourself to love, and you will find that love is there inside of you, indeed you were created to Be Love, to Express Love and become Love- in-Action, Word, Being – with All that you Are!

In truth your soul is loved by the Divine, you are forever kept, indeed treasured, the most precious daughter of the Divine, the **Divine Rose in the Heart**. So the Divine cannot breathe without being reminded of you, and its great love for you!

If *Divine love* is so immense – then how can you not be love? How can you not be loved? You are Love.

You are *Rose Heart Love*.

All that you are and were created to be just love – Pure Love.

Therefore, when you realize this, and that all of this life is but a huge lesson in loving yourself unconditionally, and loving others unconditionally, then realize that you are in highest alignment with your own soul, when you are constantly in the highest state of Love. That is why your soul undertook such a hard lifetime – to hone the inner fountains of love, and expand this love to everyone she meets, like a rose expands her beauty and perfume on all she encounters."

SOUL GROUP: The Joyful Ones

"Soul name: The joyful one who brings loving energies into the planet to raise its frequencies, vibration and consciousness.

Her tonal chord is high D, and her soul colours are a shimmering, very soft and beautiful turquoise, with very light blue, very soft sea green, with emerald green, with soft magenta and light pink, and soft crystal clear and ochre with red, violet and orange streaks and touches of gold and silver.

She is one who *joyfully emits the rays of the sun, in that whoever her life touches will feel this radiance at some level.* This shining out is not conscious at the moment, for the soul has not quite awakened to her own inner power and beauty, and sometimes tends to dilly-dally somewhat in the true expression of her soul purpose, which is to uplift and inspire others to a state of joy. She has a gentle playfulness, delighting in life, with a profound effect on others – for life is not meant to be serious and mundane, rather a dance of delight and exuberant joy. Life in its highest expression of truth, happiness and joy, which come from the depths of the heart and soul.

This whole concept of picking up others, and wanting to heal or change them stems from a previous life as a nun in a reformatory. Here all the misfits, the insane and the imbalanced were administered to by nuns with loving care, though at times they had to resort to more drastic measures like straitjackets. It was during one of these encounters that you fell in love with a patient, a young and beautiful man with an angelic appearance, but severe mental disorders. He took advantage of your infatuation to use his powers to manipulate you, which got you in trouble with the Mother Superior who tried her utmost to warn you against getting involved in this way with a patient. However, you ignored all warnings, and one day, when you freed him from whatever was binding him, he strangled you to death."

SOUL GROUP: The Golden Ones

"Your husband in this lifetime is the man who bought you to raise you as his daughter, with a fatherly love for you. So this might sometimes feel more like a father-daughter match, or a brother and sister type of union, without the fireworks. This does not negate your love, merely understand the underlying soul bond and patterns from other lifetimes, for in later lifetimes you often returned as husband and wife, or brother and sister or in some or other family relationships.

So, then those born to you, chose to be reborn with you as a mother. However, we cannot go into their soul records here without their permission, suffice to say that they chose you as mother, because you were their mother before and because they died with you in that lifetime. So, there is a karmic link there."

SOUL GROUP: The Joyful Ones

"Now interestingly, concerning the children in more than one lifetime, there was a bitter war between you both. In one lifetime you were a noble woman, married to him by force by the King of France, and you considered him to be way below your station in life. He was a knighted soldier, given your lands and castles by the King as a reward. You hated the sight of him, and then had to bear his children. So you turned them against him, until he was at war with his own sons. So, in this lifetime all of this is playing out again, and you need to finally forgive yourself, forgive him and then, in all due respect, let go, including the issue of rights in all of this. For in truth children belong to both parents, and naturally love both. Understand that there are deep wounds reflected in this lifetime, which need to be healed, once and for all.

Now, this is not to make you ashamed or guilty. Merely to define the underlying playing field. You agreed to meet up in this lifetime and bring the children into life again, so that you could finally break the patterns, and return to the highest states of love. *Now forgiveness means more than just that, it means that I truly thank you for all that you are, even those parts I do not like, and then realize that love and hate are but two sides of the same coin.* The shadow serves as much as the light. There is no right nor wrong, merely forgiveness which needs to come in, and with it a heart wide open to love. Unconditional love. Love which in truth sees only love, and thanks the other for the perfection of Love.

Often, we are too caught up in obsessively playing roles during a single lifetime, and in truth we do not know what we doing! When we finally wake up to the highest soul truth, we can forgive ourselves, let go of all shame and guilt, and then truly find that love is there, present. It was never absent. If one cannot even love oneself wholeheartedly, then how can one truly love another? And then if you look closely, you will see that the one who you have hated, was loved by others, and even by yourself at times, and that everything was not only negative. He has many lovable and endearing qualities and traits about him, for you would not have married him in the first place, if you had not seen these within him, and he within you. Indeed, you created children together! So, then, is he not equally shadow and light, as much as you are, and is he not as worthy of love as you are?

In not giving up in this lifetime, he is serving all of you. It means that he finally wants to make good what went wrong in the other lifetimes. **He**

is reminding you that there is love, and the option of love everywhere. He is therefore bringing the message that you agreed on before incarnating, that you would finally let go of all the past life woundedness, and forgive each other, allowing the infinite Divine Grace and Love to fill you – unconditional love, where you can both finally embrace each other, and see only love. Nothing else but love, in its purest form. Not lust. Love. Not infatuation. Love. Not: "You did that, and you did this". No! Just love. Without condemnation. Without finger pointing. Without anything. Just Love. There lies your greatest test in mastery in this lifetime.

For the more unforgiveness there is, the less joy there is. The more emotional pain lugged around like a huge iron ball, the more one is tied to that ball, which sucks your very life breath. Now look at your soul and your Soul Name:

Soul Name: *She expresses the wonder, the joy, the delight and the joyful expression of life spurting forth, when it is in Balance and harmony with all of Creation and in essence as this is held within the Divine. The Soul Group Name: The Joyful Ones – You are meant to express Joy!*

You are meant to delight, to find the wonder and the awe, in all and everything and everyone, and then to express this, with joy bursting like a fountain of life, from deep within your soul, and spilling over in all that you are, all that you do, and all that you radiate out to the world during an incarnation."

SOUL GROUP: The Insightful Diagnostic Ones

"This soul is an Indigo soul who volunteered to incarnate here after World War II, to bring in the massive shifts in consciousness needed at this time. Therefore, she will always feel a bit like an alien on Earth. She has had two incarnations previously – one in Bulgaria and one in Poland, when she was the sister of her mother, could well have been the half-sister, or rather born out of wedlock, for in this case she was not part of the mother's family but rather like an outsider, and treated as such, mainly because she was conceived in the First World War with a soldier, who remained nameless.

So, in that lifetime she always had a deep longing to belong, and her mother never wanted her. The grandparents more or less brought her up, forcing her to work in the farm kitchen, barely educated. However, she was hardworking, with a hunger for knowledge, so the teacher forced her family to allow her to go to school, and he paid. She stood out as a brilliant student, and aroused the jealousy of her half-sisters. This was heightened by the fact the man her sister (mother in this life) wanted to marry, or had her eye on, rather fell in love with her, and they married clandestinely. The sister was so upset, that when war broke out and the men went off to fight, she made her life a misery. She shut the door in her face during a fierce snowstorm, and she died in the snow of overexposure, pregnant with her first child.

Now, because of the traumatic death, this soul asked if she could reincarnate rather quickly to heal the wounds with her mother (sister). So, she was born to them. However, the scars of war stuck with her sister/mother – bitterness and anger, for she had been raped repeatedly by Russian soldiers, and could never open up to her husband sexually. There is a closed heart with walls and fortresses around it, and before birth, your planned parents' bickering was already programmed into you, and from the minute you were born, you were a constant reminder to your mother of the half-sister she had closed the doors on, with the consequent constant blame and shame felt on discovering your pregnant body in the snow. She had not known you were pregnant, as you had never shared that information with her. She has plenty of remorse, and additionally your soul as a volunteer soul, is super sensitive.

As a child you often saw things no adult could, and tuned into people's thoughts, which you innocently shared as soon as you could talk. This perplexed and worried your parents, so you soon learnt to shut up. Now you must remember that your parents and grandparents had been through those terrible wars, so often had to shut themselves down, just to survive. *There is so much ancestral karma to clear, with the emotional trauma of war.* This is steeped deeply into Mother Earth, where the battles took place, where there was human trauma, not only in Poland, but all Europe. *In time this will be cleared and released, but remember that the ancestral heritage is programmed into every single living cell in your body, and cell memory banks. Thus one needs to clear the* ancestral karma, *so that they can be healed and cells reprogrammed.*

You mainly chose to come to Africa, because of your soul connections to *Elysium* the first continent, bringing in those animals, and because of that lifetime in Middle Africa. Therein lies your soul's greatest calling, for it wishes to bridge the communication gap between human beings and animals, especially primates, as your soul is a guardian and keeper of them, and thus feels that innate responsibility. More than this it is unconditional love.

We are not allowed to read the records of your mother without her permission, suffice to say that the rape she endured closed off most of her deepest memory banks, which in truth is something she has to work through in soul lessons, which you cannot do anything about, just open your heart and soul, forgive and let go. Also forgive her for the way she treated you, when you died. So, there is the shadow which needs to be let go of. Knowing that in this lifetime it served you, in that you sought independence, and more of the greater whole, than if you had not had the childhood you had. It served you enormously – for in truth you learnt a lot about yourself in the deepest sense, and therefore this is expressed in that you often find that deep and unconditional love in animals, that is lacking in people. The lesson to master is unconditional love, first for yourself, totally and completely, then you can love another person unconditionally.

The answers you seek are deep inside of yourself. So often others mirror something deep inside of you, which you have not owned or loved. Instead of asking why some people react the way they do, ask what they are mirroring back to you, that you have not owned. Is it that you do not love yourself, or blame yourself, or just feel that you are unlovable? See, here lies the crux of what needs to be addressed, and all paths lead **within** you, for the shadow is always present, within all souls, as is the light. One needs both sides in balance, otherwise there is chaos within. To deny any part of the shadow or light, is to deny what is created within you, for otherwise the scales of balance, will tilt either up or down, until finally balance point is reached."

SOUL GROUP: The Glorious Ones

"This soul is not new to Planet Earth. She has had quite a few incarnations here, and this lifetime is essentially about finally working through old negative karmic patterns she created with other souls through all those lifetimes. They are all contracted to meet up with her again this lifetime, and some already have, especially the men she was karmically obliged to meet with, and work through negative karma.

In addition, there will be others who will appear, both men and women, as she took upon herself in her soul contract, to work through as much of the negative karma as she could, in this lifetime, to finally free up her soul, to go and work elsewhere in the Cosmos. It has been like a part of her own soul was tied down to the planet, because of past lives, tugging her back here, when she indeed wished to work elsewhere.

Interestingly only a fraction, one part of the soul incarnated at first, but in the last year or so, another part has integrated with the other, as the soul was struggling to get on track with her soul contract. So, you were given extra help, in order to finally wake up, and then work through what you have come to do and be."

———

CHAPTER 5

Androgyny

Androgyny is the combination of masculine and feminine characteristics into an ambiguous or androgynous form. Androgyny may be expressed with regard to biological sex, gender identity, gender expression or sexual identity.

These first extracts show how originally, we were all androgynous, and explain what occurred when this was altered. We have included a number of readings to shed more light on a very common thread running through the experiences of those who have incarnated on Earth in these times. Those souls who seek to be free of the sense that something or someone is missing, or is needed to fulfil or complete their lives.

Extracts from Soul Readings

SOUL GROUP: The Divine Blueprint Imprinting Ones

"This soul works with the **imprints** of the Divine Blueprint, which are the *sacred geometrical soul patterns*. Now soul is pure energy, often equated to Fire, or flames. Yet, each soul also has a Divine sacred geometrical pattern or blueprint, which is in essence what the Soul Name looks like energetically. It is this pattern which is read cosmically. Sacred geometry is indeed the *Sacred Divine Language* or writing in energetic form.

Your Soul Group works mainly within the first *12 Master Galaxies* with Master Imprints of each Soul Group and souls therein, and *Soul Group Clusters*, working especially with the Creations within the original 12. Thus, you work with the Divine Blueprints of the souls of animals, and mammals such as dolphins and whales. Kindred souls speak to you, for they hold the imprint of the original *Garden of Eden*, which was Elysium, in custody for humankind. They also hold the imprints of all subsequent civilizations, as their Guardians and Keepers.

Now, your soul in its highest soul form, is *Androgynous*, male and female in one form. The Divine, within the 12 Master Galaxies, created both forms, as this was the *First Creation*, and experimental in the sense that the 12 Master Galaxies are the *seed carriers*. So, all subsequent creations, other galaxies, and star systems and so forth, which do not belong to the original 12, all use the same encoding, and Divine Blueprints. Consequently, all Creation reflects what was first created in the 12 Master Galaxies.

This is particularly true with cells, as every cell in whatever life form it expresses, has the Divine Blueprints within itself, the original Creation imprinted upon them, and are still patterned based on this.

Now, the *androgynous* life forms procreate in a different way, in that the soul is **both** male and female, not just charged as predominantly male or female. You will often feel that you are **both**, in the sense that your soul is highly evolved and older, having greater maturity. Your soul belongs to *The Ancient Ones* and has an immensely strong connection to, and many incarnations in, the Inner Earth, *Agartha*.

In your home galaxy you are *androgynous,* so sometimes have great difficulty adjusting to a physical form which is just one gender. You are more balanced naturally at soul level, between yin and yang, masculine and feminine, not predominantly female or male. You are perhaps 60% more female in this life. The more you come into balance and harmony, the greater will be that balance between the masculine and feminine within yourself, and the less you will need anyone to complement or fill you up, because balance is an essential equilibrium point, with wholeness from within."

SOUL GROUP: The Codified Ones

"As for a *Twin Flame* – you are in your true form *androgynous* and therefore male and female. It therefore is simply a matter of what you prefer to be, while on this planet. In this regard, you had a short incarnation in which, with his agreement, you took over the body of a married man, but then found it difficult to handle such a situation, as you assumed your true form, within this other man's body. This led to huge disagreements and puzzlement for the woman concerned, as she did not understand what had happened to her husband! She was extremely beautiful and you were very attracted to her sexually, but had no clue what to do with all of this. This resulted in something which resembled a comedy at times, and created more confusion and pain in that lifetime, until you realized what was going on, so just vacated the body to return home again, leaving quite some chaos in your wake. She will appear again this lifetime, if she has not already done so, as a little older, and married to the original man.

When you meet her, it will feel rather awkward and strange, for she will recognize you at some level, and will feel very interested and attracted, while on another level still finding these qualities in her husband as well. So, there is some karmic residue to work through with her. It might lead to a romantic encounter and definitely a rather strange attraction, but do remember that these are karmic links you now have to rectify in some way, and will not be permanent at all."

SOUL GROUP: The Dream Encoded Ones

"You then incarnated again in *Lemuria (Mu)* and again worked with *creative dreaming in an androgynous body*. You were very happy, and did not use sexual energy, for in truth you could choose to procreate by dreaming it, and the baby would manifest and grow in an incubation tube, as one did not give birth in the way humans do now. Thus, you communicated with this growing baby, even before dreaming it, loved it into life, and into the stage where the shell of the tube (like an egg) broke open and the child peacefully emerged into new life, in a totally painless and trauma-free manner, while being held in immense love.

In that lifetime however, Atlantis arose where **two** sexes, Male and Female, existed. They wanted to control everyone through their minds, and to enslave the Lemurians, who were more advanced than them, in the 5th dimension. A *Black Magi* came to Lemuria to spread the word that God had made a mistake by giving them an androgynous body, because they were missing out on sex. (This was of course totally untrue, for the angels and archangels and Elohim all have *androgynous* forms, and are perfectly created that way). Consequently, the Lemurians became fascinated by the idea that a man and woman could have sex to produce offspring, and the Atlanteans, with their propaganda machine, of course circulated the idea that the sexual act was like being in heaven, reaching the ultimate state of bliss. So, they made an agreement with the Lemurians (who now felt excluded) to split themselves, in a water tank. You agreed to this, and then were forcefully split into two.

We now are going to proceed with the **Female** part of the *androgynous body*. As a female, now experiencing sex, was in fact something you were not emotionally prepared for, because the intense absence of the other part of yourself, caused huge pain. It was like half of you had left! And indeed, that was the case. Even having sex did not alleviate this agony! You could unite sexually for **one** moment but the rest of the time, the other half had his own free will and choice, and he now chose to engage with other females, not only Split Lemurians like you, but also with Atlantean women. He wanted to experiment with his new penis, so was not very interested in you! This induced the intense hurt of separation, and a deep feeling of loss.

Your other half, wanting to alleviate his own pain, tried to create union with other women, and you, on the other end, felt like he had betrayed and abandoned you at a deep soul level. In that lifetime, the Atlanteans totally destroyed the Lemurians in this way, and then enslaved them. You were sexually abused by Atlantean men, who wanted to enslave you, to use your creative powers for their own ends. This was so much against your own highest soul calling and purpose, that you were broken in spirit, and died of sheer pain and heartache.

In other lifetimes the two of you incarnated as halves together (as in this lifetime) and could never get back together again. In Atlantis, by engaging sexually with others, you had already created negative karmic patterns with these souls (in whatever form this took). So, you frequently met up with each other, and either married, or were lovers at some stage, but then, the old stories repeated themselves. It was like you wanted the union, but somehow the split would happen all over again.

In truth the union itself is a **search for wholeness**, namely the androgyny which existed before in Lemuria (and in other lifetimes cosmically for the soul). Now the negative karma with other souls (either through marriages or affairs) had to be worked through. Thus, when you finally got together, the old feelings of pain, of being lost and abandoned, suddenly re-surfaced, along with bewilderment. He especially, is resisting that **Unity** in some way, because it makes him feel so **at-one** with you that he fears he is losing himself in you. To some degree being with him, elicits a similar reaction in you, but it is the fear of **loss**. At the deepest level you want to cling to him, so that he does not split off and run away again.

Your first priority in this lifetime is to review the *Lemurian Woundedness*, forgive yourself for these events, and to let go of the old shame, guilt and self-hate you felt for having agreed to the split (knowing full well it violated Divine Laws). You then also need to forgive yourself (and him) and ask for forgiveness from the Divine (which has already been granted – you just have to consciously **feel** it.)

Then work on the intense feeling of separation, once the split had occurred, the betrayal and abandonment you felt when he desired other women to experiment with sexually. There was so much anger there, helplessness, and fear and guilt, especially when the three Atlantean men captured and enslaved you for their sexual needs. When this happened, you slipped into a total dream-state, hovering over your body as a means of escaping the pain and humiliation. You can also clear your sexual area of all negative hooks, cords and attachments. In addition, you need to release all old marriage vows, slavery contracts, and experiences in which you were used in a ritualistic type of sex by a certain man (whom you have not met in this lifetime for he has not incarnated). However, you can still ask for release, exonerating yourself and him for this, and others. Go deeply into the wound, find release from the emotional pain which has gathered over many lifetimes. In each lifetime, it was like you found a deep togetherness, only to then to split again and again, as if you could neither be together nor apart. So, in fact he is like your other half, the Twin, in an androgynous context.

Remember that he has free will and choice. We may not read his soul records without his permission, but suffice to say, he needs healing too, for he feels immense pain, but won't admit it. Indeed, it bewilders him. His greatest fear is to lose himself in you, but in fact it is with you that the deepest unity has come, which he cannot find anywhere else. Then fear sets in, and causes separation. Therefore, first of all you need to heal yourself, by embracing both the feminine and masculine essence within your soul – your own androgynous being which in truth you also are at soul level. Then heal the inner wounds by releasing the past trauma, as stated.

The more you do this, the lighter, brighter and more complete you will become, your dream work will emerge, with your gifts re-surfacing. Then, just allow the other half of you the freedom to find himself at deep soul level. In reality, he has never stopped loving you, he is just scared of the depth of his feelings, and the possibility of losing you again. Then examine where you may be reflecting the same emotions, for example the woundedness from Lemuria. Open your heart and soul and just send him love, unconditional love without wanting to pull him back forcefully, nor wanting to manipulate or nurse him. Giving him the freedom to heal and to find himself in his own time, is the greatest love you can give him in the here and now. Do the same for yourself. If he chooses to, and works through this all, he will come back in his own time, and in his own way. Understand, that you are free to love any other soul along the way, should you wish to. However, deep down you will always feel that search for the other half of you."

SOUL GROUP: The Wisdom, Love Light Gatherers

"*Melchior* is highly evolved and houses androgynous beings, male and female in one single body and form. Thus, your Twin Flame is not apart, but within you – even though a tiny fraction of your soul is incarnate, the rest of androgynous you is still working and living in Melchior, and elsewhere in the Cosmos. In truth there is nothing missing, for androgyny is very much present in this human body you have taken on. Humans have a rather distorted view of sexual union at times, since it is not necessary to have your twin incarnated to find the ultimate union. In your case, your other soul parts are all happily engaged in life elsewhere, in your home galaxy in androgynous forms, with in fact, no need or desire to incarnate here.

So, the fraction that is here has assumed a female body, which does not mean that you need to necessarily mate with anyone. Initially you have to facilitate the marriage between the feminine and masculine within yourself, before this can manifest as a relationship. In your case this is particularly relevant, because your soul is inherently androgynous. Now, many are mightily confused by this, thinking you should prefer a same sex union. Not so. It simply means that you seek wholeness within yourself. Like the romanticized version of wanting to be completed by a male counterpart, *the one and only!* In fact, you can love any man you choose to love and mate with because you love him and for no other reason – in your case the Twin has not incarnated, because, as an androgynous being he is already within you."

———

SOUL GROUP: The Divine Blueprint Imprinting Ones

"There is something fundamental from the time when you were newly conceived which you will have to address. Interestingly you chose your parents, in the sense that you felt they could provide a suitable platform for you to incarnate here. The soul link to your father is closer though, because his soul has incarnated with you before, as your twin brother. So, your soul wished to have this soul as father in this lifetime. Now, your mother, remarkably at the time of your conception, was not quite ready, in other words it came as a bit of shock when she fell pregnant. She did want you, but she was more concerned about the impact on her lifestyle etc.

Everything that occurred between your parents at that time, is already programmed into you even **before** birth, so there is much that needs to be released. Your mother often had mood swings during pregnancy which your father tolerated, but he also withdrew into himself, instead of seeking help. So, as a result, you were born with the innate idea that he wanted you, but that she on some level, did not. You felt this even more as you grew up, so sought his company more than hers, feeling more accepted, and in a sense that you could be more yourself in male company rather than in a feminine environment. (This has to do mainly with your own androgynous soul creation, in which you are **both** genders).

You had incarnated before in Lemuria and were one of the few souls out of a handful of Lemurians wise enough not to be split, which in the end proved to be their salvation. So that lifetime was fundamentally a happy one, until the Atlanteans convinced the Lemurians that there was something wrong with the way God had created them, namely their inability to have sex. This of course was a lie, but so many bought into that, only to experience the complete trauma and pain of losing their other half – something most souls never recovered from. You were now persecuted by the Atlanteans, so with others of your ilk, you withdrew deep into the

Andes Mountains in Peru. You later connected with those living in the inner world **Agartha**, and were allowed to collaborate with them, and move into the Inner Earth to live there.

In two other lifetimes, you chose to incarnate in a male form, but found this too harsh. You were forced into war, and interestingly we find you as one of the knights inspired by *Joan of Arc* and her visions, wielding the sword alongside her. You had an unprecedented deep love and soul friendship with her, steeped in inner knowing – recognizing something profound within each other, which resonated. When severely injured, she was there, helping you make your peaceful transition.

So, in this lifetime you are again in a female body, but in a higher sense Humanity is moving into a more androgynous form anyway, as the wounds of Lemuria are being healed. It is also important to understand that there are no real divisions between male and female, and no gender roles.

You have adopted some of the more masculine traits through smoking etc. but it is **programming**. You can reprogram yourself, and learn to love yourself, just the way you are. You were never meant to fit into a group. You were meant to stand out in a crowd and to know that the highest degree of mastery is to be able to walk one's path alone if need be. For in truth, we do not need the applause of others, but rather inner equilibrium balance and harmony – authenticity, truth and the courage to stay true to oneself, above all, and to the Divine."

———

SOUL GROUP: The Illumined Ones

"Now you were androgynous in your Arcturian body, for in the Cosmos this is one of the possible embodiments, and there are many space races that do have this form of life expression. Note this, for often your confusion comes from being **both**, and not just one at times, although you have in other lifetimes preferred to come in as a female embodiment. That lifetime was very happily spent alone, as you did not need to marry nor be in partnership, and could procreate on your own, indeed you had two children, created in tubes, whose outer encasements would open at birth. The child was fully conscious when born, having had neither birthing pains nor shock, therefore wholly and fully aware and already conscious."

———

SOUL GROUP: The Divine Expressive Ones

"You never married, for your people were *androgynous* and never paired up like we do. This is also a reason why you had your own colony, which later developed into Mu, (after the Lion Kingdom blew up), when a remnant of your people fled to the Pacific region to start anew there, (the same old factions emerging, as in the *Wars of the Heavens*).

We thus find you in *Mu* and then later Lemuria, where you continued this work, with a tuning water tank. The Lemurians had a great love for expanses of water, and their homes were often built on it. Their technology enabled them to be amphibious, and thus they interacted with the Mer people, living on land and in the oceans, with craft designed to operate on either.

This water tank was tuned into the original galaxy frequencies, so you often fine-tuned those suffering from depression, and those with central nervous systems out of sync, for water fine-tunes the nadis and meridians of the body. When certain sound frequencies were combined with the water frequency, the much higher vibrational *Light body of the Lemurians* could be fine-tuned when they submerged themselves in these tanks and you also did a type of deprogramming.

However, during that time, Atlantis had risen, and was in the 5th dimensional state, not the 7th like Lemuria, and they still coveted Lemurian technology and were determined to discover how to enslave them. They came up with the idea of brain washing by making them believe that they were missing out on the mating game – on sexual intercourse. They then sent a High Priest to divide their bodies, which some Lemurians did voluntarily, but most like you, were forced.

You never recovered from the shock of being cleaved in half by their monstrous machines – they also used water tanks. Now living in two bodies, you discovered that sexual union was not as heavenly as promised by the Atlanteans. It brought severe displacement, and the deep grief of missing the other half, who often began mating with the Atlanteans and the "halves" of other Lemurians. Many committed suicide and you were one of them. In other lifetimes you returned to try and heal from this trauma and to search for your other half – literally.

Your soul works best where she can gather together other souls for a much higher purpose, like bringing them together in the highest service to the Divine. So, you shone in that in that lifetime – you too were wounded, but it is the wounded healer who heals with insight and understanding, for those they are trying to help."

SOUL GROUP: The Shining Ones

"It was however towards the end of that lifetime that the Atlanteans, who were 5th dimensional with separate physical masculine and feminine forms, managed to convince the Lemurians that they had lost out on sex. Some actually believed such nonsense, and allowed the Atlantean High Priest, who spread such lies, to split them in half. This caused so much trauma and pain, and as the *Atlanteans now had found the Achilles heel of the Lemurians*, they enforced this, and then enslaved them. You were compelled to have the split, as they captured you, and when you discovered that sex was not as wonderful as they had led you to believe, you experienced an intense separation from your true other half. Indeed, you could never find each other sexually and in the end, he committed suicide, unable to bear the pain. In other lifetimes you continued the search for your other half, often being married off to other men, due to political or property reasons, and not because of love.

SOUL GROUP: The Winged Ones

"Soul name: She who flies in the realms of Loving Hope, Peace and Inspiration and is this expression to the depths of her Being and Soul.

This soul from Orion engaged with this planet in the Second Civilization in the Sahara, in immensely beautiful tropical lands, the land of milk and honey. Those from Orion helped the Lyrans, the Lion people to build their beautiful and reflective abodes – although the Orions were ethereal, with very high energy frequency bodies of pure light, and not the denser physical forms found on the 7th dimension. She used her ability to teleport herself in her ethereal form to work here, not incarnating as such, but acting in an advisory and creative capacity. Souls from Orion are *androgynous*, i.e., not living in two separate bodies, but in one body housing male and female as a single form.

In Orion they live in the even higher 9th dimensional state, not in dense physical forms but rather more ethereal, with the ability to project themselves into any form, whether animal or fairy, or whatever takes their fancy, when they choose to make themselves visible to those in lower dimensions. It is therefore imperative that this soul understands this, for she is unlike other souls, as her soul is essentially *androgynous* with both male and female aspects, in one single energetic form. Thus, all of the 12 flames within this soul are both male and female, not just the same gender.

It may be charged as more feminine or more masculine, if imbalanced, but this indicates an imbalance between the two sides, since in the *androgynous* form both are equal. Thus, in the androgynous form, one does not have a *Twin Flame*, although people with their very limited understanding try to insist this is the case. Rather they are in a state of completion in themselves, experiencing **wholeness** with perfect balance in that true form. So, if this soul feels that she is with a *Twin Flame*, this cannot be true. She can certainly be with one of her own Soul Group, but not with another part of her own soul, for she is androgynous in the way God created her, and cannot be other than this.

To avoid confusion, it is best to understand that *Orion* had very different life and lifeforms from Earth, with a remarkable ability to shift their light bodies into any form they wished to assume. The old human remembrance of shape-shifting comes from these beings presenting themselves in any desired form. *Trying to fit your soul into the primitive understanding of the earthly ones is short-selling yourself, because you have not truly reconnected with your soul and its very essence. So do not add unnecessary trauma and pain, by trying to be emulate an earthly being, or to fit into earthly norms, when you are so much more than this!*

So, the question here then should not be what is happening between me and my *Twin Flame*, but rather, what is happening between me and this soul who I thought was my *Twin Flame?* As I understand now, this is not the case, but is an illusion spun by assuming an earthly body for a while.

Take a moment to reflect and understand this clearly. You are NOT the physical form which you have adopted on Planet Earth. You are an ethereal soul, a winged being, who can take on any form you wish, for that is uniquely how you and your Soul Group were created! So why lament about what is happening within the very restrained human concepts, primitive human understanding, and very limited bodily forms.

Get crystal clear about this, and then the suffering which you are bringing onto yourself will cease to be!

You took on this dense bodily form temporarily on Earth. In other words, you adopted this body for a while, but were not born into it. You did a swap. You are a *walk-in,* who took over a child's body, with the full agreement of the departing soul. You wanted to assist Earth through the mass changes, and therefore before this child was even born, you had an agreement that it would go through the birthing process, then at a certain age swap with you. That is one reason why you always felt a little strange in your human form, and when you reached the age when sexual energy was stirring, for the first time ever you could engage in sexual relationships in a way you never could in an androgynous form. This is one of the reasons you sometimes have great difficulty in this area. On one hand, there is the adrenalin junkie part of you, who wants more of this novelty, and on the other, you shape shifting and projecting onto your partner, what you know is possible in an androgynous form.

When you undertook this journey onto Planet Earth, you were well aware of the pitfalls of such a life, for many winged ones got stuck in that dense human body, not comprehending sexual energy, or harnessing it correctly. So, understand the challenge here. *You are not a sexual being,* but you are suddenly experimenting with sexual energy, and do not quite know how to handle it. You use your higher power subconsciously to project the wholeness that you know full well exists in your androgynous form, onto the other person, which scares them away, freaks them out, for that is not what they are feeling **inside** of themselves!

So, the soul you are engaging with, is an old soul from the days of **Lemuria** where they were androgynous, but split into separate sex bodies. This soul deep inside knows this, and is searching for its other half, so to speak. However, you are not that other half – someone else is! So again, this is a case of projection.

In this relationship both of you have the ability to shape-shift, so you tend to shape-shift into what you believe the other might wish to have! With sexual energy this leads to even more confusion, for neither know how to handle this. You may try to amplify it, but as sexual energy is essentially the element of fire, this singes and burns you both. The heat becomes too intense and one or the other wants to run away, or withdraw because of this imbalance and disharmony with the other, especially on a soul dimensional and frequency level, for your partner is of a much lower vibration.

This does not mean that you cannot love each other – it is just that you have to truly examine your own beliefs about love, and what it is you seek in the other? Are you infatuated with sexual energy, or are you infatuated with the idea of *Twin Flames,* whether it is a reality or not? Is it that you truly do love the other, but you are not on the same wavelength and dimension here?

So, then it's important to realize that to your own soul, such things are totally foreign, and you need to give yourself the loving attention that you need, so that you can get clarity and understand who and what your soul is, otherwise you will put expectations onto yourself and another, which are unhealthy, and will distort the energies between you.

So, as with all things, where there is a will, there is a way.

First of all, understand your own ability to be androgynous. You are both male and female. You are **balanced** at a soul level. Nothing is missing. You are whole and complete in yourself that is the way you were created. You cannot be other than what your soul is. All else is illusion, including the human bodily form you are assuming for a while in order to understand what life is like here, and to do the work you came in to do, which is mainly to create a new form of life.

In addition, you have these amazing shape-shifting abilities, whether you are conscious of them or not, you still have them. So there is no effort involved, because your soul is so accustomed to doing this, it is like brushing your teeth. However, when another partner is involved who cannot do this to the level you can, it becomes overwhelming. So be aware of this, and rather use these abilities in a positive and uplifting way to assist Humanity at large, and not to increase the sexual energy potency between you, which you are doing unconsciously. This is called manipulation.

Then, go deep into your heart and soul and then ask yourself: "what is it that I would like to leave as a lasting legacy to Humankind, while I am here in this body and in this form?" Your soul knows the answer, for that is why you walked into life here. It is here on a mission. It is not about relationships at all, but rather your mission.

So sexual energy here is a by product, a novelty you have discovered, and something that is absent in the androgynous form.

As with all energy, you can play with it, have lots of fun, but it can also be used to uplift and inspire for the greater good, rather than for self-gratification, self-service and for manipulation. So, it is with all energy. In your own true home body in Orion, you know all about this. Indeed, you are a master at manipulating energy and changing its form into something else. That is how you co-create and shape-shift. This comes easily to you.

However, in human relationships, there needs to be a true searching inside for the higher meaning of love. Sometimes you might feel like you do not belong here, or feel rather bewildered by life, and that if you have someone else walking with you, then this provides companionship. Say friendship if you like – whatever. So first of all, define your own inner voice, and what it is trying to tell you.

Neediness in any form, creates more neediness, for it means that something deep inside of you feels it is not whole or complete, and not quite "kosher." This is illusion. It is **Maya**, for if your soul is androgynous and complete in itself, how can you be incomplete, not whole, and how can something be missing? What is missing is your own spiritual understanding and deeper insight into the greater Cosmic totality, and that you have forgotten how to tune into your own higher soul self, who has all the answers. You have forgotten how to have a love affair with yourself, and you have forgotten how to love yourself completely, and how it feels to be so utterly whole, that even sexual energy is completed within oneself. For in *androgynous* beings that sexual energy is as much present as in two different bodies, it is just in another form, and it is completely mastered!

Thus, when you find this completion within, and total self-love, it will raise your vibration and frequency to the point that suddenly the veils of illusion will disappear, as you remember the truth of who and what you are – an ascended master having a short time spell on Earth with a specific task to fulfil. Your dilly dallying in relationships is not serving you or the greater whole, as it is obscuring your focus and energy from your true mission. You are then literally pulling yourself down into earthly bodies, into the quagmire where you do not really belong, and which does not suit the higher vibration of your soul. Before you know it, you will be stuck like those of your ilk, who were stuck on this planet so long ago. Learn from their mistakes and don't make this one of your own.

At this crucial time in Human and Earth history it is a matter of all hands on deck, and your soul is here on a higher mission, and not for the lower self, which sometimes tends to pull souls in all directions, instead of the highest.

But you have free will and choice – with consequences. That again, does not mean that you cannot love and be loved! Of course you can, but then keep balance and remember who and what you are. Essentially there is a huge wake up call for your soul to finally understand why it is here, and what it has come to do. When you have completed that task, you will merely shed this body and return to your androgynous form in Orion! So wake up!"

SOUL GROUP: The Pearlescent Wisdom keepers

"This soul is from Orion, and came in with the Lemurian Civilization, so was naturally androgynous, accordingly there was no need to seek a partner or worry about life partners, love or sexuality for this all was within. Therefore, a state of unity and harmony exists, and one is at peace with everything. This soul chose to incarnate in the latter days of Lemuria, when she came in as a Wisdom Keeper in the capacity of a healer soul. It was understood that counselling entailed wisdom and higher seeing, in that one not only helped the soul to see truth, but acted as a healing conduit for the loving energy of the Divine. Through touch and by stroking away holes in others' auras, you were able to heal them.

So, in the beginning you were very happy on Planet Earth in an androgynous body. Then Atlantis rose, with separate bodies for male and female. Many Lemurians felt cheated, when a priest discovered a way to split them into male and female, which was a death knell, for this division resulted in intense emotional pain and a deep sense of separateness, causing upheavals and depression.

Originally you were very opposed to this change, and many who had been split came to you for healing, but you needed both parts to be effective, so you vowed you would never allow this to happen to you. Yet one day, a very handsome and comely man who had been divided walked in, and you could not heal him for his other half was indeed missing. He intrigued you by speaking eloquently about the advantages of being just one sex, and how you miss out on the sexual energy and sex when in an androgynous body, and how much he thought you would benefit by being able to experience the alternative.

So, the seed of doubt was planted, and you found yourself obsessed with the idea of him, so you decided to go to the temples for the split, which was subsequently carried out, so we are now concentrating on your **female** part, and less on the male part – which will come later.

Afterwards, you returned to the temples as a woman, and had sex for the first time with your male half. However, although the two of you now worked together at the temples, things felt discordant. Sexual energies proved to be quite unlike anything you had imagined them to be, some good and some downright uncomfortable, so this factor created tension in your relationship. Your twin then decided he was not going to stick around, waiting for you to actually enjoy sex, because when you experienced sex initially, you did not enjoy having a male member thrust into your body, and rebelled. That caused a huge rift between you, so he went off to have sex with other women, not only in Lemuria, but also in Atlantis.

Now you had been left behind, and remembered the man who started all of this. You were now in pain, feeling not only abandoned by your Twin Flame, but totally separated from the other half of you, and from God too.

The man in question showed up again, saw you were now a woman, and began a love affair, but once again a part of you just refused to open up sexually. In actual fact it was a gnawing feeling of guilt for having allowed this to happen in the first place, disobeying all cosmic laws, as your soul was also now divided. So this guilt prevented you from fully enjoying sex, and you felt completely out of sorts.

The affair did not last long, for he was bored to tears and moved on, never to be seen again. Meantime your life at the temples disintegrated, for you could neither heal nor serve, as you had done when in your androgynous body. By that time Lemuria was so divided – most Lemurians were spilt, the continent was in the process of disintegrating, and being swallowed up by tidal waves.

Your twin returned out of the blue – he had enjoyed as many women as he desired, but had found he was still missing his other half. You reconciled, but only for a short while, for you had drifted apart, and common ground was hard to find, then you both died in a massive tidal wave. In this lifetime you have been primarily drawn to karmic links and ties formed in Lemuria, and thus to the man who was the cause of the splitting, and who was your lover then.

You opted to incarnate again in other lifetimes, mainly to try and resolve the messy split with your other half, for this action had resulted in incurred karma to be worked off. However, the split, just led to more rifts. Concerning the man who triggered it all, there have been lifetimes where he appeared as a lover or husband, but always abandoned you or just disappeared. This worsened the instability which had been there from the start.

So, in a sense, in this lifetime the same cycle is repeating itself. It is best to first of all to cut all ties, as you both still use these negative attachments to stay bound, and it is not serving either of you. That does not mean that all these cords and ties are negative – the major problem is the volume of them which need to be released, so that you both are free to make life choices, without constantly manipulating each other through these cords – albeit unconsciously.

You also need to find a deep and profound forgiveness for yourself, deep within your own soul. For your soul has truly mourned the parting with her other half, from the very beginning, so you have ended up with guilt feelings, blaming yourself for all that ensued. That awful yearning for your missing half exacerbated things, you feeling that God must be so angry as to punish you. This is untrue. God does not punish anyone – souls tend to punish themselves for they cannot forgive themselves! God only loves unconditionally, with a steady unchanging love that never dies. Indeed, it was your own free will and choice that decided to split your body, and your soul(s) need to take responsibility for this.

So, until you have finally forgiven yourself, and discovered how all of this has served the greater good of your soul, something deep inside will repel any intimacy with a man.

The partner is not a *soulmate*, but rather a soul you have had karma to work off with, so therefore you have to create new and healthier patterns by forgiving yourself and learning to love yourself unconditionally. Then you will find you change inside, and if you both truly wish to, you can try to create a loving and supportive union, which will take some work. He also feels that pull to find his true other half, who was split off, so there is that yearning deep inside of him too. Honesty always pays off in the end – and knowing that any relationship needs work, and is both support and challenge. So nothing in reality is ever lost or imperfect. All are but immense lessons in forgiveness and love – unconditional love.

As for the other half of you – well, he is restless, and travelling the globe, with a deep inner void which he tries to fill with women, adventures and song. In that order. He is immensely gifted and talented, and is truly seeking answers, and he also loves to roam about the world – he has been almost everywhere! However in recent years there have been many challenges. He feels very empty, as if something is missing and so he continues to search.

So, yes, the two of you will be pulled together, and are contracted to meet each in about three years' time. Don't worry how, you will instantly recognize each other as you are **one** soul and two halves of one body, which was androgynous. There is no way you can miss each other. You will just KNOW.

Interesting you will naturally co-habit together and will feel that is right, but then will drift away from each other again, if the inner work has not been done.

One can never skimp on this work, for the more that is released within, the freer one becomes and the more one can open up to true love. For true love can only be true to the extent that the heart is fully open, with all old resentments, hurts, pain released. Truly this is a deep process. Remember that all parties involved have free will and choice, we have something to cleanse and clear throughout all our incarnations, for life on this planet tends to bring out both the best and the worst, and then some!

Do the inner work, so when you do meet your other half, things will flow together naturally, in a reunion which is blessed and will merge into that androgynous form again."

SOUL GROUP: The Relating Ones

"In this lifetime you were a princess in Bali, in what was then the Lemurian lands. You were androgynous, happy and content. You loved the people you ruled over, there was abundance, and everyone was happy, and had more than enough. There was no lack, or scarcity, no disease or anything which could disturb or disrupt. Then, however the Black Magi infiltrated your haven, to sow discord, corruption and strife, and then Atlantis rose, where people had **two** forms, a male and female. The Lemurians observed that two people could share sexual intercourse, and felt by being androgynous they were losing out on something extremely important. Observe here the first sign of *discord,* a feeling of *lack,* the desire for what others seemed to have, and they did not. When the Black Magi found a way to separate the androgynous form into Male and Female, you were one of the first to volunteer to have this done, feeling a definite lack in your life. **So you became two – male and female.** This soul which you are now, is the Female form of that soul, and you have not yet met the other half of you – you are not ready yet, for a period of time is still needed to attain some measure of equilibrium.

In your new form you had sex with your other half, and experienced bliss… but with time, you felt intense sexual attraction to other men, and especially to the man whom you married. He too had separated into two forms, you had an affair, with four souls being affected, not just the two who had divided, but another two who also had split. By that time, you had two children with your other half, and now were expecting a third child with this new man. This caused immense disruption between these men, and the other woman involved, and for the first time ever, there was conflict, a lot of pain, jealousy, resentment and blame. Your soul then remembered how this unpleasantness had not existed when you were **one** single form, so you blamed yourself for separating into two, and entered a very deep depression, so much so that you ended your own life, rather than having to choose between two men, who were now fighting over you. For you understood that this had also been repeated in the lives of all you ruled, who had followed your example.

In this lifetime then, much of this still haunts you, for, due to your suicides and great traumas, you had repeated incarnations in Egypt, Peru, Mexico, Ireland and Sweden. In all those lifetimes, the same pattern seemed to repeat itself. You learnt not to take your own life, but to live through the pain, and accept your partners loving others, or you doing the same."

SOUL GROUP: The Caring Ones

"Both you and your *Twin Flame* have been though some very tough times in this lifetime. There is sometimes fear to truly open your hearts, and to love the other in just the way they are: *shadow and light.* It is as if you are afraid to become authentic, truthful and real with each other. The masks are too much in place. Yet, know when you do the inner work, and heal at a deep level, something within you will shift. First learn to love yourself unconditionally just the way you are. You can truly only love another soul, to the degree you love yourself.

As both of you have often switched genders, you will often confuse the masculine and feminine roles somewhat, which can also lead to misunderstandings. There is nothing wrong with that – you are simply more *androgynous*, and need to understand and embrace this. Every person has both masculine and feminine within – it is just more apparent in certain people. One has to find that balance within, and then the other will reflect it, as a mirror to you, reflecting everything you have not loved and owned within yourself!

As you shift, your heart centre will open to a much greater degree, as your own deepest caring comes to the fore. Go and pamper and nurture yourself. Do what brings you love and joy, even if alone. The more you care about yourself and your greater wellbeing, the more this will expand to everyone you meet. You have so much loving caring energy within you – show this to others. Show that you care, and you will find this same caring expressed to you. Then be open to receiving it!

In around three years from now, when healed from those lifetimes and transformed, you will be drawn back together. Don't try to force it. Simply let go and let God – it will happen in perfect Divine Timing when both are ready to open your hearts and souls to each other at a much deeper level, without the old negative karmic patterns tripping you up.

Then, take it slowly. Don't jump into it. Allow a deep friendship, a deep love and trust and respect to grow between you. This takes time. Allow it to slowly unfold, as you both open your hearts and you allow love to deepen, without expectations. Without trying to change the other. Just allowing the other to simply be himself.

There is no need to hurry. There is no need to immediately co-habit together. Allow the love to deepen as you grow closer together and giving each other the freedom to be. Something beautiful will happen.

When young, the need for procreation is greater than the wisdom which age brings. Mature love is where soul meets soul, more so than just body meets body and so much more than sex, it is a heart opening, a soul opening, when sexual energy is released in extreme ways, to the highest degree. Now union becomes sacred, a deep merging, of body, mind, spirit and soul! Maturity demands a deeper coming together, for it wishes to create something very special which will generate an even deeper bond. It does not just happen overnight! It takes time and effort and a deep willingness to dive ever deeper into the realms of pure, unconditional love. It means that one experiences both support and challenges, but not giving up on the other, merely looking at ways to deepen the trust and to enhance respect as well as allowing love to expand. Such is true union, for union is meant to be sacred. Precious. Profound.

Do the inner work – you will be so glad you did.

At the moment he is going through a deep *sabbatical,* and much soul searching. Allow him the time to do this – for in the end you will both benefit. You are both very much drawn to the spiritual path, as in those other lifetimes. You can sometimes ignore such a calling – but it will always pull you back onto the path.

You are a soul who needs to express Divine caring for yourself and the rest of Humanity, indeed Mother Earth, nature and animals. You come from the Pleiades, who are the botanists on galactic levels. They tend to all of life and especially plants, trees, etc. They carry the light-codes and they deeply care about all of life and life forms in the whole Cosmos – they care for the wellbeing, not only the physical wellbeing, but also spiritual, and that of the soul. Your Soul Group embodies this caring and so do you! Embrace this caring, and become it! You will blossom forth!

Open yourself to love in all its forms and expressions, and you will find love everywhere. Deeply care about all you encounter, and you will find that caring returns to you. Live life with love and care. You will be blessed, and are a great blessing to Humanity, the planet at large and all upon her!"

––––––––

SOUL GROUP: The Sacred Geometrical Ones

"Soul name: She who brings in the codes of the Sacred Geometries and intricate knowing of the Unity Consciousness and the Divine Feminine Aspects of the Higher Unconditional love, and thus is one who brings out the deepest knowing in other souls and helps them to reconnect to the greater encoded sacred geometries within themselves.

The tonal chord is A and the soul colours are beautiful, bright rainbow colours infused with pure gold, purple and indigo and blue, with emerald green and yellow and then aquamarine, turquoise and again whitish golden orange and gold.

This soul is an old *Lemurian soul,* and thus incarnated during the time of Mu, the *fourth civilization* in what is now part of the Pacific Islands, as an androgynous soul who brings *androgyny* into being, in that, there needs to be a balance between the masculine and feminine within as with *yin and yang.* It can sometimes lead to confusion about her own sexuality, as she often wishes to express herself in a more masculine way, and then at other times feminine. Certainly, there needs to be **balance** within first, and an understanding that *androgyny* is inherent to the soul.

This lifetime is all about overcoming the pain and illusion of separateness and finding your way back to completeness again. It means forgiving yourself for allowing yourself to be influenced into halving yourself, and letting go of all the shame, blame and guilt, you felt subsequently. Love yourself into the deepest depths of your physical form, and then love yourself into a profound balance between the masculine and feminine within. In this way you will open the path to be reunited with your other true half, and he with you, and then if you both choose to, for you both have free will and choice, you can become **as one** again in this lifetime, in whatever form you choose.

Then forgive him, and forgive the Atlantean High Priest and Atlanteans. For they enslaved you, forcing you to become a sex slave. (You were the female part). There needs to be great healing in this. For the separation caused immense wounds and pain, and being used sexually was a great shock as you had never had sexual intercourse when androgynous – there was no need! See how people abused sexual energy in the sexual organs, which were in actual fact only to be used for reproductive purposes, to beget children, and are not designed for enslavement and manipulation.

Note, that in healing the deepest of your own soul woundedness here, you will be able to heal others to the same degree. It is almost as if your soul took this upon herself in this lifetime, so that she could *heal the woundedness of the Lemurian Fall to Atlantis,* to heal this in all the Lemurian souls who suffered the split. Many of them have incarnated so this work will call you from now on – more than any other calling, for interestingly the new human race in the New Golden Age will once more be *androgynous.*

This message comes with great love from your own higher Ascended Masters who work with you, Lord Maitreya and Lord Kuthumi and Quan Yin. They are ready and willing to help you to heal on the deepest levels, if you ask for their help, for they may not intervene with your own free will and choice. Additionally, you may ask the Lords and Ladies of Karma, to release the karma involved, if this serves the highest soul growth and good of your own soul and all concerned. A window of opportunity has arisen for your soul, as you have listened to your calling, and have now stepped into your soul mission and purpose, by following it."

SOUL GROUP: The Living Waters

"On Planet Earth there is sometimes a confusion with the female form, and in truth your soul is *androgynous*. You are both male and female. You are both Yin and Yang. It will surface at times in your relationships, especially when wanting to be intimate with a man, as you may feel as if your inner temple is being invaded, your own inner waters and this has nothing to do with him, but is more likely due to the fact the fact that in your own home galaxy, you do not need sex.

There is no sexual intercourse because everyone is androgynous, and one can procreate without sex. You can merely visualize the type of being you wish to create in detail, project the image through the sacral chakra into a tube, like one plants semen or a seed, and then the being will form within, it as it acts as an incubator and then, at the right moment, the child will step out, fully formed, without any pain on either side.

You need to understand, you can quite easily stand on your own two feet and be totally alone and happy. You are complete within yourself. The more you hang onto a relationship that is no longer serving your highest soul growth and good, the more you will resent the person, and feel that they are stopping you from fulfilling your soul purpose. It is as if you are scared on one hand to be independent and apart, but on the other hand, you feel he is blocking you.

This is not a healthy way to live. You need to be perfectly honest with yourself, for if you cannot share your innermost temple with him, at some stage he will start straying, resulting in more problems. Alternatively, if you truly love and wish to be with him, then perhaps it is best to do the inner work, forgive yourself and him and realize that your body is a holy temple. If you truly wish him to enter with love, and be there in love inside you, then you need to open your heart and soul. Be open and honest with yourself and him, forgive yourself, let go of all shame, blame, and guilt concerning him for whatever reason. True love thrives in the presence of mutual respect and trust, and without them, love will fly out the window. Meet each other halfway in truth, and love, and then, if you both truly wish to start again, there is no reason why not.

On the other hand, if this is impossible, or you do not wish this, then it is perhaps time to move on.

The truth is that all life starts with self-love. If you actually believe that there is something dreadfully wrong with yourself, that you are unlovable, then no matter how kind, or caring someone is, you will reject this, because you feel yourself unworthy of such attention.

Maybe it is time to see the beauty and perfection of your own soul, and to love yourself just the way you are! Dark and light. Nice and mean. Kind and Cruel. Yin and Yang, and then, to truly find your own worth. One you start loving yourself just the way you are, your heart will open. You will find that suddenly because you do, you radiate forth love, like the flowing rivers of life, and may well discover that the colleagues you thought disliked you, actually love and appreciate you! Additionally, suddenly your husband may change towards you, for he now feels more open to expressing his love, and before you know it, your whole life will improve.

In reality, you are perfectly made. Look at the truth of who and what you are at soul level! You are meant to be like the Waters of Life, flowing with the flow, with great loving energy towards everyone you encounter, and whose lives you touch in a beautiful, uplifting, and powerful, way, just like water regenerates, energizes, and enfolds you. Therein lie your soul gifts, and what you are created to do and be.

Perhaps you tried too hard to please your parents, to please others, and be the perfect woman you thought they would like or love, seeking their approval. The fact is that you tried to be someone you truly are not! You followed where others led you. Is it not time to be totally honest, take a sabbatical, to find yourself on so many levels and then love yourself into wholeness?

Perhaps it is time to retreat to a place with healing waters. You need water around you, living waters, like rivers, lakes and the sea ,as they will heal and energize you. You need to work with these waters in some form or another. For instance, a hydro spa, or some form of water therapy. Remember there are hot water springs, and all the healing therapies attached to them.

If you do, you will start feeling alive like never before and find your own inner healing powers, and start applying them. You will even astound yourself!

You are not meant to be like other people. You were meant to be your own beautiful watery soul self. Become the flowing waters of Life, whom the Celestial Waters of Life touch. You will heal at the deep soul levels, become **as one** with the Divine Source and All the living waters of life, and be so filled with love and beautiful loving and uplifting emotions, that there will be a deep rejuvenation, reactivation and transformation.

Indeed, that is why you are here beautiful star seed and beautiful soul!

Perhaps it time to finally break free and claim your own soul's truth and live it!

Yes, it will take leaps of faith.

Yes, it will push you out of your comfort zones. Yes, it will mean deep soul searching and deep healing.

You are indeed, able to be reborn and become a powerful healer in your own right, healing with the waters of life and living life, and life more abundantly, with so much love in your heart and soul and Being."

SOUL GROUP: The Caring Ones

"Soul name: The Caring One who brings that great and deep loving caring of the Divine into being and form, and thus is one who deeply cares for the greater whole and brings that caring factor into life, in loving ways.

This soul is an old soul and has had quite a few lifetimes on Earth, and interestingly enough, has had incarnations in both forms, male and female. In this lifetime choosing the female embodiment, as she wanted to bring balance into her own soul.

The reason for this lies in her previous lifetime, during World War II, as an American Soldier, in the middle stages of the war in Europe. War brings out the best and worst in Humankind, and in his case (for you were a 'he' then), he was one, who, in moments of sheer madness raped many women in conquered villages and towns. Only at the end of the war, as he lay dying, did a deep repentance come with a young army nurse, acting like an angel of comfort, mercy and love by his side. He then vowed to return as a woman, to work through his own negative karma, never to abuse sexual energy, or women again. He wanted to experience what it is like to be a woman in a much more profound way.

It is not the only lifetime where you switched genders. Some souls never choose to, but being a great caring soul, you wished to experience life as a man, just as much as a woman. You wanted to heal people through your deep caring, learning not to judge others and bringing about a healing and balance between the Masculine and Feminine.

We find you then, as a Buddhist monk in another lifetime, trained in meditation and long hours of prayer. Interestingly you had a deep and abiding love affair with a fellow monk, a teacher who was much older than you, for in such monasteries sex was definitely enjoyed, often in secret, but in fact known to all. He used you as a boy, but through it all, a deep bond grew between you. When he died, you never took another lover, but often counselled those young monks who came with stories of sexual abuse, and helped them in a deeply loving and caring way to heal in this regard. When sexual energy so repressed, it will express itself in some form, and you often struggled with this aspect – the fact that the highest kind of spiritually often brought out the lowest bestiality. It is something you struggled greatly with in that lifetime, within yourself, and others, and one which you had great courage to address within the ranks."

––––––––––

SOUL GROUP: The Loving Ones

"Soul name: The One who serves through compassion, grace and good will. This soul has incarnated in order to fulfil a prophesy made a long time ago, by a member of her tribe, who said that he would incarnate in a different body in a female form, so that they, the men of his tribe who had raped women after winning a war, could experience what it was like to have a female form and know the intricacies of what that entailed. This prophet was a leader, but had refrained from warfare, and warned men against the mindless slaughtering of opponents, and as this practice continued, he vowed to return in a female form. For this utterance or declaration, he was burnt by his own people at the stake.

This happened during the first crusade in the region of Jerusalem, and he was a survivor from the tribes of Israel, and in that lifetime suffered greatly because of his refusal to partake in slaughter and rape.

There was another incarnation in a female form at Delphi, as a servant to an oracle priestess. There was a practice in Greece of having partners of both sexes, so this gender conflict was present in that lifetime too, as she loved having intimacy with both sexes. She often acted as a mediator between lovers, and helped bring people to the temples who were in need of an oracle blessing.

In that lifetime a close bond formed with her current partner, whom she has recognized in the present lifetime. This soul was sexually involved with him, while having other male and female lovers. She always loved the freedom to experiment, however fell ill with a venereal disease, which still exists as a problem for her, as she experiences discomfort in her sexual areas now. Many sexual energies from that time, as well as negative cords and attachments must needs be cleared out – one was from this relationship, where she tended at times to manipulate the soul she is now with, to do her favours. This brought trouble, and affected her channelling and transmitting abilities.

In this lifetime she has a female body for the second time, whereas previously she revelled in having a masculine form, and the sense of power that came with it. In another lifetime in what is now known as Syria, she was a very rich merchant with many wives, and loved having sex with them all. In that lifetime too, sexual diseases haunted her later on, and therefore these need to be cleared from the etheric as well.

The lesson this soul has come to master now, is not to abuse her own sexual powers, but to bring in a loving balance and caring, concentrating first of all on **herself**. Searching for multiple partners in other lifetimes, was really a deep and profound search for the depths of her soul, which has always been there, but she always sought completion and wholeness in others, for what was perceived as a lack deep within. She also had a proclivity to use this sexual energy to manipulate others into believing that she would only love them, or be sexually potent, when they did what she wanted. Take note of this as this area must be worked on. Love never needs to be manipulated, especially sexual energy, which was never meant for exploitation or control in any form. That is abusing what is in reality a beautiful, precious and highly sacred energy.

In this lifetime, this is the greatest lesson to be mastered, first of all the deep and abiding love for oneself, finding total unconditional love and contentment **being in love with oneself,** from deep within. This love is all-embracing, and is the Divine Love in multiple forms within the soul.

The next lesson to be mastered here concerns sexual energy. To refrain from all sexual interplay for a while, would certainly be extremely healing in many ways, initially by doing a massive clearing of negative cords, ties, manipulation, hooks and debris from past lives – both as a man and woman. Then she needs to go deep inside to find the sacredness of her very own womb, reconnecting in a profound way with her own soul and Goddess self – that infinite being which is there inside. Find that deep and profound feeling of the sacredness of this space, and then understand that this is such a holy space, that one should never allow anyone or anything or energy in there, which is not also sanctified."

SOUL GROUP: The Divine Expressive Ones

"You incarnated in this lifetime as one of the first Indigo children to be born, mainly because you had cherished this planet, from its very beginning. You often incarnated here when massive shifts were developing, striving to guide those who had lost their way, back into the Light, and to teach them the fine art of Cosmic Insight, Wisdom and Enlightenment.

This encouraged you to frequently choose lives of sheer austerity, almost as if you wanted to live in some cheerless kind of isolation, in a very strict and grim manner, without true joy, which did not always serve your highest soul growth and good. In fact, it distanced you from others, and the Divine, as you felt yourself superior. You had an attitude of *"I am better than you, for I sit and pray and chastise myself all day. I am saved and you are not."* In essence this is not a pure teaching, for no soul is better or greater than another, and nowhere does it say that one should suffer self-punishment, or deprive oneself of the sheer joy of being, to reach enlightenment. In fact, the most powerful *Ascended Master Souls* all have a lovely sense of humor, a deep and abiding joy within, which bubbles over.

This culminated in a lifetime when you chose to come in as a man, as in previous lifetimes, you had been a priestess of an order in Egypt, when the Priesthood was already so corrupted, men had taken over, and abused Priestesses in so many ways. This was a spill over from Atlantis when the Black Magi feared the powers of the High Priestesses more than anyone else, so resolved to enslave them to end their powers. Now in your time these priests basically made life very difficult for women who wanted to remain pure and true to the Divine.

They abused the *Sacred Sexual Rites,* withheld their souls from the priestesses, and violated the sexual energies to feed off them, zapping the powers of the feminine for their black magic rites. You rebelled against this openly, and they hated your guts, so they cornered you, chained and killed you in a sacrificial lamb way, which was in fact high Magic.

You chose to return in the form of a priest during the time of the first Christian churches. You were an ascetic, so went into solitary confinement, living in a cave in the Sahara Desert, often spending time aloft on a pole. Yes, a pole! For pilgrims came and admired you there, and often asked for your blessing. It was a life of such severity that you fasted for months on end, and were but a walking, praying, skeleton, for there was hardly anything left of you.

Later you felt yourself to be totally superior to everyone else, and flaunted this, as your negative ego tripped you up. You felt you were a god, as these worshippers were at the foot of your pole (literally at your feet). In the end you died of malnutrition.

In this lifetime it is all about finding **balance** between the two opposite poles within. You are a very interesting combination, for your soul in truth is *androgynous*, both male and female, in your created soul structure. You never incarnated in Mu and Lemuria where many were androgynous, but in Orion, Saturn and Mercury where all souls are androgynous, although since that time, many others from different galaxies and star systems have lived there too, and are either male or female. There are many other physical forms which the Divine has created, that people do not yet know of, in star systems further away.

Now, in this form of *androgyny,* sometimes it will be your masculine, and other times your feminine side which asserts itself. You are at soul level more orientated towards the feminine in your soul creation, but sometimes being in a female body, will bring about feelings of having been sexually used, invaded, unbalanced and out of harmony, with the person entering you. In your case you will **feel** this more intensely, sensing this inequity at some point within your sexual area. It could lead to closing your vagina, or being unable to open yourself up in total abandonment to pleasure at a deeper level. The opening up will have to come through your Heart and soul centre, more than just through the physical. The heart centre links directly with the womb, yoni centre and the crown chakra and third eye. When any of these centers are not fully open and functioning, there will be blockages, something deep inside of you obstructing and separating the lower body from the upper, with you possibly being unaware of it.

The underlying reason is that your masculine and feminine side are not in harmony with each other, as yet. There is confusion inside of you, but you don't quite understand the mixed messages you give yourself. Now this does not mean you must become androgynous again, you just have to bring the yin and yang into balance and harmony, to be able to open yourself up to greater levels of love and sex and also interestingly, **service.**

There is a fundamental principle of creation to understand here, the *androgynous* form is **complete** within itself, not needing sexual energy for procreation. Being whole, comprehensive and balanced, inside and outside, has its hidden blessings, for you do not seek to be fulfilled or completed by any other. You are complete, not needing a partner for satisfaction.

In other lifetimes you wanted to be in the priesthood, never quite feeling at home in either the female or male body, always feeling you were neither one nor the other. You sometimes went into overdrive, when the austerity of service demanded in the male embodiment entailed literally punishing yourself, so as not to feel sexual energy, or to desire a woman. Though when in a female form, being sexually abused by men also had compensations."

SOUL GROUP: The Intricately Knowledgeable Ones

"Soul name: The Intricate Knowledgeable One who works with the matrix energy fields of the Divine.

This soul was born first in what was to be Mu, in an *androgynous* form. You worked as a High Priest overseeing the *Temples of Knowledge, Technology, and Wisdom*, all as one single entity. As life was androgynous, there was no sexual energy in the sense we know of as gender sexuality, hence there were no problems associated with relationships. One incarnated in total harmony and balance with oneself, and lived in a stable environment in agreement, and this is essentially as it was created to be.

In the latter days of Mu, then Lemuria (as it became), Atlantis rose, and here the human form had a distinctive male and female body. So, for the first time those in Mu and Lemuria, saw that two people of opposite genders could share sex and seemingly enjoy it. As they never had or could experience this in their current forms, they felt hard done-by by the Divine, and rebelled. Your temples had vast laboratories, and you worked with the High Priest overseeing this section. As they loved to experiment with the human form, they wanted to devise a method of splitting the androgynous form into a male and female half and also the soul. So, you assisted with this process because you felt that indeed something must be missing – for sexual energy seemed to be a life force, and something to be desired.

It has to be understood that androgynous beings feel sexual energy and procreate but this fusion takes place within them in a beautiful, balanced and unique way. However, as this method now seemed to be very deficient, this High Priest and the 12 of you on this project, then decided to go ahead and experiment until you perfected it.

However, the High Priest Council of 12 and 24 and the Elders who surround the throne of the Divine, warned you to cease these experiments, as it would bring dire calamities to your people by interfering with Divine Creation. You also would have to forfeit pieces of your soul in the experiments, as you could not create life and life forms, without giving them a soul. So, you began to create clones of yourself in female and male forms, as a type of *prototype robot*. Then the first successful division took place, as the *androgynous* form was halved in a massive tank, two bodies formed with the soul also divided, *without the permission of the Divine who created these souls.* Well, as this was successful, you were one of the first priests who received this procedure, now inhabiting two bodies with two souls.

Initially you were delighted, and revelled in the sexual energy and the fact that you could mate with your other half. However, soon the novelty wore off and a deep unhappiness, and sense of inexplicable loss overcame you. Both forms now worked in these laboratories. As more and more Lemurians came to have this procedure, you were kept very busy with the High Priests, however discord and discontent festered within your ranks for the first time ever!

With these new life forms came jealousy, as the one set of halves now decided that the spilt halves of the others, were more sexually attractive, which led to orgies. This in turn led to a total misuse of the sexual energies within the temples, and for the first time a deep and profound sense of loss of innocence, as well as the other half of oneself. You suddenly realized what had happened here and how you had acted as co-creator. You were struck by a deep sense of having betrayed yourself at some level and not only you, but also your Creator.

The subsequent strife, quarrels and unprecedented wars which broke out in Lemuria with the continent breaking up and sinking under the sea, was the final straw. Although you survived this by fleeing to Atlantis, you took your own life, for the heavy layers of guilt and intense feeling of loss were too great for you to handle.

In subsequent lifetimes you alternatively took on male then female forms – but also felt at a loss at how to deal with this. You still felt the intense grief, as if you did not belong anywhere now, and were somehow incomplete. As co-creator the karma you loaded upon yourself at the time was immense, and done consciously with full knowledge of the implications of the priesthood's actions, as it went against the **Cosmic laws of Creation**. In other lifetimes you, in both male and female bodies, just did not feel truly yourself, and in some lives, you again decided to opt out.

With the mass raising of consciousness in this lifetime, and ascension of Mother Earth, all the souls with karmic links, who caused the upheavals by the choices they made at the time, have incarnated. So, you chose the male form, thinking it would most empower you, but asked that later in life you could assume a female form. In essence this was in agreement with your *Twin Flame*, so that you could merge both parts of yourself again, and to re-find the masculine and feminine balance *within*.

However, you soon discovered that as a man or woman, you felt alienated in your body, with that deep sense of loss, of a void, and of not being one or the other, which of course is 100% correct.

In this lifetime, the other half of you was born female and committed suicide in her early teens, discovering she could just not hold her form, deciding to opt out of the agreement and is now back home, helping you to re-assume your *androgynous* form. In fact, her not being in physical embodiment at this time, assists both of you to merge totally, into one single unit again! This is an act of higher love and service on her part. You are in essence the masculine part and she the feminine, but in merging at soul level now, *the rest must merge into human form consciously.*

Your souls took on this mission as an act of working off karma incurred in that lifetime. By volunteering to undergo this merging into androgynous form *once more, you are paving the way for other souls you halved in Mu and Lemuria to follow suit.* In uniting with the "lost" parts you are becoming whole again, and therefore able to heal that sense of loss and incompletion. As you increasingly manage to do this, by becoming aware of what and why it happened, you can help to heal others by leading them to understand this principle, what went awry, and just how they can help bridge this gap and merge back into a single entity and form.

So instead of resenting this, why not embrace it with total love for yourself, and the Divine. In doing this soul work, you are healing a massive soul scar in the collective consciousness of Humanity, since its inception in Lemuria. You are pioneering this merger, immensely significant work, and will be blessed and healed in very powerful ways. If you successfully complete it in this lifetime, you will be freed up from the need to incarnate again, and may assume duties elsewhere in Sirius, in the mastery which you truly have there. This then is your highest soul calling and the greatest there is. You do not need love outside yourself – all is within and in you, you **are** all that is."

———

CHAPTER 6

Guidance and Healing

Extracts from Soul Readings

THE SOUL Group: The Sounding Ones

"The fear is deep-rooted, and comes from both lifetimes when the *Black Magi* took over, wishing to infiltrate the *High Priesthood,* in order to obtain the secret codes and keys, and most importantly the crystal keys and skulls which each *High Priest* had in their possession. However, they have all been relocated to the ethereal, so those which are floating around are all replicas, as the *High Priesthood* created them to prevent the actual ones from falling into the wrong hands. In the process many High Priests and Priestesses were killed to obtain them, and many women were sexually manipulated. For once they stepped into the arena of sex, they knew how to control them, and they would reveal their secrets by hooking into their sexual fields. In this lifetime you have attracted to you those men who did just that to you in other lifetimes, and are still hooked into you. You will have to cut all the negative cords and attachments to them, for they are draining away your power, and preventing you from moving up into the higher states of being, where your soul can be free to serve, unencumbered and unrestricted – not pulled in different directions."

———

SOUL GROUP: The Ten Thousand Lotus Ones

"The sexual centre is the powerhouse of a woman, particularly as it connects to the feeling centre – the emotional body, and as such is the sacred temple where she experiences the most feelings, as it connects directly to the heart. If the heart is closed, her sexual centre will be too, from years of being hurt.

If any man enters the most sacred part of a woman without love, to just use her temple, and is not present in the highest state of love, she will know this, from deep within. Therefore, she will subconsciously feel used, her heart will close up as will her sexual centre, in some form or another, and discomfort will arise, indicating issues of emotional pain, low self-worth, shame, guilt and blame.

What most people do not understand about sexual energy and the sacred temple held within a womb, is that there are negative cords, hooks and attachments to the person who uses another in sexually abusive ways. This may result in subjugation and or domination, then these negative cords, attachments, hooks, and ties will remain there energetically. Every time someone enters with anger, with negative energy, it leaves this imprint in the sacred temple, often introducing dis-ease, as subconsciously women will *know*, and intuitively sense and read his energy. Such a person can drain one by zapping energy like an energy vampire through these cords. One will feel drained for no reason, or feel used in some way, which cannot be explained logically, or put into words. Indeed, this all happens energetically.

These hooks, cords, attachment and ties can be carried over from other lifetimes as well. (*This also applies to men, and will culminate in prostate problems, etc.*)

So, it is best to call in **Archangel Michael**, and ask him to use his mighty sword of light, to cut these negative cords, hooks and ties from your sexual areas. When you actually become aware of them, and start to psychically feel into them, you may be surprised at who is on the other end. Sometimes even family members who were abusive in some form or another, not always sexually. He will continue the work until the area is cleared, radiating his purifying energy into the area. It would be wise to do this exercise, to free your temple and yourself.

It will help you immensely. (You may need do this every time something triggers within you, related to sex or intimacy, or fear of opening your heart or yourself to even having sex) in order for you to heal in this area. Especially when a cyst develops, this can signify running the same old movie, nursing old hurts, and points to the need for forgiveness of self and others. You will also need to ask Archangel Michael to release you and all others from old marriage vows, contracts, oaths, vows, dowry and slavery agreements, business contracts, etc. and hand over all outward signs of these, such as rings and bracelets.

Allow this to be cleared over many lifetimes, to free yourself and others. Then learn to love yourself, love your body, love all that you are, just as you are. Touch your sacred temple and send it love until you feel your love for yourself in all areas, the physical, emotional, mental and spiritual bodies, to the point where you can open your heart to feel the *thousand petal lotus* of your heart opening to its fullest, inviting the *Divine Mother* in to flood your heart, soul, mind and being with pure, unconditional love. You can call upon her anytime, she will always be there to hold you in pure love, day and night. Then ask her to heal you and open you up so that you can love totally love yourself again, and when healed, you will attract the perfect match who will love you just the way you are, as you love him just the way he is."

SOUL GROUP: The Caring Ones

"Interestingly in the lifetimes which followed, you were predisposed to being born into powerful aristocratic families, owning vast tracts of land and were sold off to the highest bidder. Thus, loveless marriages ensued, with men involved in power struggles and political intrigue and during one lifetime, you even ended up accused of high treason in the Tower of London, where you eventually lost your head, although you were innocent.

In this lifetime authority figures, or even family members, husbands or male authority figures, may sometimes trigger soul memory banks of times when you were literally used as a pawn in their power plays, especially so because of your considerable dowry fortunes. You were played, courted or rejected, depending on land and power concerns. This will sometimes evoke a deep-seated sense of insecurity: "*Do you love me for my sake only, or for what I have? – this will mean body, possessions and land etc.*

You will need to work deeply on your womb area, for as awakening occurs more innate soul memory banks will trigger, needing healing at the deepest levels here.

Every time a man enters a woman, without love and uses her body, (she will feel used) negative cords, hooks, ties, and energetic links are established, which often last over lifetimes. It brings about discomfort in the womb area, often subconsciously. As soon as Humanity takes the heart and love out of anything, they tend to sow pain, and their own despair. One actually has to cut those cords, hooks ties etc. with the help of *Archangel Michael,* and release those who are on the other end. Additionally, old marriage vows and contracts, dowry, political contracts and agreements, oaths, vows etc. also need to be let go of, and the angels holding you to them dismissed.

In your case you were once Queen, and as head of state, state contracts and papers, and oaths of alliance need to be released, including outwards signs of power, such as rings, crowns, tiaras, bracelets, brooches, etc. This mean deep healing and releasing which will finally set you and all souls involved free, with an understanding that your physical body is a sacred temple. Love it in its deepest sacredness, and then forgive yourself for everything – let go of all shame, blame and guilt – even that felt in other lifetimes, when you were used by men and raped, and when you felt intense shame for your own body and how it had been violated. In one lifetime in a Puritan society in America you fell pregnant after being raped by a much older married man – you were a mere fifteen years old, and he was an elder whom no one dared to accuse.

You were forced to confess your sins to the entire congregation, and were literally branded by him afterwards, as he declared that no other man would ever have you. No one dared come to your defence, for all feared him. In that lifetime you felt righteous bitterness, anger and shame, fearing you had done something dreadfully wrong, so God was punishing you. You died in childbirth, having given up on life.

So, there needs to be a deep letting go of all shame, blame and guilt and a forgiveness for self, followed by pure, unconditional love. See yourself as a true Daughter of the Divine God and Goddess, and so loved, just the way you are! And in truth there is nothing to be ashamed of, only to love! You did nothing wrong. These were but lesson in loving grace and forgiveness and unconditional love!

During the time of Atlantis, the patriarchy dominated, when men were taught to shut out their heart and live in the mind, so many were forced to become what in truth they are not. Forgive them and find that deep caring unconditional love within you. Set yourself and them free, and healing at the deepest levels in your womb area will come.

At this stage of your life, when you are stepping more and more into your beautiful soul maturity, these memory banks need be dealt with, to allow you to awaken, becoming ever lighter, as each one is healed, and you find that deep reconnection with your own beautiful soul!"

SOUL GROUP: The Golden Ones

"In this lifetime the tendency to be very religious and serve in convents, was carried over and developed, so first of all it is time to release all previous dowry agreements that have been made. Essential vows are to be released, especially those regarding chastity, as in your Italian lifetime your husband tried to control your sensuality by insisting you wear chastity belts when he was away, and when he neglected to do this, you immediately had an affair. So, they must be removed by *Archangel Michael,* and all unpleasant residue released. You also took vows of poverty, abstention, to live in harsh conditions, like in convent cells where you had pneumonia, self-punishment for sins, celibacy, along with a marriage vow to God. All must be dismissed and dissolved, along with the Angels keeping you to these vows.

You have an amazing ability to find deep inner wisdom and to flourish doing any work, such as counselling with your insight, patience, love and wisdom. You would also do very well in reading people's energy fields, assisting them to release any obstacles to living happily, giving words of wisdom for them. You can be trained to read the *Akashic and the planet's records* if you so choose. This, combined with laser crystals in healing, or as recording crystals, will make for very successful work.

However, your soul is very sensitive, and it would help to work with your womb area, and your sexuality, and observe how this translates into feeling in your body. Feel into the base and sacral chakras to release all blockages there. Explore all your insecurities, your feelings and beliefs of lack, scarcity, low self-worth, low self-confidence, your hang-ups, and whatever else lies buried here.

So, delve in there and cleanse and clear all old soul memory banks. This is significant, such as in that lifetime when you had a child from your lover, and you in desperation decided to become a nun. The warped and twisted Mother Superior had awful things done to your private parts, in an effort to ensure that her nuns could not pleasure themselves, or have secret sexual experiences with each other. You were severely mutilated with infections that lasted for the rest of your life, which drained your resistance to disease, and so you died of pneumonia. It felt as if the very essence of your womanhood that had made you a vibrant and healthy woman, died when this happened, and you suffered severe pain there for the remainder of that lifetime. It is time to release all the trauma, pain and shame, guilt and self-inflicted punishment of that lifetime in particular.

If you truly wish to work on your inner self, learn to love yourself totally and unconditionally, and be open to love, you will be able to have a beautiful, healthy and committed partnership. Please be willing and open to understand that you need to be very discerning about who you let in to your sacred space, as you are so sensitive, and tend to pull out all the stops for the man you are with. Healthy boundaries are necessary, with absolute trust, respect and a very deep caring, so that you can feel safe and secure and loved. Sometimes it is best to walk your path alone to heal first of all, before you can truly love, as you will then raise your vibrational frequencies, and attract a higher-level calibre of man who is on the same life path and on the same wavelength. For your soul this is imperative."

SOUL GROUP: The Joyful Ones

"Soul name: She is the joyful expression of the beauty of a heart and soul filled with love and joy that bubbles over with elation within the soul. Divine Joy that is the fountain of all life and being, for Joy is one of the greatest gifts of the soul itself.

This is a soul who did not need to return to Planet Earth, but chose to do so, for she was your sister in a past life and wanted to be your daughter in this one. There was always a close bond between you, and in one lifetime you came in as twins. Thus it often feels like she owns you at some level, and resents anyone taking that space. However, at the same time she is a very loving being, filled with joy, which spills over as she relates to her siblings, but also to life in general, and to all whom she meets.

This soul has had some very tragic lifetimes, often traumatized during times of war, highlighting the brutality of men. So, when she grows into puberty, and the first blossoming of maturity, talk to her about the passages: growing into a woman, sacredness of the womb and sexuality, so she can understand this at a very deep and profound level.

Otherwise, she might sometimes shrink from men, due to fears from lifetimes of rape and abuse, when she lost her joy. These will surface in the years of awakening, so encourage her to wait for the right soul to come along, rather than being indiscriminate. For this soul this is vital, she chose you as her mother to help her overcome her fear of men, for when the Goddess withdrew with the consequent trauma, she vowed never to return, unless the Goddess did, so she could heal in this regard, and help others to heal as well, by bringing joy and delight back to their bodies, their own sacred temples. Also, to help them recognize their *Goddesshood*, the blossoming joy of womanhood, at its most sublime, namely that inner beauty which bursts through in jubilant expression of their sexuality.

So here is the gentle guidance required, for in ancient times, girls were led through the rites of passage by older tribeswomen. One celebrated birth, the first blood, the passage into puberty, the full blossoming into adulthood, the passage of union or partnership, pregnancy, birth, motherhood, maturity, the bourgeoning into full and beautiful maturity at 60, and then at 70 the full and total honouring as Grandmother Elder, the Wise Woman, the Sage.

Guide her through this process, for she will need that. Don't let her buy into the hype, the false programming that women have been subjected to, told it is acceptable to have sex with many men. For a woman truly in touch with herself, this will be false programming, for her most sacred place and power lies connected with the heart, womb, vagina and clitoris. If she allows any man in, who does not love her, or who does not arrive with the best and most loving intent, she is violating that sacred space, and she will feel desecrated to the core. This soul in particular will feel this intensely, as she came in to heal Humanity, to lead women home to purity, and the holiness of their own sexuality with the right partner, to share the joy, the sheer bliss and ecstasy – so here again, that joyful expression of Divinity lies at the key of all sexuality, and thus is a beautiful way to experience the Divine.

Interestingly, she is here to bring in the keys and codes of joy, for joy in truth is one of the highest expressions of the Divine itself, for Divinity bubbles over with joy, taking so much delight in His/Her children and Creation. Happiness is so much part of the Divine, that to be in the highest states of sheer joy and gratitude, and to count your blessings, is one of the highest ways of serving – indeed it is the purest souls who will know the truth of this in its highest forms of expression and innocence. For truly, joy is contagious, likewise the delight, which fills life with light and love – the *joie de vivre!*"

————

SOUL GROUP: The Wisdom Keepers

"This soul works with the wisdom, love and light of all ages, and the threefold flame of Love, Power and Wisdom held within the heart energies of the *Divine Feminine,* and embodied in the *Goddess of Wisdom, Sophia.* She also holds the patterns of the *caduceus* within her, as well as that of the flame and fire of that threefold flame, which expresses itself in blue, pink and gold in the centre. She therefore contains the codes and keys of the celestial wisdom which are not earthbound, and she is here as a *Wisdom Keeper Soul* attached to the Soul Group, *The Wisdom Keepers.*"

————

SOUL GROUP: The Loving Ones

"Interestingly. this soul has immense soul connections with the Ural Mountains, with the *Northern Inner Cities of Agartha,* the *Inner Earth* (where her soul often incarnates, and has done so recently) and also with *Malta,* where her soul was very involved during the *Lion Kingdom* on Earth.

The soul is one who *needs to have her inner eyes* opened in order to fully function, often feeling distress in her body, when they are not fully opened. Thus, there is discomfort in her womb area, or the area associated with it, due to it closing, as there is no heart/soul connection, along with her not allowing that deep love for her vagina, clitoris and uterus, and everything that makes her a woman, as these work together as an *inner eye.* In ancient times female oracles or psychics, knew that this *inner eye* must be fully open, along with the heart and third eye energy centers, in order to achieve full awakening and awareness, and to be a fully conscious instrument for the *Divine Feminine* to work with and through

You were then an acolyte at the *Temples of Aysis* in the *Ural Mountains.* There was a huge Goddess energy centre there ages ago, where you worked as an oracle priestess, and loved this work.

In those days you trained from the age of five, and were an ordained priestess only after many stringent tests and initiations, becoming a priestess when all inner eyes were activated. You therefore learnt to honour the womb area, and everything which makes you a woman in the physical sense. Your heart centre was totally filled with unconditional love, love for self, others and for all of Creation, including Mother Earth, as well as the third eye, which is that of the seeing, hearing and knowing, which functioned together as mentioned above. One could not serve competently without this alignment, so predictions made were very accurate, and priestesses literally served fulltime in this capacity, and were disciplined and focused. Marriage and children were not permitted, and that lifetime was the happiest you ever had on Earth.

Next, we find you in a very ancient and huge city which housed the temples of the *Divine Goddess*, of which now only a tiny remnant remains in Malta. You served then in the Temples of Love, where the priestesses were *oracles*, but also partook in the ancient sexual rites with male counterparts, within strict temples rules and laws, trained in the highest use of sexual energy, and only engaged in this with one chosen as *the Beloved* from the same ranks. Therefore, he was the perfect soul match for you, physically compatible, and on your frequency band. You only merged on certain days, nights or times of the year, within hidden chambers, to do specific energy work together in the highest possible service.

At this time, you truly became one in *total unconditional love* with great respect, trust and full knowing of what you wished to co-create together in great love. So, this was carefully contemplated and worked through *before* engaging in physical union, meditating together with deep and profound soul level communication, ensuring their partnership was steeped in tenderness, respect, trust and great loving intent to create only the best for the highest good of all concerned, and the Divine.

Such union is only possible if the negative ego steps out of the way, and one is fully present with the heart, soul and physical body fully aware and conscious in the highest states of union, bliss, and ecstasy, so **Oneness** can be reached. This far surpasses anything currently known to us, when often lust, self-gratification and gymnastics are more important than any contemplation of sacred and sanctified union.

It was during the latter days, when you were nearing the end of your life, that the destruction and wars started. It was deemed necessary that you guard the temple altars against an enemy faction wishing to destroy and violate them. You defended these altars from a rampaging mob, who had forcefully entered and lit fires to destroy them. In an attempt to prevent this, you set fire to the outer ring around the altar with the other priestesses, but before you knew it, they had raped you all, and as you lay there bleeding, these men threw you into the altar fires where you burnt to death, greatly violated and defiled. In later lifetimes this resulted in you often feeling immense discomfort in your sexual areas, with an innate fear of being raped and burnt."

SOUL GROUP: The Crystalline Ones

"And then, remember that *you attract many souls in your lifetime.* Some will be companions, some lovers, and even the one you wish to settle down with. However, at this time in your life, with the immense soul mission your soul assumed, it is best to first become what you undertook to be. Truly step in and activate your mission. If you have a love in your life, then know it cannot stand in the way of your full activation at soul level. You cannot become encumbered with a wife and family at this stage. It is vital for you now to step up – you have a whole planet and soul commitments to fulfil. Your dilly dallying is not serving anyone – least of all yourself.

The only way to live a mission is to grab it like a tiger by its tail and then to *live* it – to *become* the tiger, and to truly go out there and do it. In this lifetime just a tiny fraction of this soul is incarnated. This means that *his higher evolution stays in the Milky Way Galaxy attached to the Federation of the Great White Brotherhood, who are assisting the raising of consciousness here. He thus works with the Ascended Masters Maitreya, Lord Kuthumi and the High Lord of Arcturus and Sirius so it is wise for him to start to consciously working with them. He works with Archangel Metatron, and can tune into these Masters and Archangels to truly activate his own soul and his soul abilities.*

This soul essentially works with crystals, using them correctly in the *Crystalline Grid System* in the higher healing of Humanity and the planet, and knows which crystals to plant where on the energy grid, to bring in a higher understanding and use of them."

SOUL GROUP: The Shining Ones

"In this lifetime in essence there is a return to innocence and purity, releasing the nightmare of that lifetime. It is the cleansing and clearing of that past life memory bank, and the magic which was done as she was sacrificed. Even now certain symbols and objects like swords, daggers and knives will invoke deep fear in her. A *deep healing has to occur with her relationship to men.* In this lifetime she chose the same father as she had then. She had a deep inherent resentment towards him, as she felt he had forced her to go to the castle, which subsequently caused her harm.

However, he nearly knocked the castle doors down, demanding that she be freed. For all his efforts, he was stripped of his bakery, his home burnt down and his wife was raped, while he had to look on. They were homeless and your mother died from wounds inflicted by the men. Your father died of pneumonia, a broken man, after having to live in the forest, mourning the loss of his business and family – a fugitive who never recovered from the shock of losing you and knowing your and your mother's fate.

Regarding this relationship with your *mother and father, it is the same family again, with many old scars, but nevertheless there was deep love there.* The shadow of that lifetime often caused communication problems. So, indeed there is much pain here to be released, understanding that at the depth of these beings, there was just love.

So, here is the opportunity to return to purity, and to the state of truth and love which first involves forgiving yourself – releasing of all shame, guilt, and feeling unclean and unworthy. It must be released to the core, for truthfully what happened in that lifetime was not your fault – and no one could have foreseen what happened. For even your father remembered the man as a nice youth who sometimes came to buy bread at the bakery. Yet, the crusade he returned from brought out the darkness in him. So, no one knew about this, least of all your family. The tradition of the land owner deflowering the bride was ancient and feudal, just the way things were done at the time. It was not your fault, nor your father's, and the man who did this was in such pain, that the darkness pulled him in at that time.

A deep healing needs to occur here, let go of trauma and pain, and most of all, forgive yourself for being desirable and beautiful in that lifetime, and go deeper to forgive all those men, and let go of that ritual death."

———

SOUL GROUP: The Loving Ones

"In subsequent lifetimes you were not involved with the mystery schools, having lost some of the innocence required to be pure in this regard. There is thus much debris to be cleared from your energy fields, and your heart and soul need to be purified. With the awakening of your kundalini something deep inside of you has triggered to remind you of your participation in the Mystery Schools. You asked to be initiated again, perhaps not consciously, but *subconsciously, and thus you were led to this channel.*

So, there is a great deal of learning and remembering to do. You will be put *through the initiations in the inner planes by the Goddess herself and Isis,* if you should ask for it, and they may take unexpected forms, which might be non-physical. However just open yourself up to all possibilities, understanding that at the same time you will have to refrain from sex *with other partners for a while, to regain your purity.*

This is to teach you to go deep within, to open the heart and soul to truly learn to reconnect with the *Divine Mother,* and the *Divine Goddess* principle deep within. It means a deep nurturing and honoring of the womb, the pelvic bowl where the power of the Goddess within you lies. You must understand that this is so sacred, and so precious that you should not allow anyone into your most private places, who does not come with utter love and great respect, with the intent to create something beautiful and profound with you. It means honoring your body to work through all the accumulated emotional pain and baggage from previous lifetimes and this one, finding forgiveness for yourself and others and then to be so open to love, that love literally flows through you, and into every single soul you meet.

With you more than any other soul this is imperative because your soul name says it all: Soul Name: *The One who is the greatest Love in presence, when she is fully focused and aware.* When you are fully present and focused in a pure and open loving heart, feel this love to overflowing, unconditional love for self and others and are fully aware of the power of Love, you become a great catalyst for positive change in the world and all around you. You literally become the loving energy that changes everything it touches. That is how powerful you truly are at soul level.

Yet, all love starts from deep within. And it is total unconditional love for self and others. If the heart energies are not wide open, then the kundalini energies will harm more than they bring love. Remember this.

As for your Twin, he needs to first clear some of his karma and liaisons with other women from the time of Atlantis and elsewhere, before he can reach this state. There needs to be an awakening deep inside of himself, with a complete opening up of his own heart and soul. During the time of the *Essenes,* he retrieved some of this, but later closed his heart again, and went off on a totally destructive spree, turning against his own people and their inner teachings and persecuting them. So there is karma to clear.

So, just be aware of this, and only allow total union, when he is completely in his heart space with **pure love** and **deep respect** for you, fully present and united in what you wish to create here. It is imperative that you go deeper and deeper into yourself and your own soul memory banks to remember what has been taught. Don't look for that in any book that people may have put together – these mystery school teachings are so sacred that they cannot be relayed in this form. The more you **live** your Soul Name, the more your heart will open and the more you will shift into the power and purity of the love you in truth are, and radiate this love into every one you meet, transforming lives through your love."

––––––––

SOUL GROUP: The Loving Ones

"In other lifetimes you had a total dedication to heal the hearts of others, helping them to keep them open. You allowed men to keep you and use your body, but never to engage with your heart. When making love it was as if you stepped out of your body, watched yourself performing the ritual of union, making men wild with desire and passion, but kept your heart and soul aloof from it all. You acquired much wealth and status that way (albeit in some quarters you were shunned by society).

In this lifetime you will be challenged by both. The man will trigger this within you, as he has been contracted to. In essence there is much love between you, but also distrust is present from other lifetimes, for he was often your lover, but shared you with other men. All of this has to do with an ego trip of that soul. Essentially it comes back to his own heart energies, and him being unwilling to engage the heart. He plays at love, but cannot allow himself to truly open up his heart and love. As he is your *twin flame* this will be the greatest challenge for him to overcome, and also for you, for your heart is open and his is closed, because deep down he fears the power of a woman when he loves her.

As this is not a relationship reading, it is just to make you understand that in this lifetime you are called on again to do higher healing work on yourself first of all, by releasing past life trauma, in order to open up the heart energies to reach the stage of complete unconditional love for yourself. You need to forgive yourself for what happened in Egypt, because deep down you felt betrayed, not only by him, but felt you had betrayed yourself and your standing as a temple healer. So, there is much to be released there, including how you allowed men to use you, and you used them, without engaging the heart and soul. So let there be healing there.

You have immensely beautiful and profound abilities to anchor in the *Cosmic Heart Ray*, and so much to give in this regard. If you work with these as you did in Atlantis, something deep inside of you will trigger. You might find that you love working with rose quartz, rose oils, energy healing, crystal bowl healing etc. while focusing on the heart energy centre, and electromagnetic currents. This will give you so much joy and the Goddess, the compendium of angels of Love and the Archangels will be delighted to help you do just that. They have been nudging you for ages, however something in you believes that this is no way to make a living.

If you would establish a love temple or sanctuary again, and truly set about using these amazing gifts, you will feel vibrantly alive as your creative energy explodes, and as you find innovative ways of making everyone feel that immense unconditional love from your treatments. In addition, you will transmit the *Goddess heart energies* into the person, activating the *Soul love Keys* and *Codes* at the same time. These treatments will become so popular that you will open your own *Love Treatment Spa*, and it will be a rip-roaring success story! You might even branch out in developing you own love-filled products, selling and using them in your treatments. Don't be afraid to intuitively experiment – just let this happen and then see how you become vibrantly alive, enthusiastic, creative and inspired.

One of your Ascended Masters will start arising as she is working with you in the inner planes and is none other than *Aphrodite* herself – not according to legend, as Goddess (although she's that too) but as a High Priestess. Indeed, you will find the more you work with the loving energies of rose quartz, the more something deep inside of you will be ignited, and you will just love it.

In this lifetime, she has also met up with her past life husband, and wishes to break or mend the karma she had brought upon them both. It is necessary to tell this whole story, for deep down there is mistrust, and also the fear of being hurt – of something not being quite in place and not understanding where this feeling comes from. It is necessary to understand here that both souls truly love each other. He is not a twin soul, but rather a soul mate, and there is karma to resolve. Both souls agreed to incarnate at the same time, to resolve this karmic link.

It is best to do karmic clearing of anger, hurt and pain. Also simply sit and think through the vows. Do these vows still serve in this lifetime, and then, if vows are made, are they applicable? Is this love, one that honours the other? Is this authentic? Is this in integrity? For see, these are the lessons this soul has to re-master in this lifetime, as this is the last lifetime here.

The penalty of betrayal of the *Priesthood Oath* is still active, and true happiness will elude her if this is not resolved. In this instance, she must resolve or ask for release of that oath, if she chooses to release marriage vows. Her heart will guide her towards the right steps. When all those karmic emotions are worked through and healed, then this relationship will flourish in a different and higher state, with a greater love than before. Yet, only if this is authentic and true, from her heart and soul – for his soul has also suffered, having committed suicide. He has his own soul issues to work through, which to a certain extent has already been done. See this then as a process, and work with this."

———

SOUL GROUP: The Illumined Ones

"She will meet up with the Magi, in the next few months and years as she has already been in his sphere and felt an enormous pull towards him. Yet, remember what happened in that lifetime – what he was then, he still is now, and this is the way he still operates. Then listen to the alarm bells and don't fall for it again – because more instant karma will have to be resolved.

He is a high-profile person, and his exterior is one of charm, and what he pretends to teach looks all good and polished on the outside, but look deeper and you will find that there is no heart. Heed this warning then, knowing that your soul is strong enough to resist that charm and manipulation. To your own self be true!

Your Twin Flame will come into your life at a much later stage, for he also has issues to work out with another soul he is currently married to. Both of you have plenty of karma to resolve before becoming close again. Yet, this will only be much later in life when both are ready to evolve. For this twin flame relationship is more than just physical – it is transcendental, and the twins of this soul group have a very special calling. Yet, this can only be partaken of when both parties have learnt to balance vital aspect of themselves, so such a union can truly reach that transcendental stage.

First work to resolve the karmic issues between you and this beautiful soul in this lifetime. For here your true blessing lies. Deep down you do know this…. Yes, it is not easy, but remember that the scars and wounds of the soul lie far deeper than physical ones. It is also teaching you integrity, authenticity, staying true to your Higher Self – lessons you are regaining in this lifetime, which are vital for the true empowerment of your soul.

This is your chance to regain what you lost in Atlantis. For on the greater karmic scale, that was the only time your soul truly faltered, yet it brought beautiful lessons too, and you learnt about integrity and authenticity of living and staying in the greater Truth. So, see the blessing in once more winning the trust and love of the soul whom you sold out before. He does love you unconditionally, and chose to incarnate, so that your link can be resolved and the soul wounds healed, so you can both step into the evolved state and mastery that awaits. He will finish his sojourn on this planet a few years earlier than you, for his soul yearns to go back to the Pleiades, to serve there. So now is your time to resolve these issues and to gain peace and healing for your own soul and relationship."

———

SOUL GROUP: The Knowing Ones

"Work on releasing the shadow, and understand that it is good to voice what is there inside of you, and there are many ways of expressing this. If you cannot openly talk about it, then write a letter, but communicate. He will often pull back from you, if the old programming of that lifetime is triggered somewhere. Help him to release – for what he saw and experienced wounded his soul, and he never knew how to express or heal this. He often reached out to you for sex, because that was the only place he could lose himself in you, and feel that softness and the love that you are. He loved you so much that he sought that, for it helped to still the nightmares, even if just for a moment. So, help him to heal, and help him to love and forgive himself. He never forgave himself in that lifetime for killing others, and now is the time to release this once and for all."

SOUL GROUP: The Sounding Ones

"In this lifetime in your own healing work you will be asked to remember these higher healing techniques, especially with the pelvic bowl and womb areas of women in particular. Your calling this lifetime is to amplify your sound healing so that it soothes women, releasing the after effects of sexual abuse, being treated as sex slaves, being abused as children, and treated as worthless by men, for thousands of years. It includes teaching women to once again honour their wombs, and keep that space clear and clean. It helps to dissolve disease and *dis-ease* in that area, to bring in beautiful self-healing there – in that women learn to honour the Goddess inside of themselves, by nurturing their wombs, and loving that sacred space, where the power of women is held. Thus, they can restore their feminine power, and not allow just any man to violate this sacred space, and misuse sexual energies. In essence this is a solitary time of your life, because your soul wished it to be so.

Your soul wants to bring the gift of sound healing back to Humankind – as you do this and truly work with this, it will be amplified and the sounds of the Cosmos and lost chords will be transmitted through you. Your energy systems need to be crystal clear, especially your womb area, for this is the power house of women. Clear out all negative hooks, cords and ties from all sexual partners, understanding that as you heal yourself in this regard, you heal others.

You are then especially called upon in this lifetime, as your soul has taken on itself the mission to heal the wounds of *Mu* and *Lemuria* – the wounds of the androgynous form being split in half, and the consequent pain of loss of the other half, and intense search for it. Again, this includes misuse of sexual energies, and the whole bundle of pain and discomfort people loaded upon themselves by allowing that. You in essence took this immense task upon yourself, to bring healing and balance back to them. Therefore, this time is about finding that inner wholeness, and the balance between the male and female **within** yourself first of all.

This means embracing and transcending shadow and light, to move into the truth of who and what you are. In essence your soul is androgynous and you work with the angelic realms. In Mu you were one of the *Elohim counsellors* who took on form. The split of the male and female introduced immense pain into Creation at that time, which you have come in to help heal. As much as you seek that other half, that other half is there within you. The Beloved is there within you. The more you seek the Beloved within, the more the Beloved will reveal himself/herself to you with profound experience with sexual energies in this state – for the sexual energy is an energy force all on its own. It does not need a physical body to express itself. This is what was not understood in Mu, and what you foresaw at the time. You are a highly evolved soul, and it is extraordinary that you came in with this specific mission."

———

SOUL GROUP: The Graces

"She has Mother Mary, constantly with her, as well as Lady Nada, and the Divine Mother herself. See here how loved this soul is – how they are all surround and help her. They are also with her twin, who as said, is already in a different soul state, just the physical body does not wish to let go. She will benefit a lot from going to a therapist, who can help her to release the karmic residue, and a Reiki healer will help her to balance out the debris, hooks and attachment to the man, and the karmic link. This soul reading will already help her to step into her Higher Self – the wise woman, who heals others through Grace. Once this is done, the arthritis will be alleviated and she will blossom into a second flowering of life."

SOUL GROUP: The Crowning Creations

"This soul is finding that having a dense physical form on this planet, so far removed from the much lighter ethereal form she has on Venus where she is over 12 feet tall, is somewhat burdensome. She also finds it cramps her style, for she loves to fly free and unencumbered. Emotions get in the way, and trip her up, and then all her best intentions seem to fly out of the window and sometimes she moves into anger, frustration or even pain and confusion.

This soul has to remember that this is what Humankind created for itself, so it now has to create a much lighter and higher state of being. In essence, as she is a volunteer soul returning to blaze a new trail for the *Human Collective*, then first of all, that impetus has to come from very deep within. It is no use to pay lip service to this, for your soul is so pure at its core, that it will not tolerate impurities, and you will have to work through these very quickly as they occur, or else you will just turn off your own light and love from deep within. Your soul knew that before being born, so it is just a matter of remembering this. So often you intend to love, but feel threatened at the core, because of the way you try to get this across to others. It is almost like a part of you does not understand why people just do not get it! They lack that openness to receive love being emanated like sunlight. So there is that feeling of being let down, when people don't understand that you are giving them love, and you feel rejected.

First of all, learn to step past the ego little one. You are here to love and to radiate out love, like a diamond which does not resent anyone, neither asks why it must shine, it just does, because its core identity is this love. You are love at the core, and you cannot be other than love. If you believe anything else about yourself, then you are buying into the illusions Humanity spins around you. Get back to the core of your soul, and there you will always find the truth. Then love yourself totally and unconditionally.
You are super-sensitive to any negative vibes and emotions, especially violence, jarring music, or anything which is violent or harsh. Switch off televisions, phones, radios, and don't allow yourself to look at anything

violent, like movies, or video games. You come from a planet where all of this is unknown, and because of the calibre of your own soul, you are damaging yourself to the very core by even allowing such things in your orbit. Switch off all jarring and loud music, and get back to high frequency and healing music. Don't pollute your space with it, or allow others to pollute it for you. Especially with foul language and expressions of that kind.

Think of all your bodies as sacred and sanctified ground. Think of your home space as sacred and sanctified. If you like dedicate it to *Lady Venus* and purity, and don't allow anyone, least of all yourself, to violate that in any way. Don't allow negative vibes and feelings in there or anyone into that space, who is not on the same frequency wave as you.

You are also super sensitive to any form of drugs or alcohol, and even medical prescriptions. Let go of those, for they will harm you in ways you cannot even foresee. You are so sensitive that even one single dose of drugs, or alcohol can move put your whole atomic nervous system into total disarray. Don't allow this to happen. You are greatly harming yourself, and this leads to depression, dark nights of the soul, feelings of separateness, and being unworthy. You do not need that in any form in your life.

Fill your space with crystals, use singing bowls, and lift the vibration in every way you can. Play uplifting and high frequency music, have chanting and use candles and incense. Make the whole space inside and out, one single celebration of the Goddess. Make it the purest and most sacred place you can create with -everything you have, and then see how your whole life changes.

Then bless all you encounter with words of love. Bless everything — food, clothes, spaces, people, animals, plants with love. Use your hands and infuse love through them. Become a love transmitter. Everything you touch, all whose lives you touch bless them with love, sprinkle love upon them, and more of the same. Become a love transmitter, and radiate this forth like a rare, beautiful and precious diamond.

The more you do so in everything you do and wish to become, the more your own creative side will open up. You will find ways of honoring the Goddess, through love circles, through teaching others to open the petals of the roses of their hearts to allow the Divine love, pearls and perfumes to come into their hearts and being. Celebrate the Goddess, and make sacred places for her. Bless children and teach them love. Allow them to grow into the love they are at the core, and to express the beautiful talents and abilities they come in with.

Bring in the loving and sacred union, in which one loves the other with a pure and open heart, without needing to possess, to own, to control, to manipulate, to take or demand – teach the higher ways and pathways of **love**. When love becomes a deeply ingrained habit, then society at the core has to change, for it cannot exist in the old forms any more. Blaze a trail of pure love – teach that, and become that."

SOUL GROUP: The Energetic Aligning Ones

"Understand something very important here. You come from a star system where the life forms are very highly evolved, therefore sexual intercourse is on a very different and very high energetic level of exchange. In your own home planet, one does not just mate for the sake of mating, but is very careful in the matching of frequency bands and soul purpose, and therefore union is considered holy and the sexual energy is used in many sacred ways as a creative force, and not just to beget children. This is something Humankind has abused in the past, so it was taken away from them.

Sometimes you ignore your own better judgement, and you tend to allow people into your energetic fields, who jam things up and create havoc and so there is no use in doing energy work. Sometimes you are not aware or conscious of it, for you have the tendency to merely step out of your physical form, and watch this happening with some bewilderment. You over compensate by withdrawing to a level where no one can communicate with you, and then suddenly when you feel better, off you go again. What is happening creates total imbalance because you allow people into your physical form and energetic energy fields who should never enter because their own energies are totally out of sync, and of a much lower vibrational form. The same applies with your living spaces, where you practice your healing, and sometimes even beyond that.

What you have to learn first of all is *Balance*. Remember this is one of the first times that you have ever incarnated upon such a dense planet as this, so you are going to go through learning curves, but you will not be able to help the new generation of kids that are emerging to cope with life, if you cannot cope with yours. Again, you are one that paves the way for others, this is a task you soul took on. So, if you are not balancing the output and inflow of energies into your physical, emotional, and spiritual bodies, and all your energy systems, you will shortcut yourself, and your system will jam up. Then you panic and make the wrong decisions, and the whole cycle starts again.

Get very clear about your own abilities, and the boundaries you need to set. You are not meant to be like a normal woman, who only wants to get married and have babies, or just sleep around. That is for the lower vibrations. That does not serve anybody – least of all your own soul, for you are very sensitive and empathic, and then things jam up and short-circuit.

It is no accident that you are drawing mentally unhealthy men into your fields. The outward form may be perfect, but what is inside is not. This does not mean that they have to be perfect, but look inside – at the heart and what truly motivates them, for many want your energy, as you exude sexual energy (most times without being conscious of it) which makes them want what you are putting out there. They want to feel good by zapping into it. Some are fascinated by the way you can heal with energy or transmit it – they want that power. However, behind it all there is not the intent to serve with integrity, or to use this in higher service. They want this for themselves. So be realistic here, and become more discerning about whom you trust.

Yes, the last few years have been an inner healing journey. This has brought with it an intense awakening, but she will go through a number of inner initiations of her order in the next few years, therefore she will be challenged in those parts of herself she has not yet mastered, and in her own healing skills, as these have to be tempered with wisdom and higher understanding, which she has not yet retrieved fully. It is thus an initiation phase for the soul which will take time, as she will only be given as much as she can handle at one time, and no more.

Know that you embody all women who came back to bring in the higher healing of the female energies especially, and even if there have been traumatic past lives, now is the time to lay these ghosts to rest, and to stand in your true feminine power, which is always steeped in immense love and wisdom. It is the **Sophia**, that threefold flame which burns through all the dross, and moves into the inner core and purifies. You have that flame of purification – use it. Do not shrink – but start moving more and more into it for this is what you gift others with.

You will learn to step up and more and more so into your mission of higher energy healing with immense insight and wisdom, as you help to heal the collective feminine, and the male aspects as well. This is the higher healing that the 12 and 13 have come in to do and they are all incarnated. There is not one missing and there is but one single flame.

Know that these next few months and years will be ones of immense inner and outer changes, in that the more inner initiations you pass, the more you will change in the way you live your life and heal people. Women especially will flock to you for energy healing, and you will be like a huge beacon of *Higher Healing and Wisdom* drawing them to you. This is where your mission and higher calling truly steps in.

She is not like normal people, and it is time she realizes that. She will never fit the norm for she is not meant to. Deep down she knows this, and therefore she has to remember that there are not even a handful men on the planet at this moment who are truly tuned in on that frequency band. Therefore, clear your sexual energy fields and pelvic area. You are far too sensitive, and your energy system is one huge transmitter station – so anyone you let into your sexual area will jam your frequencies, and then your own higher healing abilities will suffer.

In this time of your life, it is not that you cannot have the love of a man – if that makes you happy then there is nothing wrong, but you have to be more aware of whom you let into your personal energy fields. All those initiations which you are going to go through in the next few years will be very challenging for you to experience, and still keep a man happy. You will fall over him all the time, and this is a choice of your lower or higher soul self. Your higher soul self truly does not need a man to validate you – you are immensely powerful when you are reunited with all parts of yourself, with a power to heal others steeped with great wisdom and discernment. When you step into that power there truly are no earthly men who can match you in any way."

———

SOUL GROUP: The Loving Ones

"You work in the inner planes with *Aysis* herself, as she in truth is a manifestation of the *Divine Feminine* and works with the *Fires of Illumination* from the 7th Central Sun and also that of the *Brother and Sisterhood of the Thousand Petal Rose of Illumination* and that of the inner and hidden mysteries. She is Pure Love, Pure Knowledge, and Pure Wisdom. She will appear you as pure Light and Love, which are blinding, and you might sense the perfume of roses. She will initiate you in the inner realms with *Lady Nada, Elohim Vista*, and *Quan Yin*. You will be asked to use the purest rose oils for higher healing work. They open the heart centre and rose petals of the heart and soul, so that one can experience ever greater levels of pure Divine Love.

Your soul, more than any other, wishes to serve in the highest possible way. You are very intuitive – please follow that, for this reading will trigger many soul memory banks, as important keys and codes have been activated within you, which will empower you to do the work. In many ways, this will be pioneering work you will be called to do, to bring in or rather return the knowledge that all higher healing has to go through the heart and soul centres, and flow into the living cells and into *all* the bodies, so that vibrant, radiant health can be found."

———

SOUL GROUP: The Infinitely Loving Ones

"Yes, he is a *twin flame,* also from *Arcturus,* who has incarnated with you and we may not read his soul records without his permission, but he loved you so much that he did not want you to come to this planet on your own, knowing how hostile and dense it is. However, he has had greater problems in adjusting to life here than you, and with him there is sometimes a deep resentment about having to be here at all. He wants to literally be able to fly free and change energy forms, and just do what he does in Arcturus, and then wonders why everything is going haywire within. So it really has nothing to do with you at all, but with what is churning within him, as he does not know how to voice this, and often runs away from it.

With the crystalline forms that you both have, one should be very very careful where you go and more importantly what you eat and drink, and nowhere is this more important than with taking drugs – you are committing suicide if you do that, for your body cannot handle them, nor alcohol in any form. It is poison for your system and clogs things up, jamming all your frequencies and vibrations, and then the transmitters from Arcturus which help you to stay tuned in, cannot function through you.

So, in this case it is not that love is not present, indeed love has been present for all eternity and in Arcturus you just know love and harmony. There is nothing else. Planet Earth is just different however, and—the environment, as pointed out, and life in general will disrupt things for you, if not monitored carefully. In this regard understand that because you both are natural transmitters, you need to keep those transmitter channels clear.

The work you have both come in to do together, is to be crystal clear transmitters of love, light and joy. Indeed, that is the essence of all Cosmic Beings. However, if inner stillness is not sought (yoga, meditation, long walks in nature, healing music, healing environments and food etc.) then your frequencies will jam, you will be at each other's throats because you are not living your life congruently according to your own highest soul calling and truth.

So, there needs to be inner housekeeping, with awareness of your own ability to heal with the Arcturian Love and Joy Machines, understanding that you need to be crystal clear transmitter channels."

––––––––––

SOUL GROUP: The Intensely Loving Ones

"This is the real thing, and it is here that she needs to be open to allow herself to be led. When she feels and sees herself doing things like using her hands in unconventional ways, and not in the ways she has been taught, then allow this to happen. The teachers that she had, although they were very good souls, are or were not of the same calibre and high vibration as her own soul. When she truly reconnects with the other 11 flames of her own soul, and her 143 other soul mates, within her soul group on the soul level, then this will amplify. Meaning that she will be able to channel higher healing techniques which will be different from what has been known on this planet up until now, and will be able to adjust her own higher healing accordingly. In the inner planes you are now working with *St. Germain,* with *Hilarion* and *Rekovsky.* In addition, the *High Lord and Lady of Arcturus,* and the *Arcturian Master Crystal Healers,* are all already there assisting you.

You just have to ask them to step forward, so that you can communicate with them, and feel their palpable presence around you. As you form part of the *Arcturian Higher Healing Team* who work with this soul group, you will find it easy to allow their energies to merge with you, and guide you in your work. In fact you often go to their crystalline chambers to heal during your sleep state when you have been too stressed out, or could not function properly. You may call on their healing for yourself any time – they are there to help you in every way…

You are in your last incarnation on Planet Earth, and have come to complete your journey here. You will not come back, for your skills are needed elsewhere in the Cosmos. Your family are waiting for you there – your true husband and star children. Deep down you have always known this, and that is the truth."

———

SOUL GROUP: The Caring Ones

"You had lifetimes in America with the Native American people, where you were trained to reconnect with Earth, to listen to her speaking, and to communicate with spirit, animals, plants and trees. You were, in those lifetimes, often trained as a shaman and in the art of drumming. You listen to the drums talking, tuned into the song of *Mother Earth* and the songs and spirits of the ancestors. You had an a-tune-ment with Mother Earth, which was amazing. You went on vision quests and communicated with the wolf, deer and bear spirits. You felt the Mother moving beneath your feet, and knew beforehand if there would be harsh winters, or droughts, and communicated this to the people. You were often that caring, loving voice for all those who could not voice things, and those who needed that caring loving touch. In those lifetimes you thrived, for you were fully tuned in. It is time for you to remember.

It is time for you to speak up for those who cannot. It is time for you to touch with great caring and love, those who have never experienced loving and caring touch from people, plants, trees and animals. That is why you are here. You have such beautiful caring in your heart and soul, although you often tend to close your centres, moving through life like a robot. You will amplify this by taking any kind of drug or alcohol, even a trace of any substance – like psychedelic drugs. Your body will reject it, and your emotional centre will shut down. Some experience this through sex, suffering deeply every time someone connects to them sexually, without loving intent – this leaves blockages and a black sticky residue which clogs up your centers. This is all meant to shut people down and keep them prisoner – so stay away from toxic people and substances and toxins in any form! Your body is super sensitive, and your soul even more so!"

SOUL GROUP: The Graceful Ones

"This soul must do the inner work before the outer will manifest. As much as she seeks to know more in the interim, remember that your soul has free will and choice. The choices you make and how you choose to live your life, ultimately affect how your life unfolds. Therefore, you may have soul contracts and a soul framework to work within, but remember that you choose the experiences that you attract into your life, by your decisions and choices. There is no one who manifests what you attract into your life except you.

We have given you all the details that you needed in your last soul reading. In the end you are asking for directions, when this is not what it is about. It is truly about your own soul, and how you choose to empower or disempower yourself. All knowledge leads back to self, and one can share with you your whole history as a soul, but until you do the inner work, and truly and honestly seek to bring your life into higher alignment with your own higher soul self, nothing is going to change or happen.

Look at your *soul contract* like a map. When travelling to a distant destination, you can use the map, but can chose at any time to hesitate and dawdle along the way, or stay where you are, or use side roads and by-roads, or get lost, or just not bother to move on. In the end it is all your soul's freedom to choose.

You belong a beautiful soul order, with all the tools and attributes for living a truly beautiful, profound and soul empowered life, yet, no one else is going to do the living for you. Not your twin flame – for even if he appeared now you would not be ready for him. Essentially you would believe that if he just waved a magic wand, everything would be fine. Life is not like that, and as much as you yearn for him, it is not going to happen.

The story with your sister was related to you to show that this has been a repeated pattern over many lifetimes. This means pain is being held within a soul wound which is festering. You may talk it away, shrug it away, and say it is only family, but in reality, she has come to teach you beautiful lessons. The lesson you have not quite mastered in certain lifetimes, of standing in your own highest truth and power, and not allowing her to do that to you. Stand your ground, shield yourself properly, refuse to be intimidated, and everything else will change. You do not need to get into a war – just learn to stand up for yourself, and say enough is enough. This will bring healing for both of you. The deep inner insecurities, and profound lack of love, present in both of you, needs healing. Heal the inner patterns, and the outer will heal. Sometimes it is more authentic to cut ties with family members with great love, teach them boundaries, rather than just wallowing, and sabotaging both of you.

The more you work on releasing, the lighter and brighter you become. You cannot skimp on this work. It has to be done. Cultivate a deeper and more intimate relationship with the Divine, and the Divine Mother. Ask with all your heart, soul, mind and might how you can serve. How can I enhance the lives of others? How can I be like a beautiful rose, and truly make a difference in the lives of all who I meet?

If you take the focus off self and onto the higher soul self, who came to this planet first and foremost to serve, then you will not seek that twin flame as if he is going to be the sum total of your existence, rather you will make yourself that, so that when he arrives, you can dance the dance of completeness, as you will both be complete, without baggage to lug around. You can tango *ad infinitum*, without having to constantly go and release more slights, pain and hurt."

SOUL GROUP: The Transmitters

"The question then is: Do you truly wish to bring love, light and upliftment to others and relearn how to be a transmitter channel of the purest love, light and intent, which will be needed as the planet moves up into the higher states of consciousness, and a new way of life? For the new way opening up, will not allow life which does not use and transmit love and light. Darker matter and form cannot exist on such a high vibration.

If this is the choice, then there are many options open. He can see where his heart and soul call him. Does he wish to learn to be a transmitter channel, to reconnect to the earth energies, and the *Web of Light* to bring the ancient, true and powerful methods back to the planet for the higher good of all? Then he will have to do much work on his inner soul self, and choose to work with *Archangels Raphael,* and *Metatron,* who is the Archangel in charge of Africa, and *Lord Serapis Bey,* who holds the keys and codes for this continent, specifically Egypt. Yet here absolute *purity of intent* and authenticity is demanded, for one cannot work with such powerful ones who are in the Light, while trying to serve the Darkness.

Should you cling to darkness, you will tend to self-destruct. If you choose rather to use your powers to manipulate, and abuse this power, as was done in Egypt, then you may work on the same wavelength as many who rule the planet, but it will not serve your higher soul growth. For what is not of the Light, is barred from the higher planes of existence and consciousness the world is moving into.

One can take substances and try and enter other worldly realms, but this is a world of darkness and fear… Once the substance leaves your body, then all the old fears and dragons are still there to confront, and this is ultimately the road to self-destruction.

Your soul has so much light and beauty, and immense power to do good and uplift the planet and Humanity. If your truly start tuning into the love and light and seek the *Divine Mother* with all your heart and soul, and are prepared to walk the *Higher Path* of love and light, then you will be assisted in many ways. Your soul will blossom and grow into a new state of being, and you will be an inspiration to others. You will show many how life can be lived, following your heart and soul. This is fundamentally a path you will have to follow on your own, away from your family.

It is not an easy path, as you will be put through many tests to purify your soul, and bring you into alignment once more with your own *Higher Soul Self* – the beauty and purity of it. Should you choose the lower path of the masses, it is not congruent to your own highest calling, and deep down you know it. Unhappiness and self-destructive tendencies only come when out of sync with your own soul, and its commitments before incarnating here. To serve the lower self and darkness is only a path which leads to more and more unhappiness, unfulfillment and abuse of substances, power, and whatever else.

The soul you raped in that lifetime is about to appear in your life again, as you have karmic ties. She is pure in heart and soul, and beautiful inside. However, there is a test here. Will you do what you did in the last lifetime, or learn to let love unfold as it should, by giving her the freedom to be, and to live her life as she chooses? If she does not choose you, then leave her to it."

———

CHAPTER 7

Soul Mates and Twin Flames
(Part 1)

The following are extracts from readings done by *Judith Küsel* on *Soul Mates and Twin Flames,* that will help clarify the many aspects and possibilities of these relationships, which are a very important part of our lives. Indeed, it is important to understand Twin Flames – the search for them, incarnating with one, and how they fit into the Divine scheme of things. This vital knowledge, helps one to live a balanced life, and to ascend more easily into the New *Golden Age* which is upon us now, as predicted and covered in Judith's other works.

SOUL GROUP: The Illumined Ones

"Subsequently, you know what happened, in other lifetimes he simply forced you into marriage or bondage, and then proceeded to tap into your energy force. However, in *Languedoc,* your father (as in all other lifetimes, he was either your husband, lover or father) came to protect you, to re-engage the sexual energies to break his power. In Languedoc, he could protect you while he was alive, but as war broke out, he could not do this anymore and the dark one came in as a tutor (as in this lifetime) and proceeded to use you. However, your father observed this, so had you sworn under oath not to reveal the secrets to him, nor anyone else. Subsequently you were married to your cousin, who also tried to inveigle those secrets from you, and sold you out by disappearing.

Though you never betrayed anything, and controlled the sexual force with *ancient rites* passed onto you as protection, which made him leave, thinking that by departing he would force you to surrender your power and knowledge. Your father died, yet continued to protect you from above, and in the process his friends, colleagues, and your uncles who were the founders of the Templars, through Philippa, your mother, came to your rescue.

So, in this lifetime, you first had to clear the karmic debt with the dark one, see through him, and sever the ties, which is now done. He will try and win you back, for he uses sexual power to enslave and entrance others, which you inherently sensed and resisted. Your saving grace was refusing to have sex, and walking out. He is married to the other one, not because he loves her, but because she runs his brothels and sexual enterprises, selling herself to powerful men. That is how he really runs his business. The teachings are but a front. You now will meet up with your Twin, who will have the power to protect you and hold this one at bay. You will reignite that sexual power to work in tandem. He knows this.

You will also be involved in returning the *Temple of the White Flame*, and the other temples to this planet. You will gather the High Priestesses, and he the High Priests, and proceed to repair this planet. The dark one will try to re-establish his hold on you, but now he will be blocked. He will find his energies flagging, becoming very ill. He will not last as long when separated from you, for he has used up his life-force enslaving others as always, through the body and mind. Unless he gets hold of another group member, he cannot evolve in this sphere... although he will try.

Dangerous this one, as always, he works under cover... and slinks around. You will be reunited with your significant other soon, and will go into partnership in business, and a very happy marriage. You will be inseparable and he will protect you, shelter you, set up the School, and work with you. You will have to reunite the twins and soul partners of this group, to purify and cleanse them. This is your work now. We are telling you this, so that you can be prepared. Pack your bags and get ready. Great and dramatic changes are occurring ... yet it is time. You will be blessed in manifold ways, and you will not have to worry about anything anymore. The abundance you seek is yours, and you are now being brought back to where you truly belong.

Let this then be your work:

Bring the twins and soul mates of the Illumined Ones back together.

Let the women cleanse their pelvic bowls, and the men their hearts and sexual centers. It is best for the men to flood their sexual centers with golden light, consciously seeking to raise that energy in a double helix form to cleanse their groin area, working upwards to the heart as the energies clear and return to the base. Open up the sexual energy centers in *Australia* and *New Zealand,* and from there out to the rest of the world. Reintroduce the ancient sexual rites, open up the crystal chambers which you will both be led to find. Purify the souls and cleanse them. Prepare them for higher service, and assist them to find and assume their crystalline bodies.

Reconnect them to the Divine Source, and the soul contracts they made before this time. Reconnect them to their soul calling by doing soul readings for them. We will assist you. The Earth's Energy centers will be cleansed and cleared, as you function together… often unconsciously, finding that all comes together as it should. Teach and write. Write your book from scratch. We will help you for there is vital information withheld from you, while you are still involved with the dark one. Soon you will leave. He is already activated and ready to receive you. He has known this since the day he first was led to see your photo. He is ready, willing and able to assist you. You will have to go, but what you will get in return is immeasurable … Go in peace little one. I am with you."

———

SOUL GROUP: The Illumined Ones

"His soul is a volunteer soul from Andromeda, here to assist with the healing of the *portals* and *energy grids,* and the planet's *Web of Light,* with his close connections as a Commander of the *Intergalactic Fleet.* He chose to incarnate in a volunteer capacity, to assist with the ascension of the planet, and to help crystals to heal the energy grids, animal and plant life and Humankind. He will work best with the elementals within the crystals, once he has trained his mind, as then he will be able to request help in erecting buildings, healing and in harnessing the high frequency energies.

He has the ability to teleport and to practice telekinesis, while also telepathically communicating with nature spirits and other beings. The relationship goes back to *Andromeda,* as he is her other half, who brings out her illumination. He has been searching for her, even thinking he had already met his twin – she was not, but is a soul mate. He has been searching in the wrong places … Great open heart this one, but also very stubborn, and he is at times rash, as he struggles to work here within a limited framework, when his own power is boundless. He also has the same royal background in Andromeda as you – this can come across to others in the wrong way, which really is the "right" way!

He was drawn to expand his know-how into other countries, following his love of life with his open heart, which has led him to connect to women, but not always the correct ones. He is very deep and spiritually empowered, often feeling himself to be an alien and this is correct. He does not belong here. He has had incarnations in Atlantis so is associated with the *Temple of the White Flame* – which he now has to tune into, by reconnecting with this entity – as you both work with this flame, and helped construct it. You know where the remains are, yet he does not…

You will link up for you have to, and the passion between you will be as before, and will include a remembering of the ancient sexual rites, with the help of crystal caves and so forth. You will then help heal the energy centers and portals, travelling widely. Abundance will pour in, and you will be much in demand.

There is great power in union, and this is why you are being brought together at this time.

There is thus the call to move now, becoming increasingly stronger in the next weeks. This is not a time for shrinking, but rather a time to step up the powers and to spread healing everywhere. *The Temple of the White Flame* is rising again, and you need to finish your work there, but this time in tandem and he is a catalyst and brings great powers to do so. Here is a union of souls who need to work together, and they will."

SOUL GROUP: The Illumined Ones

"In reading about *Twin Flames*, something deep inside of her awakened, but it was the remembering of the mystical marriage she experienced as *Hildegard*. For if the masculine and feminine within merge, it *is* a true coming together in sexual union as equals. However, in that lifetime, there was a *Twin Flame* incarnated as a Bishop, administering her convent. He often acted as mentor and guide and they had a love affair, only in their light bodies. So, let us look at this further.

Profound love grew, you were much younger and he had a gentle wisdom, tempered with an inner strength and vision that truly reminded you of the Divine Father Principle, with that utter truth and integrity that stood out above all. The temptation to become lovers was constantly there, but he always brought you back to the initiations and their higher meaning, guiding you through it all. You made a desperate attempt to get him to commit to having sex, but he merely reminded you of the uncompromising lessons of truthful integrity.

So, you entered these dense and dark chambers without a light, for the initiate had to find their own inner light to find the keys, codes and activations necessary to progress into the next chamber. You had to navigate your way through 7 chambers until you finally emerged through the *Eye of Horus* and into the light again. *So, you had to die unto yourself, to find life more abundantly.* You came through five, when fear set in, followed by terror and a deep depression and despair. You lay there hovering between life and death, when *Archangel Metatron* appeared, and in that moment, you were given a vision that lifted you up into the realms of the heavens and higher seeing, with that mystical sense of being carried through all this horror into a state of *supreme unparalleled bliss*. You journeyed through into the light, and there was much celebration, for you had now stepped into the higher priesthood.

You were identified as his *Twin Flame* (had been since the beginning, and hence he did the initiations with you) were permitted to partake in the sacred sexual union, for which you had been trained for more than 7 years. You had found the knowledge of the sacredness within, and experienced the mystical within, before honoring the sacredness in the other and undergoing the mystical union of *Twin Flames*, which is that of only the Illumined Ones. Thus, a bond was forged between souls that indeed was forged in eternity.

You have had a man in your life who has been in and out, sometimes as a dear friend, a teacher, mentor, and sometimes not being free to pursue this (freedom is relative to the circumstances, thus not only in the context of relationships). There was a deep bonding and mutual interests in the mystical, or hidden, and you were on the same wavelength. Nevertheless, he was married and not one to cheat on his wife and children, so loyal in his own way. But there was a deep yearning in you to connect more deeply and although you made this clear, he withdrew and hasn't been seen for quite a while now. This will change – you will be drawn together again, and this time the relationship will develop into something very intense and profound, as you both are more mature and aware. *This is your Twin Flame.*"

———

SOUL GROUP: The Illumined Ones

"In this lifetime this twin will be in your life, if not already present. He is a tall, slightly stooped figure, very Nordic blond, and if his hair turns gray, it will be white-gray. He wears glasses, and always looks as if he has been poring over books most of his life, as indeed he has. He is highly learned as a lifelong student of *Medieval Architecture,* and *Symbolism.* He keeps his deep interest in the *Knights Templars* carefully hidden however, including their secrets, the secret language of symbolism and the Goddess sites. Indeed, he often visits and worships at them, lecturing there if asked. So, he is active in that whole sphere, and is a very quiet poised man, who does not immediately stand out in a crowd, but his inner illumination shines through, hidden from those who cannot see, but revealing itself to kindred souls.

You will immediately know who this is, and it might well be that at first you both feel a kind of a shock on meeting, like a part of you is recognizing another part of you, and this uncanny *knowing* – you will just **know**. You both have certain symbolism in your auric field programmed in at your request, to read in each other as confirmation. You pledged in that lifetime to do this, to both continue the work, and that your love for each other be ignited once again.

He loves solitude, studying, experimenting, walking the ancient pilgrim routes of Europe, and just researching. So, as said he is not the loud type, very quiet, until you ask him questions that stir that heart soul and passion within, and when trust is there, out comes the intensity, the truth and beauty, the incredible knowledge of this soul, and he becomes animated and alive. So, never take things at face value – your soul knows, so trust and go with this.

You will discover that you are so in-tune that you start reading each other's minds, and communicate non verbally. You practiced this in that lifetime and others, where fear of persecution was always there in the background, when the ignorant simply did not understand, and what they did not understand, they feared and persecuted."

————

SOUL GROUP: The Illumined Ones

"She has met her *Twin Flame* in this lifetime and they have incarnated together, as well as many others *Illumined Ones*, to help to hold the Light for this planet, as they were involved in its creation from the very beginning of time. Thus, his soul name reflects this, as his name is *"The Illumined one who brings the joy and happiness of the Divine into Creation."*

Although *Twin Flames* meet in this lifetime, this does not always mean that they will be together in physical form. As the *Illumined Ones* are very highly evolved beings, and formed part of the Angelic realms in the beginning of the forming and creation of this planet, they often continue to work in this higher lighter form rather than in a physical one. This is largely due to the fact that they are so highly evolved, that even in that light body they appear to not be in one place all the time, but are see-through and translucent.

Often during incarnations here, they appear other-worldly, reflected in the wisdom of their shining eyes, and youthful appearance, even after reaching middle age in this body.

Then, when they meet, yes, it is very, very intense, sparks flying, air crackling, as their energies merge, contract and expand, and they will feel intensely moved. With twins from the Illumined Ones, often these energies are too extreme for the physical body to absorb at one time. Then one often shrinks, even when feeling this intense attraction, not feeling quite ready yet to engage in physical union with the other – but they are, in any case never apart in the soul body.

In this case the man is not ready for union – because in this lifetime he has soul commitments, karmic links and karma to first resolve with his wife.

These two souls, were one of those twin sets who incarnated here at the time when the holes in the *Web of Light* needed fixing. During that time, they participated in the ancient rites to facilitate this, as their collective flame helped steady the grid. Notwithstanding in that lifetime things went awry, for she was entangled with another man who was just after the sexual power that twins emit when in union. As he was not from this soul group, he had no business trying to gain such power, but he seduced her anyway. Later she broke up this relationship and reunited with her twin, but still had a karmic cord with the soul who had seduced her.

In the meantime, there were others also wishing to destroy their power, and sabotage the repair of the web of Light, desiring to possess the grid's power for themselves. They created and spun intrigue, and, having just lost his twin to another man (albeit for a while), he decided to experiment and was involved with the soul who is now his wife. When this relationship did not work, he left her, using some underhanded methods, so now has this karmic link to resolve, before the twins can link up this lifetime. This also concerns other lifetimes, in which he was inclined to use this wife's soul for his own purposes, veering off course from his own mission. All of this is hindering his progress now, as he is caught up in dramas not only from those lifetimes, but this one as well.

In the wider sense, twin souls are never apart – and even when they do not or have not had sexual intercourse in the physical form, they will unite, and the kundalini energy will be immensely strong – as their souls merge in different ways during the sleep state. However, as much as the soul contract is there to unite in this lifetime, and it is her last, it is not always possible to reunite *Twin Flames* during a lifetime on Earth. As in this case, basic fear and manipulation holds him back from cutting the karmic ties with his wife, and even if the pull to this soul is there (and it is), he is entangled in the web, which initially was his own making, and then later hers – however this is a web which only he can undo.

Sometimes souls simply get so involved in the drama on this planet, and in their own agendas in the physical form, that they forget their own soul and soul's mission. In this case, yes, he has forgotten and is unwilling to open himself up spiritually, or at the soul level. Yet this is his own soul choice."

SOUL GROUP: The Illumined Ones

"Thus, the point of these experiences is to wake him up to his higher soul self and mission, as he is highly evolved, and a *Messenger soul*, as he is one of the Illumined Ones chosen for this task. He volunteered to return to assist with the massive shift in consciousness, and wished to do so with his *Twin Flame*, as the *Twin Flames* from the Illumined Ones, when they merge as one, bring amplified light waves into the planet, and the fires of purification, transmutation and illumination. He agreed at the age of 38 to be ignited, and woke up to his understanding that he was here on mission, to bring in changes as a messenger as part of the Chosen Ones, for the Illumined Ones indeed were chosen by the Divine as emissaries of Light – thus Illumination.

Often though he tended to forget this by being side-tracked with world issues, and the business of daily living, growing lax in the matter of completing his soul mission, to bring in the fires of illumination, igniting all those whose lives he touched in some profound way. As his own vibrational frequencies became too low to merge with his twin at that stage, his soul asked for the illumined flame and fire to descend to lift him into the higher States. *During that Near Death Experience another part of his soul merged with the incarnated part and is now working with him – thus the shift. So now the mission is amplified until such time as he leaves the planet."*

SOUL GROUP: The Illumined Ones

"This has been a tendency since his first incarnation on Planet Earth, a mercurial character, with amazing genius and attributes, who is able to change whole galaxies – such is the power he has to change the very nature of souls, by emitting tonal or vibrational sounds, and combining them into a musical scale. He has in previous lifetimes (he is a very old soul) used this ability in a good and uplifting sense, by raising the vibration of entire nations and planets, to bring them into a higher state of being.

However, during the lifetime in Atlantis when he was a Magi trained in the power and use of vibrational sound, he came across a *Black Magi*, who greatly influenced him to use his gifts to control others. So sound was no longer used to elevate. He found that he could win the adoration of people by tweaking sound, to make them do what he wished – at first this was innocent, but was later stolen by the Black Magi Leader for his own purposes.

In that lifetime and in others, he always had a close and sometimes stormy relationship, as said, with this individual. In a sense they do complement each other, yet not always in a beneficial way, as he had a tendency to manipulate and use her love for him to get his own way.

In some ways he is a taciturn character, who loves to be adored by the masses, and again not always in the right manner, controlling people's minds with his music, and what he puts out, and how his shows are staged. Take note here little one, that those who often obtain fame and fortune on Planet Earth, are not always the most evolved or have the purest intent, amongst souls. Adoration by the masses sometimes corrupts, because of the temptations that accompany this, and the addictive sense of control. Music can do just that, and he knew that and acknowledged this in the state in which he had to meet with the Lords of Karma to become aware that he had failed to master this soul lesson. There is no right or wrong here – just lessons to be grasped.

He often was very lonely with all the adoration in the artificial world he had created for himself, and thus this relationship was a special one to him, even though he very much tried to control it. Once more this is a carryover from other lifetimes, and something that these two souls have a history of. Intense attraction, love and soul mate feeling, belonging and being, but simultaneously owning and thinking he can manipulate the other, by using this love as a two-edged sword. Love is something few ever truly understand in its deepest sense, so sometimes that eternal dance, becomes a dance for balance between two souls and here this is the case, always on the edge between two swords, sometimes uplifted to extreme heights, and then other times feeling cutting pain.

Once again, the two souls knew this before they incarnated, and the lesson was to stop this dance, or at least to find equilibrium, and reach the stage of unconditional love and acceptance, which in a greater sense it did. Yet again there was manipulation, strings pulled, pendulum swings to both sides. (*I'm getting the message from the Divine Beings in Halls of Records that this is closed now. They will only give so much information and not more. When they do this, they consider this closed. Sometimes only so much information will be given, to contribute to your own soul's growth and no more – for it is something that you have to learn or master – as this forms a part of your own soul contract.*)"

SOUL GROUP: The Illumined Ones

"At the moment there is a tendency to be intertwined with souls who do not serve his highest soul growth. There is a *Twin Flame* there who he sometimes acknowledges as such, and other times just flees from the intensity of the flame of love between them, as he feels too exposed on an inner level. Again, this is because he lives too much in his mind, and not so much in his heart. Yet, at this moment everything is a learning curve, so instead of pushing her away, let her know of your deep inner conflict, gently tell her that you wish to reconnect to all aspects of your own soul, and truly learn how to step into your own power, before true union can occur. In this, let love bring a freedom to be, where both souls can prosper and grow into their own higher power and full soul potential, and then when both are empowered the relationship will grow into a new and profound union, such as only the union between those of the Illumined Ones can be. *Sacred geometry comes in to play here, for the sexual flame ignited has to be channeled into the 6-pointed star, the Merkaba field, in order to reach its true beauty of expression, which then leads to ecstasy, bliss, euphoria as the flames reconnect to the energy fields all around it via the conduit of sacred geometry.*"

SOUL GROUP: The Illumined Ones

"When you met this man in this lifetime, both your soul memory banks were triggered, but he is totally involved elsewhere in another relationship, of which you are unaware. That is his own karmic pattern to work through, as he is in his last incarnation – so are you. He is not truly free to be with you this lifetime, and there is no need to come together, for you do at higher soul levels every single night, and actually are never apart, for you are the same soul. *You can never be separated from your own soul, nor soul group, nor the Divine, for one part of your soul is serving the Divine in the sacred Central Sun of the Illumination and the 7th fire.*

We will not go more deeply into your other incarnations, as this is more about him and your relationship there. In that regard, your life here and now is all about learning to stand on your own two feet, and not getting sucked into religion, for 99% of them are fragments of male egos. Therefore, they wrote the feminine out of their religions, and placed her in a subservient role."

SOUL GROUP: The Illumined Ones

"In that lifetime in Atlantis she was in partnership with her *Twin Flame*, also a teacher and higher guide, although he worked mainly with the more mature young adults, and their intrinsic genius. He was a brilliant mathematician and musician, and thus taught these sciences. However, in the latter days of Atlantis, tension arose when he adopted the *Black Magi's* teachings and abandoned the true path. Actually, they then led separate lives, as he was asked to leave the school because of his radical shift to the mind, instead of the heart and the soul teachings of those who stayed true and pure.

They also encountered each other, during a lifetime in France and Italy, where he worked with the great philosophers and teachers of the Renaissance. You you were a daughter of a nobleman who sponsored these teachers, and fell in love with this young man, when he first appeared. You asked your father if you could marry him, but this was denied you, and instead were married off to a cousin, the man you are currently involved with. You then took him as a lover, bearing his children, behind your husband's back, which caused a huge uproar when discovered. So, in essence he banned you to a different region in Italy, where you lived the rest of your life without either man. This pattern has tended to repeat itself somewhat, however in those lifetimes, you were always drawn to teach in some form or other, and always soul teachings, wanting to remind people of their soul, and the vital heart-mind connection. Here you were often in direct confrontation with the men in your life, causing conflict and you were torn between love for them, their behaviour and what they created.

In this lifetime thus your inclination is not to trust men very much, and you tend to be attracted to their minds, while at the same time feeling repelled by them. The more you delve deeper into the truth of your own soul and your heart connections there, the more you will discover that you will move into a higher understanding of the *cosmic truth*, and your soul will remember how and what you taught. Indeed, you will read or listen to something and just know that it is true."

———

SOUL GROUP: Illumined Ones

"Yes, he is the *Twin Flame*, but he is not aware of this because he is struggling to adjust to this life, after the walk-in. The higher frequency energy of his own soul is struggling to adjust to the denser life, so he also tends to shut himself down from emotions, because he hones into the energy fields of others. He might not do this consciously as yet, but is doing it nevertheless, instead of placing a protective bubble around himself, to filter out anything too negative or dense. It will take this soul some time to adjust, and sometimes his over exuberance to help others does not serve his own highest soul good. She is far more acclimatized to Earth, and is there to guide him through this awakening and adjustment phase, and to remind him of his emotions, yes. But there is a drawback here which originated in *Atlantis*.

There he worked with these energies in the High Priesthood, overseeing the acolyte and priesthood initiations, as did you. You were involved with the ancient sexual rites, with the awakening of the sexual energy centers, for there are reminders of the serpent energy raised in the womb. However, as he tended to live too much in his mind, along with some High Priests in that lifetime, he was influenced by the *Black Magi*, flirting with mind control boxes. Nonetheless to his credit after being warned that if he continued along that path, he would forfeit his position within the Temple, and as you begged him not to fall for their manipulations, he managed to stay true. However, he did adopt many of their teachings secretly. Later in Egypt, he started to use them in more ways than one, and you were in a dispute with him about it, when you caught him controlling the minds of his acolytes.

This greatly perturbed you, so you asked *Isis* for advice. Concurrently he withdrew his full presence during sex, (that inherent manhood, which is more than just a penis, but all of the soul, mind, and spirit and well as body, and a deep honoring of the woman in sacred union) and just used her to access the energies, and manipulate them. Isis told you to withdraw from sexual rites, and to work on your own sexual energies, and also to remove any negative hooks, cords and ties that he might have put into that area. Some were actually found, and this perturbed you enormously, as you realized that what had started in Atlantis, was manifesting into form in Egypt.

Again, you confronted him about it, because he was throwing tantrums because you were not engaging in the sexual rites. There was a confrontation. He admitted to being fascinated by the idea of being able to control the minds of those he taught, for it made his task so much easier. As this went against all the rules of the priesthood and especially the *High Priesthood,* as well as the laws of love and cosmic laws, you felt in your heart and soul he was untrustworthy, so withdrew completely from his presence. Later in life he regretted his actions, only after being basically demoted from teaching and training the acolytes, and being asked to leave the temples. He then joined the *Temples of Amun,* and had a near death experience which jolted him awake.

So, to work off the incurred karma, he lived in the desert for 12 years, where he prayed and meditated. Yet, he never regained his position, and you trained in the sexual rites alone, learning how to attain that peak energy without a man, creating an immaculate conception, as only a High Priestess could do, after many years of intense training. In that a son was born whom you loved, but your twin heard about him and tried to get to him, for he felt that he had been cheated on by you, not only out of sex, but also of fatherhood. Still, you succeeded in keeping him safe, and refused to have anything more to do with your twin. In other lifetimes he has often taken on the role of lover, or mentor, or husband, although in Salem, as your husband, he more or less detached himself from your public burning.

In France however, he supported you all the way when you were tortured by the Inquisition, and were dying at the stake. In some lifetimes there was great love between you, and all worked out. But in others, where you were both severely challenged, he shut down emotionally (the mind control story) and he sometimes *shape-shifted into an emotionless* being. It frightened you.

All in all, this is the time to relearn unconditional love. The sexual energy between you will always be immense, having shared those rites and taken oaths to keep them sacred and pure, within the context of the higher service work being done. The years of training were for specific reasons and advanced service. So, there is once more the challenge to find each other in equal and sacred union. In that yes, you are triggering emotional responses stemming from past lives when he was under the influence of those who wished to separate the mind and heart. (*Atlantis/Egypt*).

He is brilliant in what he does, but without a heart connection, which needs to come, otherwise the higher work will remain undone. You are a catalyst for each other, opening your heart and sexual area in response to meeting him, because he *is* your other half, who shares these ceremonies. The challenge is to find the right balance between heart and mind, trust and mistrust.

Your suspicion was awakened after Egypt, and those memory banks need to be dissolved. If you truly wish to find each other, you need to be able to work together body, mind, spirit and soul. It is not enough for him to recognize Source energy, and his role as co-creator. So, the basics are there, it is just a matter of learning to love yourself and the other, as yourself. Thus, there will be turbulence, and also fear. Fear lurks. It concerns those lifetimes, when despite amazing sex, the deepest parts of you were unacknowledged. So essentially coming together is the first act of forgiveness, letting go of the past, revoking old marriage vows and oaths, and clearing out your sexual area, as you still have negative hooks, cords, ties attached there, hence the discomfort triggered by those memory banks."

SOUL GROUP: The Shining Ones

"This other man is a soul mate who has spent quite a few lifetimes with you here, and is one of the reasons you are back, as he was your husband in three of them.

We find you both in *Atlantis* in the *Temple of Light,* you as a priestess who worked as a transmitter channel for light, and the light quotient. This is a profession or calling now unknown to earthly people, and they were highly trained to work with and anchor in the light energies and *cosmic energy light rays.* They were transmitters, much like a satellite transmits information, transmitting light frequencies from the *Great Central Suns.*

In that lifetime you did very well and were very powerful, until this man walked into your life – you were so smitten and distracted from your mission, that you even left the temples to marry him, for priestesses were not allowed to marry. That minute you ceased doing what you had come in to do, and married life just did not serve you. Indeed, a type of love-hate relationship developed, which manifested as *"can't live together"* and *"can't live apart"* infatuation. This pulled your energies into all kind of stress states, and completely shut down your transmitter channels, so you developed a deep unhappiness and resentment towards him. This created thunder and lightning and conflict, and you fought constantly, but then had sex, which allowed him to manipulate you any way he wanted, for he was involved with the wrong crowd – those using sexual manipulation to gain control over women to enslave them.

In that stormy relationship you totally lost your own powers, and succumbed to his exploitation and control. Indeed, eventually you felt like you had wasted your whole life, just for him.

In the last lifetime spent in Spain you felt called to walk the Camino on a solitary pilgrimage. On a very lonely stretch in the high mountains, you had a wake-up call, when the *Goddess of Lightning Light appeared* to ask you when you would return to the truth of your soul, and serve her again. She touched your forehead, you fell into a trance state with far-reaching visions of these lifetimes flashing past, and gained further understanding of your actions. Also, your true *Twin Flame* appeared in all his splendour, reminding you that the beloved was in truth him, and not the man you had married."

SOUL GROUP: The Radiant Ones

"In this lifetime your soul chose to work through your negative karmic patterns with those souls you incurred them with, and to meet later in life, where you would have the opportunity to finally work through your old karmic negative patterns. In the next few months and years, it may well be that you will be given the opportunity to do so, depending on each one's free will and choice. As in other lifetimes he tended to break free, and it may well be that issues of trust and other patterns will come to the fore, which often created pain and strife in the past. In truth, this will be the greatest challenge, which will need to be addressed and worked through.

It's possible that this lifetime will not bring about that final merger. It is about dissolving the old negative karmic patterns and creating new, healthier ones. Remember that a lot will trigger what went wrong before, so that you both can transcend these patterns. Oftentimes souls, when incarnated on Planet Earth, do not wish to do the inner healing work, or to shift. There cannot be a definite answer as to how and where such a relationship will lead, because free will determines the outcome. If a soul chooses to harden their heart, or not to dance with you, there is nothing you can do about it, but master the fine art of unconditional love for the soul, just the way he is. Your soul's greatest challenge in this lifetime is to live your soul radiance, your mission and purpose, without allowing him, or any other man for that matter, to dim it. In as much as you allow a man to run your life, you will find that the old negative karmic patterns will repeat themselves.

You are a highly intelligent soul with immense healing gifts, particularly as far as assisting other souls back into harmony and balance, and lighting them up from deep within. However, it is a matter of *"healer heal thyself"*, in order to become a great healer. *The Radiant Ones* hold the *Radiance keys* and codes of the Divine, as is displayed by the Inner Sun. If clouds block out the sun, one cannot feel or see that radiance. Often clouds are all that is obscuring the radiance, the emotional baggage, which is hindering or blocking one living one's soul purpose, and calling on and serving the Divine. This meeting was there to remind you to stand in your own radiance and soul power, and not to allow anyone to overshadow or close you down in any way.

As this reading has to do with your Twin Flame, this will not be elaborated on, but your own inner knowing will provide the answers.

Love between twin flames never ends. It can never evaporate, even if in lifetimes on Earth, it seems like it has. Love loves eternally – ad infinitum. So, even if things are not worked through in this lifetime, it is not to say they cannot be worked through in other lifetimes, parallel lives and Universes. When an old soul like you incarnates on this planet, it is mainly to work through the karmic patterns created in lifetimes here. In other parts of the Universe, these patterns may not even apply, for there you are together in every way, and are never separated as such. Planet Earth is one of the toughest schools of initiation in the whole Universe. Therefore, life will spin illusions. When one is totally immersed in soul empowerment, one will start looking past the illusions and see only the truth of Pure Love. *Pure Love* is the mastery of *unconditional love* for **self** first of all, and then for the other!

All of life on this planet will lead you back to the core truth of unconditional love."

SOUL GROUP: The Light Bearer Souls

"This soul is an ancient soul with many sojourns on Earth, also traveling intergalactically, a cosmic being who is not very earth-bound. However, at this time a tiny fraction, indeed truly a fraction of the soul is incarnate, the other soul flames are working full time in highest service in *Andromeda*, and also in the Counter Galaxy as mentioned, and therefore are also not incarnated.

As this soul has had other incarnations here, there first of all needs to be an understanding that the different parts or flames of the soul have incarnated in different phases. So, the fraction of the soul now incarnated, has not necessarily the same recall of her sojourn on Earth – for remember a lower soul self, and each of the 12 selves or fires, will often operate separately, and have different incarnations simultaneously, and therefore the 12 will be as one, but each one of the fractions, is also different.

Now think of the human body, the arms and legs all form part of one single physical form, yet each functions differently, and thus each has a diverse role to play within the greater whole. The records your soul is tapping into, are the lower records attached to Earth. You will only tap into those parts of your soul incarnations here on Planet Earth. Remember that different parts of your soul may have incarnated, thus the part now incarnated, might not be the same part as you are tapping into, when reading the records. That is why one has to have discernment when reading your own records, pertinent to this planet *only*, for you are missing the entirety. You are only reading a tiny fraction of what is truly your soul's book of life, for it is not in highest alignment with the **whole**, as found in the *Super consciousness Energy fields, as held in the Central Suns, and the Central Sun your soul belongs to.*

So get this crystal clear. There is nothing wrong with reading Earth's records, It is just that the complete picture is not presented, and therefore what you are receiving is not reflective of the greater *cosmic whole.*

Now the soul as incarnated here, came in to do specific work, to literally be like a *beacon of light*, showing others the highest pathways of Light and Love. But in order to do this, she herself has to be lit up first, and ignited from deep within, living her whole life as one total dedicated to the highest possible Divine service.

In your case it is imperative that you understand this. For your soul has strong ties and links with the *Ancient Crystal Temples of Inner Light* held in the first civilization on Earth (*as recorded by this transmitter*) and later on returned during the time of the Lion Kingdom, and then later in Avalon. There she served with total dedication in these temples as a priestess.

It was known that to serve completely, one did not marry or have a partnership, as this was a distraction from service, with energies pulled in too many directions at once, dissipating the quality of service, especially in those days, where one constantly worked with light and sound frequencies, and balls of energy.

It took total focus and dedication.

During the time of these kingdoms many *Twin Flames* incarnated together to do specific service work, and yours incarnated, to do precise energy work with you. This is very high technology, it was pure *sacred sexual union*, based on energy work, which needed to be carried out in the highest possible service. So one experienced intense and stringent training on how to access the highest sexual energy, with great love, harnessing it while in union. It was not at all how people now perceive sex, as indeed they have sunk lower than the animal kingdom, abusing and misusing this God-given gift.

Highly trained in this knowledge, you performed the ancient sacred sexual rites with your twin, but only at certain times and during certain periods, as directly ordained by your temple rules. You were both dedicated to the highest service. This ensured that the love, the tenderness and the greater union was preserved. Likewise, there was truth, respect and the greatest unconditional love for each other **as equal** partners, equally empowered, in the Divine Masculine and the Divine Feminine, becoming an act of worship, and a total rendering of highest service to the Divine.

Now, understand that was unique within that time frame, and it worked perfectly. However then came the second and third fall of Humanity, with their misconceptions of partnership and love, and whatever else they had created without the Divine.

So, in that lifetime your twin fell under the spell of the Black Magi, disguised in the *Druidic High Order* (in the beginning men and women were equal, with like powers) and they began to abuse the energies, and hence created a rift between you. There was so much pain observing him having sex with multiple partners, and additionally, he wanted to control you through your sexual energy centers. (A person can create negative hooks, cords and ties to zap energies from you, feeding off them, as was the case here.) So in the end of that lifetime there was great anger and bitterness between you.

This soul part of you did not incarnate for a long time, but his part did. He often acted in ways which created more karmic patterns and karmic debt to pay off, with other souls. However, we are not allowed to go into his soul records without his permission. It is imperative that this is understood, for even you may not go into his records without his permission, even if he is part of your own soul, as this would violate Divine Law.

So, after many sojourns elsewhere in the Cosmos, you both decided to incarnate together again, to heal from the divided lifetimes. However, and here lies the snag – he has far more negative karmic patterns, and so more negative karma to clear with all his sexual partners and lovers in other lifetimes, when you did not incarnate.

So here again, you are reading only part of the story and not all of it. There is nothing wrong with recording that part you are tapping into, but understand the law of free will and choice we all have. He can choose not to engage, have other partners and go his own way, or to be awake, aware, and reunite with you in physical form.

So, what you most often recall and experience, was that previous connection when you worked as one in highest service. That incarnation was in the 5th to 7th dimensional state in a much higher vibrational light body, with a keener insight and understanding of what true partnership and union meant. That takes dedication, utter honesty, truth, authenticity and then a great deal of respect, not to mention true love.

What is happening is that through your memory bank, you, have energetically engaged with him in his other soul state, his higher soul self, which he does not consciously remember when in his normal state. On the other hand, a part of him does subconsciously pick up the sexual energy etc. and is engaging with you telepathically – but the man as he is embodied, is not consciously aware of this. He is *unconsciously engaging with you*! For he is not aware and awake. He is just not on the same wavelength as you.

What this pertains to is that even if you send him your memories, he cannot see clearly because he is on a different frequency band. To him they are but ramblings, and then he plays with you, through the sexual hooks, cords etc. which are still within you, for they carry over from other lifetimes until released. Deep down your soul knows this, and therefore would rather walk alone and be sexually inactive, because she understands the highest paths of purity. This is your soul's memory and higher understanding coming through, and therefore you are being true to yourself, and your highest soul calling and purpose.

Your soul understands that the highest pathway entails keeping your own sexual powerhouse crystal clear as a woman, and to walk the highest paths of enlightenment on your own, instead of being abused and misused.

Now, there is underlying truth here, not yet consciously understood. You still think of ultimate sex and final partnership, but within a 3D understanding. It is time to switch gear. Your soul wished to incarnate to work through the negative karmic patterns that had been created, then to return to the original state of purity. Therefore, your path is not for the masses, as in truth, you have nothing missing. For your true *Twin Flame*, the one who is consciously aware and awake, is not incarnate. He is very much with you day and night, as a higher guide and you meet with him during the night when asleep. Often you confuse the two in your recollections. He is a high Master, so had no need to incarnate, and chose not to, for he has no negative karma as he has never incarnated. (Meaning that part of your soul).

So, in fact he is always with you, his love for you has never wavered, and is totally pure. Deep down you know this. Now, in this lifetime your wish was to finally clear that karma with the soul part, who is **one** of your other soul parts. Nevertheless, you cannot force anything. You have to just allow him his own free will and choice. If he does not wake up in this lifetime, then that is okay. For there are other lifetimes and parallel existences, in which this can be resolved. That your soul knows too.

On the other hand, there is nothing preventing you from having a partnership and beautiful union with a soul mate. Many of your own soul group are now incarnated. However, you must be open for it, and at the moment you are hung up on one individual, and cannot see clearly.

There is a beautiful like-minded soul who has been hovering on the edge of your life for some time, wishing you would finally notice him. He is a dear friend, genuine and true, on the same wavelength as you – but you tend to push him away, being focused on the other. So, love is there, it is just that you are not noticing it. Indeed, if you truly wish to have a partnership then it will come, perhaps in a totally different form than you imagine. Much of what has been put out in the media as *Twin Flame* love, is not the truth. It is but a hype. Look for the truth deep inside of you. In this lifetime you can only resolve the whole, if the other is willing to engage. If not, then understand that you need to give him the freedom to make his own choices, and to go his own way, and that is the greatest gift of unconditional love you can give each other."

SOUL GROUP: The Glorified Ones

"Soul name: She serves with Light, Love and Glory the infinite cathedrals of the God/Goddess, and sings praises to them.

This soul is a *volunteer soul* come in to glorify *God/Goddess* with the essence of her being, and therefore chose a lifetime on Earth to do this, maintaining an attitude of worship, no matter what illusions or delusions life here spins. In that task, she often takes on challenges to test her own resilience and ability to praise God, and be grateful in all circumstances.

Many of her life trials were drawn to her, and all form part of the *Soul Challenge Contract*. It is therefore to bear witness to the way she relates to other people, her nearest and dearest, her family and friends, but also to those who are not so. As they will reflect like a mirror back to her what she has not appreciated and recognized within and out. All are part of the initiations in the inner planes, where she works with *Jesus Christ Sananda, as Ascended Master, with Mary Magdalene, with Mother Mary and with Quan Yin as her higher guides.*

She had a lifetime in Egypt with the Mystery Schools, and also in Judea, in Jerusalem, where she was a temple maiden, who served from the age of 12 with *Mary Magdalene.* She married a disciple of the Mystery Schools, following Jesus and later accompanied *Thomas,* to spread the gospel in Asia. So, there are strong connections there which have come, or spilled over into this lifetime.

The *Twin Flame* as Thomas, has not incarnated in this lifetime, for he has completed his sojourns here, and evolved within the soul group, where he acts as a *Higher-Ranking Master Soul,* who guides other souls within the soul group. He therefore appears to her in energetic form, and often leaves messages or communication in symbols, to trigger her soul memory bank, just to reassure her of his continual presence.

They agreed to this in that lifetime when they were travelling in Asia, for Jesus went to Asia after rising from the dead. He had the greater benefit of his teachings, and you both went onto China and Japan. *There were many exchanges and also moments of sheer oneness. You vowed that whenever one of you incarnated without the other, that you would still be energetically with each other and leave symbols and signs, which the other could read.* So he does communicate with you in such a manner, and you are always with him in your sleep state and he acts as a higher guide. You knew this before you were born, and agreed to this in principle, knowing that this lifetime would be your last and that you would not return here, but rather go back to your home galaxy and work in the outer regions of the Cosmos."

SOUL GROUP: The Glorious Ones

"You incarnated this lifetime, with a strong desire to serve Humanity, so were not so focused on relationships, but more on higher service work, as in other lifetimes, you tended to become entangled with men, through dowry agreements and sometimes affairs, but in living this, you were never able to truly live out what your soul came in to do and be. Even in those lifetimes, you felt that you somehow failed, and resented men for having made you what you were.

In this lifetime therefore, you met the very men with whom you had created negative patterns in other lifetimes, where they used you in love affairs (in two you were the servant girl, and existed for their convenience right under the nose of their wives, and could not say anything for fear of losing your job). So, there was karma there to resolve.

Your soul yearns to be of the highest service, and to truly step up and into your mission in this lifetime, without being dictated to by men. This is one reason why you attract unavailable men, because subconsciously you do not want to be bound in a relationship, along with the karmic patterns which need to be worked through."

SOUL GROUP: The Glorious Ones

"In essence you are a volunteer soul in your first incarnation on Planet Earth. As you come from a star system which is very much more evolved and highly ranked than this planet, you have to understand that there are only a handful of people who can match your frequencies and vibrations here.

This is one of the reasons why your *Twin Flame* has not incarnated, for he is too evolved, and only a tiny fraction of your soul has incarnated. It was impossible to have more of you here, for your high energy fields and soul frequencies would not have allowed you to take on such a dense human body as is presently found on Earth. Your true light body is pure crystalline, and ethereal, and not familiar with such a heavy form. You will often feel weighed down or impatient with this body not moving fast enough as you are used to shape-shifting and taking on whatever form you want, to teleporting and doing telekinesis etc. That comes naturally, for that is what you can do in your true existence.

There are some soul mates incarnated, but not many. Remember you are a *volunteer soul* come to anchor in the New Golden Age, in fact to build and create it. So you have come to raise the vibrations and frequencies all around you – much like the sun warms all it touches. That is what you are! You are a Sun child. You radiate forth and ignite! You are fire!

Yes, there is a soul mate who will enter your life a little later, and who is also one of the *Sun Children*, very bright, and already healing others by transmitting his energies. Nonetheless he is living in a different state from you, and becomes so engrossed in what he is doing, that he is not much interested in anything else, for he does remember who and what he really is. When this one loves, he loves forever, so he will be true to you, no matter what.

As for your current partner, if you wish to love, then love by all means, it is just that you are not of the same soul group, although he is also a volunteer soul. That is what attracted you to him, for you remembered him from an outer planet, you visit from time to time, and also because he is a crew member of the Intergalactic Fleet, and works there in his sleep state. That was what drew you together. You will have to work harder to make the relationship work, for your fiery vibrations will be a bit much for him at times, and you will become impatient. So, there will be challenges. Again, it is all about learning to understand who and what you are, and about the body's energy fields. If your own energies do not totally match another's, there will be short circuiting. Imagine trying to install a mismatched program into a computer – it jams, because there is a conflict between them, until the computer packs up.

Well, that is what is bound to happen if you try to mate with someone with different cosmic programming. Something tends to give. Again, little one, you have free will and choice, and this human body, and all its energy fields is alien to you. Therefore, you tend to be confused sometimes, which is okay. You are learning and all you are experiencing here; you are transmitting back to your Twin Flame and home planet. So, in fact you are here on special assignment. You always knew that it would be challenging, and that you would have to adjust, but that does not mean it is impossible. In fact, it is an adventure!"

SOUL GROUP: The Glorious Ones

"Her *Twin Flame* has not incarnated, he is working with the fleet, and is with her in her sleep state, as a guide, helping her with her being and work. There is much love in her heart and soul, and she always wished to express this in many ways. So, she will draw to her loving experiences, and men who will love her, even if not of her own soul group. There are very few of her soul group incarnated, as most work on the outreaches of the Cosmos, where new galaxies and star systems are being formed, where mathematical equations and geometric patterns still have to take on form, when new planets are being prepared for habitation, or life forms. Thus, the Glorious Ones assist as co-creators of the Divine Source, the masses are formed, and the first places are built to reflect this glorious accord. The congruence in the structure which is eventually erected, reflects the harmony of the Cosmos and beyond."

SOUL GROUP: The Graces

"This lifetime primarily was about honoring soul contracts with both these men, because of karmic ties and links which had to be worked through. When this was done, the soul was freed up to leave, whether physically, or another form, it did not matter. Therefore, your husband's time on this planet was complete, and he wished to return home to his own galaxy, the *Bear Constellation*, for his calling is now in the outer reaches of the galaxies, where he has much soul work to do. He is excited about this prospect, having resumed his true soul body and form. So, he is very happy where he is now, doing the work he loves so much and delighting in his true 7th dimensional body and form, so much lighter than his earthly one ever was. So, he is just feeling happy and content, although he does send you love, and is present with you many a time, even if you do not see him."

SOUL GROUP: The Graces

"This soul will have to open herself up in this lifetime to truly experience *Grace* in all forms, for others, but most of all for herself. The Soul Group was created to experience loving Grace that the Divine offers to all of Creation, but first and foremost to experience this, and then to **bestow** it on others. It encompasses forgiveness, but goes beyond forgiveness, where one experiences grace-filled moments, understanding the perfection of everything, to only see, feel and know **Love** – unconditional love. That is supreme grace in its highest form and expression.

Before incarnating this soul undertook to work through all remaining karmic links with certain souls, and to live the giving and bestowing of **grace**, as this is her last incarnation here, or is supposed to be, as her soul group wishes to work through all karmic links, and to move away into a more evolved *state of being and serving.*

So, in this lifetime you are drawn together once again as husband and wife, to learn unconditional love – how to cease manipulating sexual energies and truly see only love. Your soul wished to break the negative patterns of those other lifetimes, and find that state of sublime *grace of all ages in love,* deep inside. Initially this meant to have gratitude that he had assumed the role of abuser, to teach you to love and validate yourself so strongly that you would no longer tolerate these awful conditions, but would stand up and love yourself unconditionally.

Deep within you know you are worthy of honoring yourself, your body and your energies, to experience fully the greatest love of all for yourself, and to walk away. This unconditional love will show you are worthy of love, enough to release all shame, guilt, and feelings of unworthiness, to find that sublime self-love, which is that higher state of Grace. Then to find the same for your partner, seeing the bewildered and wounded man within, who only wishes to be loved for who and what he is. He undertook to teach you to set healthy boundaries, to claim your own power, and mostly, to find that loving grace for yourself first and foremost, and then for him, breaking this pattern of abuse. Fear prevents you doing this, and therefore the other man in your life also came to teach you another beautiful lesson.

Here is another soul, who is the *Twin Flame* yes, but he too, in past lives has always played with the feelings of those he loves, using them for his own satisfaction. Thus he married the soul with whom he had plenty of karma to clear, for he had literally enslaved her in other lifetimes to control her, and use her in any way he wished. So, until he finally masters the lessons of unconditional love for himself and the woman in this lifetime, and finds the strength to honestly stand in his own love, and not manipulate or control others, he will not be free. He is accusing his wife of *black magic*, yet it is he himself who is doing that, by controlling her, and being abusive in many ways.

See, with you he plays the angel, but with her the exact opposite. He has astral sex to gain access to your sexual energy centers, and to feed off them. Often you will feel drained, or lethargic for no reason, because he steals your energy, so you need to cut all negative cords and ties with him on all levels. So here the lesson is to love yourself so much and validate yourself enough, to be whole and complete inside yourself, loving yourself totally, so you will attract a loving complete partner into your life..."

SOUL GROUP: The Graces

"However, it was during a very rare sojourn away from the Temple premises that she met up with this soul, who is now her husband. It was love at first sight, although there was an intense inner struggle as they were not allowed to pursue this, for it may have diffused, diminished and depleted her energies required for her temple work, as she well knew. He was not free to enter into a relationship either, as he was an administrative priest, building temples and other sacred places with geometrical shapes and patterns. Nevertheless, he was madly in love with her, sending her messages, so they met secretly, and in a moment of utter madness, had sex. She fell pregnant with the child which has now been returned to them.

However, temple rules and regulations were rigidly strict owing to the *Black Magi* infiltration through sexual means, so no exceptions were possible and he had to leave the higher priesthood, to be a temple acolyte. They cohabited for a while, but he was occupied elsewhere, and travelled so much that they drifted apart. A deep bitterness built up inside her, having lost her status and power in the Temple realms, and been abandoned to bring up the child. He returned and there was some attempt to heal their rift. He died in an accident on a building site, and left this earthly plane to return to the soul realms. She was urged by the High Priestess to return to the state of grace, by accepting the grace of forgiveness and to bestow the grace of forgiveness upon this soul. She died in a huge tidal wave which hit the temple complex, which sank under the sea.

The child has come to her for the same lesson, as he often felt himself to be the pawn between his parents in that lifetime, which has tended to repeat itself in this one. He is a master soul from the same soul group, come in to teach his parents the art of grace, of unconditional love and acceptance, and most of all the art of loving despite appearances, to return to the core of love itself. All of this, great and profound lessons in Mastery, and once grasped, this soul will be free to truly step into her life's mission for her later years, which will be teaching others the art of bestowing grace through the gift of forgiveness and unconditional love."

SOUL GROUP: The Graces

"You had three lifetimes as a shining light to others, and then landed up being punitively persecuted. In one lifetime, you were a *Cathar Parfait,* when the Inquisition tortured you on the racks. In this lifetime they have returned as tormentors and you worked off that karma, but there is still some residue there, requiring forgiveness and grace. Especially because your chief oppressor and torturer, is a family member this lifetime, who was that black magician back then, so there is a great need for forgiveness, but with the highest states of Grace, for he has opened up your higher healing abilities, whether you are conscious of this or not. Thus, you owe him a deep gratitude and unconditional love, knowing that you have worked off your karma, so he has no power over you.

The same applies with the woman in question, you also met her in this lifetime and she taught you some valuable lessons in how not to get sexually hooked. Claim the lessons, see the blessings, and allow her to be set free, for indeed she served you with great love, as she and the other man were contracted into your soul agreement to fulfil these roles, which they aptly did.

You were freed up to meet your *Twin Flame* in this lifetime, after a few lives of both having had other partners, and needing to work off karmic residue and negative patterns with them this lifetime. Please bear in mind that your Soul group, the Graces, wish to finish their involvement with Planet Earth, to move into a higher state of being. This is your last lifetime, in which you have undertaken to endure such a hard life, as you wished to work through all your karma, karmic links and negative patterns. You were warned before you incarnated that you might be taking on too much, but you were confident that you could do it."

———

CHAPTER 8

Soul Mates and Twin Flames
(Part 2)

SOUL GROUP: The Loving Ones

"Your *Twin Flame* has incarnated, and is slightly older, but not yet in your life – he will come later. He is not free at this moment to be with you, for he is relearning to open his heart, and to love, and is currently travelling in South America, in order to find his own heart and soul. He is attracted to the south because the heart centre of the Earth is in the Southern Hemisphere, and he feels the reconnection there. He is training to be a shaman, which will keep him busy and away from you for some time. However, you always meet him in your sleep state, both working on the planet's heart centre, along with the cosmic heart.

After these *rendezvous*, you often wake with a sense of being completed and sexually satisfied beyond anything ever experienced in human form. This occurs, for the higher your frequency and vibration, the more intense the union becomes. At first your mission is to work on yourself, and empower yourself at heart and soul level, to facilitate this work with women and children. It will take about a year or so, and then you will be led to travel, so do that, for it is in your travels that you will meet him. He is about the same height and eye level as you, but is darker skinned, Latin American. He is a man of immense heart presence, and he will remind you of the condor, for he is very similar to one.

He knows who you are, and is keeping watch over you, wanting you to empower yourself at soul level to step into your calling. He cannot truly link up with you if you are not empowered, for otherwise there will be an imbalance, and this loving union is all about balance."

———

SOUL GROUP: The Loving Ones

"As far as the question of your *Twin Flame* is concerned, there has to be an understanding that sometimes souls are here on this planet to fulfill specific missions or tasks. You had to first find that path again, step into higher service, in order to work truly unencumbered, without splitting your energies in many directions, as can happen when committed to someone. Women especially tend to sacrifice their own missions to please the men they are with. In essence your own soul is *androgynous*, male and female, as you hail from a part or parts of Creation that chose this specific form.

In Lemuria you were *androgynous,* and one of the very few who never split into male and female. It is good to remember this, and to cultivate the masculine and feminine within yourself, to be balanced. In reality when both are in balance, you are whole and complete on your own, not needing a man to fulfill you on those levels, for this becomes unnecessary, when you are really tuned in. However, there is the matter of a *Twin Flame* – bearing mind that there are *11 flames within one soul, and therefore, other parts of you are still working and being, in different parts of the Cosmos.*

Your *Twin Flame* did not incarnate, as he/she is busy working on a special project in a new galaxy forming in the outer reaches of the Cosmos. Another part of you is working in Sirius, another in Venus and yet another part of you is busy with energy work in the Pleiades. So all parts of you are very much engaged in working to the fullest."

———

SOUL GROUP: The Loving Ones

"In essence this is an old soul, returning to Planet Earth to finish off her karmic links, as her own soul group wishes to ascend. There are many karmic ties to Ireland, to the lands lost under the sea, the Celtic lands of Northern Spain, Brittany in France, and also to Nova Scotia in Canada. In all these lifetimes she was involved with the *Druids* in one form or another. In the beginning they were very pure, later on they too were tainted, as they lost that inner knowing and wisdom of the Ages. Although they were custodians, the veil of amnesia set in, transforming them into a different species altogether.

The first incarnation came in those lands lost at sea, before Atlantis rose. This was an ancient land and, in that time, and in that region, it was called the *Land of Mists*. It was a colony for the first civilization on Planet Earth, consisting of a group of volunteer souls who agreed to partake in an experiment to see how they would adjust to life here. The *Druidic Order* was first established by women, for they ruled in their own right, and therefore could choose the person who would enhance their lives, and there were no squabbles or wars. It was a beautiful and peaceful place, in the snow-capped mountains, with emerald green forests and azure blue lakes. Life was good, and you were so happy then. You were a *female wizard* trained in the art of manifestation, shape-shifting, manipulating energies and changing forms.

In that lifetime you never aged, but at some stage merely decided to return to your home galaxy, taking your leave of Planet Earth.

Many thousands of years later you felt yourself called to incarnate again in that part of Atlantis which was offshore from Ireland, which sank into the sea. You were in training again as a female wizard in the same arts. You practiced white magic, manipulating energies, using what was natural, and merely changing its form.

There was strife, war and bickering as the *Black Magi* gained control over Atlantis. The islands you resided in kept their energies pure, their ancient knowledge and practices secure, with no threat of possible abuse from the Black Magi, so they decided to surround themselves with a massive shield. Henceforth they were shrouded in a mist, and only those who knew the keys and codes could penetrate this shield, thus all islands were protected.

However, you went on urgent business to Northern Spain, to assist your sister who was under siege. You were so powerful you could change energies and energy fields, working with the energy of the Goddess herself, so you quickly set sail.

As you arrived at their abodes in a sacred oak grove in the Pyrenees, you understood their concerns, for the Black Magi had built a temple right in the forest, and were using laser beams to destroy all life forms. A torrid battle ensued, and you came in direct confrontation with the Magi leader, dark haired, and small in stature. Nevertheless, what he lacked in size, he made up for in power, so in the subsequent altercation, you brought down lightning and thunder to strike his head. He managed, by some fluke to deploy a laser, which destroyed the oak grove and Druid temples. You were also killed in this onslaught.

After that you had many lifetimes in Ireland, to try and rectify these events, always drawn to healing, or to working with energies within the Druidic community. In one of these lifetimes, you were captured by a Viking Chieftain, and taken to Nova Scotia and so began a strange love affair. You considered him a barbarian, despite loving him in your own way, and as he allowed you the freedom to be (within limits of course) and you helped him with your powers. You settled and had children. You loved living in this relatively new settlement, feeling called to start the ancient Druidic traditions there. However, a massive tidal wave wiped out everything, and you all drowned.

There are two men who will play a role in your life, the one is the Black Magi who brought the wrath down upon you, and the other the Viking, your *Twin Flame* who has already crossed your path. There will be a great love between you, more subtle and more profound, in the sense that in this lifetime he might not be free to have a relationship with you in the normal sense, owing to his past life karma with another soul. So, best to work on loving and accepting yourself fully, using your innate abilities and knowledge."

SOUL GROUP: The Loving Ones

"This soul works with the heart energy center and chakra as part of the *Sisterhood of the Rose*. For that reason, she works with the Goddess in the inner planes in all her expression and forms, as she is sometimes remembered and manifested here on Earth: *Mother Mary, Mother Amina, Mother Teresa, Isis, Athena, Artemis, Quan Yin, etc.* In whatever form you find you relate to, that is how she will express herself to you.

When the *Divine Feminine* was suppressed by the male principle, the *Sisterhood of the Rose* took it upon themselves to hold the light and love steady for Humankind and so never left, but rather withdrew into the inner planes of existence. They often took on great pain themselves, to keep this flame alive and to hold the rose intact. Every single tear ever shed has been counted, and every single pain has been crystallized, as one day they become that crowning glory for Humanity, when the balance is finally restored between masculine and feminine on Earth.

In this connection you often found yourself bearing the brunt of male arrogance, and suppression of the feminine in other lifetimes. However, in Ancient Greece, you were part of a city state governed and ruled by women. Indeed, they had an island where they ruled supreme, and were often remembered in legends as the warrior-like Amazons, but this was not the truth of their being. They worshipped the *Divine Feminine Goddess,* with temples dedicated to her in a matriarchal society, where land rights were held by the female lines, with women in all the high positions. Men were subservient, there to guarantee there were offspring, and women chose their men freely, ensuring they could also fulfil the role of supporting them.

Within that society, women sometimes abused their powers, often enticing men to the island, under the pretext of free sex with as many women as they liked, but in truth they had to succumb to their whims, and were second class citizens, especially later on when their lives became as much a game of survival, as a worshipping of the Goddess herself.

As a priestess you had the power to perform the *annual fertility rites,* where men were chosen to impregnate the priestesses. Most did not wish to be under feminine rule, and tried to leave, and some were captured to defend the island. A fierce warrior captain seized from such a ship came into your orbit, and indeed, he was in the prime of his manhood, as hard as nails, and spun his fancies around you. You wanted this man, and to have his child, as you desired a son just like him.

However this proved to a challenge, for as much as he was a good sexual match, he broke all the rules, and for the first time you found that love was rather like a battle ground. For indeed, he brought you "to heel" in a manner you were not accustomed to, eventually gaining sexual control over you, as he enticed you to do his bidding, and not the opposite, which was the norm.

This created somewhat of a dilemma, since instead of you having the upper hand, as needed, he did. So your fellow sisters reprimanded you for breaking the rules, as he had created havoc.

You saw that the only way to solve this, would be to give him the freedom he wanted to return to his own people, but now your love for him was part of the equation, and you could not let him go, without part of you leaving as well. (He was your *Twin Flame.*) However, you could not leave the island as it was your home. Nonetheless, after he got himself into enormous trouble, and was nearly killed by breaching something very holy and sacred, you had no other choice but to help him escape.

However, you could not let him go alone so returned with him to his people, where he was a ruler prince in his own right. Once home, he changed beyond all recognition, and ignored you, treating you as one of his concubines in his harem, which did not sit well with you. All your rebelliousness exploded with the force of the fierce fighting freedom you had always enjoyed on your island.

Love became a battle field as you clashed, almost killing each other in the ferocious arguments that followed. With that he had no option left but to ban you from his abodes, so you returned to your home which had changed hugely, as the original leader had vanished, and a stranger was now in her place. The women had become warriors, fighting a losing battle against the overwhelming forces of the men ruling the countries and islands around them.

It was as if your heart and soul had been torn asunder, and that is when you first understood what love meant – and that hate and love were sometimes much akin to each other, and with this insight, came a great resentment against men and their rule. However, with female rule restored, and the accompanying jealousy and undercurrents present all the time, you also realized that women without men, were incomplete."

SOUL GROUP: The Loving Ones

"In those lifetimes you often ended up married to a soul who is your *Twin Flame* who was a trained shaman, healer and teacher, who will enter your life in about three years' time. He frequently goes on expeditions into the Amazon jungle to collect medicinal plants, and to study the ancient tribal healing methods. He is very adventurous, with a lovely kind of quirkiness about him, and enjoys wearing one of those slouch hats, squinting at everyone from under the brim. When he laughs his whole face crinkles up and his beautiful brown, velvet eyes complement his longish dark hair, which is speckled with grey."

SOUL GROUP: The Loving Ones

"When you had the NDE, two other parts of your soul incarnated, and merged with the part which incarnated as a baby, so the push to serve is now greatly amplified. You do **not** have an embodied *Twin Flame*, for he did not wish to incarnate, having already worked through his karmic patterns and ties to this planet. You came in with the specific mission of traveling this path alone, to work through all the remaining karma and to serve Humanity at large, with all that you are.

This is not to say that you cannot have a loving relationship, but it is not written into your soul contract at this time, for you are first and foremost here on special assignment, and quite capable of standing on your own two feet to complete it. Should you wish to have a man, there is nothing stopping you, you have free will and choice, just remember that it might bring in karma in some form, or rather negative patterns which you will also have to transcend. As your soul group wishes to complete their mission, it might mean that you would have to return, without their support. Soul contracts are but a framework, and you still have free will and choice with ripple effects, and as one sows one reaps, even if lifetimes later."

SOUL GROUP: The Loving Ones

"There is attraction to the soul she is engaging with now, which is due to her beautiful loving heart not always being discerning about who she opens up to, for in her own home galaxy, it is a matter of partnering for life, with immense love. That is why the experience of separation, and multiple partners are unknown, for love has many expressions, and the choice of a partner is for life. People have forgotten this, and believe you can have numerous partners and experience sexual energy in several forms – yet that brings boundless pain and repercussions, which eventually causes more pain, karmic ties and links. Until people learn to first love themselves and the Divine completely and utterly as self, they will always seek that love and validation outside, and not within. This places unrealistic expectations on the one you wish to love, for he cannot make you happy and content, as these states lie within.

Deep down your soul knows this, for in your home universe, you do have a *Twin Flame,* and he has not incarnated, whereas you have done so on a few occasions. So, he is keeping the flame steady, and you visit him in your sleep state, where your relationship is as loving and supportive as always. You know the state of utter, beautiful and profound sacred Divine union, which is only felt by two souls truly loving each other from the depths of their soul, and being in total balance and harmony. One is not too much or the other too little – they are each complete on their own, but then become a greater whole in union.

At this stage of your life, you feel societal pressure to be in a relationship, such as your friends have, so you feel excluded, tending to offer too much and thereby depleting your energy. You consequently are in a constant battle with yourself, which spills over into your relationship with your parents. Sometimes we confuse infatuation with true love. Infatuation sometimes means you are in love with love, or the idea of love, infatuated with the idea you need another to feel complete and whole, to fill up any sense of feeling incomplete. It is also an illusion that often creates the notion that when you lose yourself for another that this will make them happy, or vice versa. All of that is illusion, and not the truth.

Understand that sexual energy is not comprehended to the fullest extent here, for it does not even require a body to experience it, as it is an independent energy, and often infatuations and physical attraction can play havoc with hormones, when there is not an equal meeting of vibrational frequencies."

———

SOUL GROUP: The Lovingly Wise Ones

"This is very much a learning curve in life for this soul. She has to learn to go deeper within, as said, for the path of others is not for her. When she is being taught, she often feels that something is not quite right, or is missing. That is because it is not right for her – it might be right for the teacher, or for the others, but it is not the right way for her. This is most important, because her soul and her own work with the *Names of God* and the vibratory frequencies, comes from inner hearing and healing abilities.

She is here to bring back this type of healing, and thus is a pioneer, so the listening has to come from deep within. She is on the right track, but not quite the right path. She should start learning or reconnecting with the *72 Names of God*, chanting them, first in her own tonal chord, and then experimenting with the music scales. It would be also good to experiment with the *Ankh*.

You do not need teachers – they will confuse you; your teachers and guides are there inside of you. *Thoth* and *Ma* are working with you, as is *Apollo* and *Lumina* the *Elohim, St. Germain* and his teacher *Rakovsky*. You are being instructed by *Archangel Raziel* and *Metatron*. So look, you have all these beautiful beings there to help you, to remember and to guide you into remembrance!

When you start this chanting and work, you will be drawn to another group who work with sounds, and the 432 kHz frequency. *Within this group there is a man, bald at the back, greying or with greyish brown hair, and big soft brown eyes. He looks a bit foreign, but is not. He has a tendency to touch the bridge of his nose from previous lives where he was the cantor of the names of God, and used this finger to test the vibrations of the sounds.*

In this lifetime he is a healer musician, and is also experimenting with the Names of God. From the minute you meet, you will be fascinated with each other, as he is the man who went to meet you in Ethiopia, who died in Atlantis, and is your Twin Flame. There will be a shared delight in finding each other, and in working together again. You will enhance each other perfectly."

———————

SOUL GROUP: The Infinitely Loving Ones

"Oh yes, he is a *Twin Flame,* also from Arcturus, who incarnated with you and we may not read his soul records without his permission, but loving you so much, he never wanted you to come here alone, knowing how hostile and dense it is. However, he has had greater problems in adjusting to life here than you, and carries a deep resentment sometimes for being here at all. He literally wants to be free to fly, change energy forms and just do what he does in Arcturus, and then wonders why all goes haywire within! So, it has nothing really to do with you at all, but rather with his own struggles churning within. He doesn't know how to voice these, and often runs away from his problems.

Being composed of crystalline forms, such as you both are, you should be very, very careful of where you go, and more importantly what you eat and drink and particularly you should abstain from taking drugs any longer, for you are committing suicide if you do. Your body cannot handle them, nor alcohol, in any form. It is poison for your systems clog up, all your frequencies and vibrations jam, and then the Arcturian transmitters which help you to stay tuned in, cannot function through you.

So, in this case it is not that love is absent, indeed love has been present for all eternity, and in Arcturus you know only loving harmony. There is nothing else. But Planet Earth is just different, and it is the environment and life in general which will disrupt you, if not monitored carefully, understanding that because you both are natural transmitters, it is imperative to keep those channels clear.

The work you have both come in to do together, is to be these crystal-clear transmitters for love, light and joy. Indeed, that is the essence of all *Cosmic Beings.* Nevertheless, if inner stillness is not sought (yoga, meditation, long walks in nature, healing music, restorative environments and food etc.), then your frequencies will jam up, and you will be at each other's throats, because you are not living your life congruent with your own highest soul calling and truth.

So, there needs to be inner housekeeping, done in awareness of your own ability to heal with the *Arcturian Love and Joy Machines,* and an understanding that you need to be crystal clear transmitter channels."

SOUL GROUP: The Greater Loving Ones

"Your souls have been drawn together since you shared past lives in Egypt, when he was a priest, acting as an astrologer and numerologist, often visiting the temples to consult the oracle for his own higher guidance. You became very close friends, which developed into an intimate liaison, both dedicated to your work, combining your skills which made your work very sought after.

In this lifetime that moved into marriage and as such, it would be to both of your advantages to delve deeper into the mysteries, for working together in this would result in amazing events, as you trigger deep remembering of the soul. There is however, another side to this story, which occurred in a lifetime when you were in his harem. He was a Vizier to the Emir of those lands, and was presented with women as gifts. Nonetheless, you hated harem life with its politics, intrigues, fierce competition, and rivalry between other wives and children.

On your arrival you were an immediate threat to the head wife, who had jealous tantrums, and persecuted you with her poisonous words. In a noteworthy argument, she literally poured arsenic on you, causing severe damage to your skin (which is now erupting due to your current location). In your recovery time, you felt a deep resentment and anger at such treatment, and the fact that this man had not stood up for you, but cowered before her. Your revenge was to put on weight, so as no longer to be a threat to her, and to ensure he would lose interest in you. *So, this is where your present weight stems from, and this soul memory bank needs to be released. In fact, you gaining weight did not actually deter him much – he loved you in his own fashion, but was still dominated by his first wife.*"

SOUL GROUP: The Gracious Loving Ones

"Often your relationships were submerged in a search, seeking the Ideal, however it fell short of what is there in your own heart and soul, in the form of true soul connection and companionship. It also occurs in conjunction with your own dedication to higher service, which never made it easy for anyone seeking to be in a relationship with you. You found long ago that sex for the sake of sex is not an answer, if it is empty, and devoid of a deep soul connection.

In fact for a short time, you did find someone who shared this with you, however she always felt she could never quite measure up. During those times you tended to withdraw into yourself, to seek higher meaning, pushing others out, which all stems from the time you were tortured during the Inquisition, when you had to withdraw deep inside to detach yourself from the unbearable physical pain. You need to release that karmic memory bank from your emotional body and spinal cord memory bank, so that this idea of being tortured for what you know, and for who and what you love, can be dissolved once and for all, otherwise this pattern will continually repeat itself.

You also need to *forgive the darkness* for what they did in Atlantis, and at the time of Inquisition. Often *Dominic* waved the bible in your face, singing *psalters* while you were literally being pulled to pieces. You need to release the intense hatred that welled up in your heart and soul, it was truly appropriate, but is not serving your soul any longer. This is also why the *dark nights of the soul* are there like clouds. Dissolve this hatred, as your soul wishes to be in higher alignment with its truth, which is pure love and grace, which always comes with forgiveness of others and self, for having caused the laser to bounce off the shield.

There is such immense love, higher healing and knowledge that your soul is returning to the planet at this time. With the releasing of the past shadows, something very deep inside of you will trigger your soul memory banks, and you will sometimes do unconventional things, and work miracles. This is because in essence your soul works with energies and energy fields, and knows just how to heal others through the proper use of these energies."

***

SOUL GROUP: The Beautiful Ones

"For herein lies the key ... Your relationships tend to fail, because you are so intense one minute and then withdraw in the next, it is a matter of you feeling the beauty in one moment, simply dancing with exuberance and a beautiful expression of your true nature. Then in the next instance you withdraw into that other world, leaving the person in a state of limbo, not quite knowing how to love, or dance with you. So, it tends to be you dancing to one tune and your partner(s) to another, thus you clash.

The man you connected with loves those of his own sex, and has sometimes had problems adjusting to life here – he is lost in the way that he does not quite know whether he is male or female, and there lies his own struggle. Yet, there are also other hidden things, which he is concealing deep within. Such souls have to master their own paths and worlds, so it is best to sometimes simply leave them to overcome this on their own, and not intervene with their free will, leaving them to discover what needs to be nurtured and found deep within.

There is a younger man waiting in the wings, and he is your *Twin Flame*. He has dark hair, beautiful blue eyes, a sensitive face, and he is a dancer in another country to the north of you. He has great beauty and passion in his soul, and loves to live life with exuberance, with a true passion for expressing and healing with his dance and music. He plays the violin with his long-tapered fingers, with gypsy blood running through him. His hair is curly and he is intense – very intense, and is the partner who truly will enhance you, as he hears the same music, and dances in step. Combined you will create magic– a true beautiful magical dancing vibration, as your talents and abilities merge, healing many by teaching them to dance to the tune of their souls, and listening to the music within."

SOUL GROUP: The Beautiful Ones

"As far as relationships go, you have not incarnated here before. You acted more like a higher guide from the Pleiades, where you have soul connections. When Earth was first created, by those from the *12 Master Galaxies*, you were part of that team, here to create beauty, and she was the *Crown Jewel of Creation* when completed. Those who flew past in the Motherships and other craft, would often just stand in awe and wonder at this beautiful planet

Alas she is no longer that, for Humanity created ugliness and discord. Thus you have come in to recreate. Yet, always what is within, will manifest on the outside, and nowhere is this truer than in relationships. If all is stormy and dark inside, that is what will manifest on the outside.

You tend to love, and then insecurities pull you into creative uncertainty, sometimes doubting your own ability to create beauty and harmony. If you truly wish to gift yourself at soul level, then it is time to nurture that inner child deep within, and allow it to feel so loved, so filled with beauty, and so lovable, that this is what manifests outside. **If you feel loved from deep within, feel validated from deep within, beautiful from deep within, then you will radiate this outwards and it will manifest in your relationships.**

Your first love was a soul mate, who helped to create beautiful Planet Earth. You work together in the *Intergalactic Federation of Light* with *Jesus Christ Sananda, Lady Nada, Lady Portia,* and with other *Ascended Masters* like *Paul the Venetian,* to create beauty and harmony – so here kindred spirits meet. However, it was your own insecure belief that you were unworthy, or not beautiful enough, that brought this relationship to a close.

There has since been inner growth and more maturity, so it served its time and purpose. Your *Twin Flame* is not incarnated at present, mainly as he is very highly advanced and is much occupied with creating a new planet of beauty in the outer regions of the Milky Way Galaxy. He works for the *Intergalactic Federation of Light* and you have three children in the inner planes, whom you visit every night while asleep and have a beautiful, loving and balanced, blissful relationship with him, which is also sexual, and therefore a sacred union.

In this lifetime you will find that something deep inside of you knows or remembers this, and therefore all relationships with any man in this lifetime, soul mate or not, will feel inadequate."

———

SOUL GROUP: The Joyful Ones

"She will often draw men to her who sense this inner power, and are sexually attracted to her. Even so, she always had a deep mistrust which stems from a lifetime in *Atlantis*, when the *Black Magi* coveted her powers, sending their lackey on many occasions to seduce her, but the strong love bond between her and her *Twin Flame* kept her untouched, although she witnessed many temple priestesses succumb. In this lifetime this will manifest as an aloofness, which is really her own higher soul self, guiding her to the inner knowing not to compromise her highest truth and wisdom for just a fling.

One of the men she is currently in a relationship with, or is there hovering around her, is a man who is often in the role of a mentor. Lately this has become more intimate, however it is a strange hide-and-seek game. Both are hiding like two sparring partners in a fencing match. He is hiding many layers of being, like a layered flirting with the dark side, mixed in with reality. That is intense shadow. He often pretends to be all light. Deep down you have sensed this, and thus withheld your deepest self and just played along.

Lately this has bothered you, as he is somewhat obsessed with you, sensing you are deeper than first thought, with an inner power he lacks. He was a *Black Magi in Atlantis*, and one you confronted on many issues. In this lifetime that shadow is not as intense (for he has had a number lifetimes since then, paying karmic debts), but it is there, carefully hidden. He belongs to certain secret societies where atrocities are still committed, unknown to the lower ranks. So just be careful of this one. He is not what he seems. It might be that he is a colleague, so just play it carefully. What he truly wants is your inherent knowledge and power, which he knows is there, for he is very psychic, although he carefully hides this.

There is another man in this milieu who is the quieter type, not open with his deepest feelings, sometimes friend and lover, and other times on the outside looking in. He has a deep and profound interconnection with you through many lifetimes as one of your soul mates, but mostly travels his path solo, because in essence he is *androgynous,* and always has been. Sometimes he is not quite sure whether he prefers males or females or both. The yin/yang within is sometimes out of balance, so he often seeks your company when he seeks the more feminine aspects of self. He is a deeply sensitive soul who can channel music.

Sometimes there is the interplay between all three of you, as karmic links play you with that back-and-forth between dark and light, which may be there to awaken you to your greater mission, or roles to fulfil.

There is another man who often acts as a mentor, or friend or whatever he chooses to be, and is currently going through many changes. He hovers around but not seriously, as he is in a relationship, and is more like a platonic friend. He has been a mentor in previous lives, and is assuming this role again.

At this time, it is wise to first be crystal clear about what you want and where you wish to be. If you wish to be true to your own *higher soul self,* then changes will come. For deep down there is a yearning to move more into being an orator or inspirational speaker, or even a life coach, or something similar where that innate wisdom and knowledge can help others. That in itself is a blessing, and more will flow from it, and you will make it a success. If you try and get back into nature especially into a sacred oak grove, to just sit and meditate and ask for higher guidance to come through, it will.

You have, interestingly enough, *Merlin* as one of your higher guides and *Thoth, St. Germain* and *Serapis Bey,* all working with inner knowledge and wisdom that is currently still being withheld from Humankind. Merlin is the one in charge of the sacred groves, often by your side, trying to pull you to them. You work closely with *Sophia, the Divine Wisdom* in its feminine form, and *Lady Nada,* who works closely with Serapis Bey.

You also have a great connection to standing stones and stone circles, which the *Wisdom Keepers* of the planet programmed to reveal their knowledge to those who truly seek. Again, this is there in your soul, to reconnect with your inner soul self – listen and write down whatever guidance comes. There is immensely powerful information you can tap into, for it is there inside you. Your soul knows this. Heed this. It is important.

Interestingly your *Twin Flame* has incarnated further north, and is still in Russia. In fact, he has lately been drawn to the Ural Mountains to work here. He not only looks a lot like you, just taller, but he is an engineer of sorts on assignment. He found himself suddenly being able to speak publicly, so is gathering groups around him while in the process of resigning from his job, and assembling a *School of Wisdom,* or something similar. Remarkably his soul has strong ties with *Dostoevsky,* as he was one of his disciples in a lifetime prior to this.

If you take a trip to the Ural Mountains, in tune with your higher soul self, you will find yourself drawn to each other, a happy reunion of souls who have always loved each other dearly, whether you decide to be together or not. That is your free will and choice. If you chose to stay together you will be immensely powerful orators, and will touch the lives and soul of thousands as this will be a ministry on its own. In this then there are strong ties to these mountains calling you but again, it is your free will and decision whether to heed this or not."

SOUL GROUP: The Joyous Ones

"Your *Twin Flame* is the *High Healer Lord of Arcturus* and goes under the name of *Arctus.* He loves you so much that he is with you day and night, and acts as a higher guide for you. You constantly reunite with him at night while you sleep and experience blissful unions there. So, it is not that you lack this beautiful and profound love – you have it, just in another state, or higher existence of your soul. This is the truth of love as deep down you know this, and no earthly man will ever be able to match up to him, for they just simply are not at that level, and would take too long to get there. So, there will be challenges with human relationships for you, for most men on this planet are not so evolved and struggle with their own egos, and sexual self-gratification, not always acting from the state of pure love. So, when challenged in this way, understand that sometimes it is better to walk one's path alone and know that nothing is ever missing, rather than to invite more unsuitable relationships into your life."

SOUL GROUP: The Cosmic Joyous Ones

"As you have never experienced this before in your other lives (where souls have a committed partnership with their *Divine Other* happily for life, living in harmony and bliss), you will be challenged here on Planet Earth to find the same. Your *Twin Flame* has not incarnated, because you are both so highly evolved, but he is with you as a higher guide. In your sleep state you are reunited with him, and receive all the love and attention and sexual pleasures, that you cannot find on Earth. So, love is not absent in your life – it is merely that you know a higher state of love and being."

SOUL GROUP: The Joyous Ones

"As for your twin – he has not incarnated this time round for he felt that it was not necessary. He worked off his karma here in his last lifetime, when he also incarnated without you, as you were elsewhere. He is a highly advanced master soul, and works mainly on *Pegasus,* so is very involved with the horse energy there. As one of the leaders in this star system or galaxy, there was no need to incarnate, so it was decided you would incarnate to work through old karmic ties and links, and to assist with the anchoring in of the return of the Goddess, and the Goddess energies. He acts therefore as higher guide, and goes by the name of *Art-u-vian-u-an.* He is a very high-ranking soul whose frequencies and vibrations are higher than any soul on Planet Earth. You often meet him in your soul state in sleep state, and also in the higher Goddess Councils over which you both preside."

SOUL GROUP: The Joyous Ones

"There is a new soul in her life, he is not her Twin Flame, but rather another fractal of her soul, manifested into a form which he assumed when he took over, or rather was a walk-in to the entity which houses his body – more like a merger. He is one part of your soul, which, within the soul group context, energized and merged with the soul who occupied the body. Your soul has 12 flames, and in this regard, he has one of the other flames or fires of the soul, like a twin, but only one single shard of that – so with 6 of the flames being male, this means that five are still not incarnated, and therefore this is just one single fraction of the soul fire.

Your soul has more *female parts* incarnated, which, in this lifetime through steady integration of the two other flames during initiations, has amplified your mission, but then he is just one – so that makes *four shards, three feminine and one masculine.* So, there is no equal balance, because the other male parts are holding the guidance. This concerns your own soul mission, which is to amplify the female energy, so that the Goddess energies can be anchored in, and therefore does not really need that male energy. You tend to get yourself tangled up with the male energies, not always serving your highest soul growth and good, often preventing you from stepping up in your own power to fulfil your mission

The so-called manifestation of what is part of your own soul, albeit a fraction in male form, is merging with the entity or soul already occupying the body. It was done with permission of both. We are not allowed to go into this soul's record, even if a part of your own soul, without his permission. Suffice to say, that if you truly wish this merger to walk this path with him, then that is permissible if you both agree, with an understanding that to truly have pure love, you must go through the fires of initiations, so all that no longer serves the highest soul growth and good may fall away, especially at this time when there is a massive shift."

SOUL GROUP: The Joyous Ones

"You have been with a *soul mate* (or are for that matter, if he is the father of your children, or of that family) and you share much in common. There is love yes, but firstly joy has to well up from deep inside, with no false expectations that the other should fill you up, or give you joy, etc. No. You have to be this unto yourself, with your inner joy turned on. *The twin* is interesting, for you have met him a few times, fleetingly in this lifetime, but both of you were engaged elsewhere. Immense energy was released between you, but you shied away from it all, each going in their own direction again.

You might remember, or you might not. He is at this moment in Europe, struggling between his mind and heart. He is a psychiatrist, or someone who works with the psyche, but his heart and soul are not yet engaged. He is searching for truth and answers, and his mind often gets in the way of his own intuitive knowing. This has to do with a past life where he turned against you, as you warned him of betrayal within his ranks of Druidic Priests (Avalon) and he, in turn accused you of betrayal. You were outraged, and the pain caused a rift. When he deserted you and the rest of the priesthood who remained and stayed true to the *Law of One*, it was traumatic, and he eventually destroyed himself.

You will not meet him again until he finally listens to the call of his soul, and embarks on reconnecting at a deep soul level, listening to his inner knowing. That is his soul lesson to master, and not yours. Yours is to stand on your own two feet, and stay true to your innermost heart and soul, getting the needed work done, even if alone for a while, or with someone else, like the soul mate, as there you have free will and choice. If you are really on the same wavelength with another, then it does not matter if he is a soul mate or not, it is just an opportunity to learn ever greater levels of love and joy, to keep your heart open, and to understand that every single soul brings lessons and gifts.

When you do meet your *Twin Flame,* it will be very intense and filled with emotional charge. You will literally scrape the edges off each other, to expose the best and worst. There again it is a matter of finding the **joy** inside, not seeking it in, or with him. You will at last know that love is eternally present, never absent, it merely changes form. This might however manifest later in life, as said he is still struggling with his soul lessons, and the more he resists them, the more they will persist. So here then lies the greatest opportunity of your life, to truly live your soul calling and purpose. You have such a beautiful and profound gift to bring out the very best in other people, to spark that inner joy, that inner love, to inspire and teach others, and to reach them deep within.

If you bring this light heartedness, this joyous expression of the life force into all that you are – a *joie de vivre,* that bubbling of joy from deep within, you will attract people to you, who will want what you have. You are quite a magnet when you allow your soul to shine through, and that Divine Joy to break through. It is beautiful, and is a supreme gift you can bring to others. So then become that Joy which changes and ignites the *Human race* and brings them back to the first time, when they effortlessly lived this within the *Law of One,* and when they knew peace, harmony and abundant life. You are here to help heal the pain of Humanity, and bring them back into their highest joy and love. However, this work first has to start deep within yourself, before you can truly gift it to others."

———

SOUL GROUP: The Moving Spiraling Loving Ones

"In Atlantis, when you first decided to bond and have a family together, you stood on the edge of a cliff, overlooking the sea. There was a sacred oak grove behind you, and you both had long hair, standing there with your hands and fingers intertwined, as you pledged eternal love, and how you would always find a home in each other, even when far apart. You said: *"I love you soul of my soul. I love your body as my body, and I love you no matter where the tides of life may run, or in which dimension and forms of existence our souls choose to be, our love will eternally be there. And let us never forget that love is free to roam where it wills, like a stream flow where it wills, finding paths around all obstacles. So let our love likewise find paths around all impediments and hindrances until we flow into a single stream and the river of life once more. So there is your love."*

———

SOUL GROUP: The Solar Ray Ones

"The lesson here is that both souls are created equal, and empowered with solar rays. However sometimes when incarnated, one can tend to shrink, and not stand in their highest soul power and truth. In relationships, you may want your partner to become like you, or start feeling needy as if you were incomplete on your own. *Now one solar ray does not say to another, "Complete me!" It knows that the others, although looking alike, and radiating forth in a similar way, are each uniquely made. Each is created to be itself, but distinctive in its own light.*

When souls are born, they may start believing that they are imperfectly made, and something is wrong. That is illusion. That is not truth. Then they believe the other is imperfectly made, and wish to fix them. That is illusion and not truth. In fact, there is nothing wrong with either self or the other. What is wrong is warped seeing, and believing such falsehood.

These viewpoints come from a lifetime together in *France*, in a period of great enlightenment, but also of great woe. You were a nobleman, with the Sun on your family crest, for your family held the long and ancient lineage of the *Solar Sun children,* who lived in the ancient lands where you currently live. Well, you were born with the mark of the sun under your right breast, indicating you were ordained to be trained in the *inner mysteries of Apollo,* as was done in the royal families under a secret mantle, for the church had declared war on anything that they had not proclaimed as the truth. You were thus sent at age five to train in the Ancient Mystery schools beneath the Pyrenees, with the Ancient Ones, living in the inner cities.

At twelve, you were trained to be a knight in the family tradition, but also as bard, troubadour and poet, again in the ancient mystery tradition. You were not trained to go to war as such, but rather trained in the higher ways of Humankind, for in reality you were being prepared for the priesthood – but this could not be done openly, because of the hostile opposition of the church.

At sixteen, you married your *Twin Flame,* preordained by the elders, and she was ten years older. You deeply resented being forced to marry, because of settlement agreements, and although you knew that the Ancient Ones held careful record of all births and signs, something deep inside of you rebelled. She was not pretty in a conventional sense, but was very learned and trained in the mystery schools of the Goddess principle and sun female lineage. She was an only child, and very well educated from her father's vast library.

Subsequently you made her life a misery, tormenting her by flaunting your love songs and poems in the love courts, openly pursuing the objects of your affections, and seldom being at home. The crusade against your people was launched and for the first time you had to seriously go to war to defend your castles. You loathed war and the destruction and something deep inside, recoiled even more at that. In the interim four children were born, and she publicly became a *Cathar* believer (which you all were in secret), so you now feared not only for the lives of your children, who all were burnt at the stake, but the Inquisition.

You were seriously injured with a sword through your hip, and she nursed you back to health with such love and devotion, that even your hardened heart softened, and true love was born. However, the war called you back into action, and desperate times descended, with thousands being burnt alive, and the Inquisition taking care of the rest. You lost your castles and were homeless. You both were forced to seek refuge in the interim at Monségur, but as fate would have it, as your love for each other knew no bounds by then, she was separated from you, caught and subsequently tortured and burnt at the stake. Your sorrow was endless, as was your deep anger at the crusaders and the Inquisition. You yourself were then betrayed and tortured, and burnt at the stake.

In this lifetime you will find that much of that lifetime haunts you in one way or another, for you were at first not appreciative of her, and then went the other way."

SOUL GROUP: The Solar Ray Ones

"In this lifetime your challenge will be to find true love, despite all illusions created by your mind, or the quest to find perfection, when love is both challenge and support. You will not only be challenged in the relationship, but also in the way you handle life and how *you reconnect to the inner teachings of the Sun*. Your awakening process has to do with love in your heart and soul. It is the fire of illumination in your own soul, and the challenge to find union, despite all the illusions you spin in and around you. Your soul asked for this during the period when you were tortured, for you felt that God had deserted you. You also felt that you at last loved, and this was taken away from you, so you hated the church with a vengeance. You also felt that you had forsaken your own people, from losing your castles, unable to reclaim them and witnessing your people being burnt *en masse*.

So, here is a deep awakening process, in being reunited with your twin. It is as if your whole soul has to find itself again in the very core – deeper than the mere testing of truth, but the truth of the heart and soul and being. It is the inner initiations in the inner circles of the Sun, and then the highest pathways of illumination. It is therefore a great initiation into the higher truths. Your soul cannot be other than that, for it is illumined. What is not of the truth in your soul will be burnt, and what you pretend to be truth, will also burn you.

Thus the challenge here is to rise to this, and not to shrink.

You will have to find a deep and abiding love for Humanity, for yourself, and only then will love extend to your twin. You will only be able to love to the extent that love ignites your heart and soul and being. Anything less will singe you. For you chose this higher path of illumination before you incarnated, wishing to burn off the karmic debt and anger. You desired to be brought back to the purity and essence of the truth of your soul!

So, in this regard no matter what your twin does or does not do, it is your highest pathway that you have to find and be and become. Only in doing that will the fires of your true heart and soul ignite, and you will at last be able to love and be loved in equal measure, and find true love with her. For she will be put through the fire of initiations herself. With every test you pass, the fire of love will be ignited more and more. So, this is a union of fires, the fires in the furnace of truth, integrity and being authentic and real. No holds barred."

———

CHAPTER 9

Soul Mates and Twin Flames
(Part 3)

SOUL GROUP: The Oracles

"The love bond will grow when both are awakened to this fact, understanding that nothing is by accident but rather by a grand design. Meeting again in this lifetime was to give both of you the freedom to be and express yourselves without the fear of persecution, even if others to do not understand or support, trust that what comes now will be for the highest good of all.

Some souls chose to have an experience of both the masculine and feminine. Some soul chose to be just feminine ... some souls are both masculine and feminine and are androgynous. The Creation is truly vast. It does not matter what body one is in, for it is merely an outer shell. It is the soul that matters – the rest is just a tool of expression. It is humans who tend to label everything.

The Creator does not label, but loves all of its Creation equally. One cannot always choose one's family. Sometimes more than one soul, from different soul groups are drawn to the same parents. They may have karmic links, or the parents had the correct energies, or could give the souls the experience they wished to have. Therefore, not everyone in the same family will have the same values, or karma, or soul calling or expression.

One has to learn to stand on one's own two feet, and not let other souls intervene with one's own soul's mission. Often these souls will be great teachers in this, for they teach how to love unconditionally.

———

SOUL GROUP: Those who bring Structure and Form

"Now, an earthly man will have a hard time to compete with what you have in your true Twin Flame, and you will always feel at some level that the man in your life does not quite match up your ideal. The man you are currently with is a soul mate – not of the same soul group, but of a cluster soul group as explained by the transmitter in her book *Soul Empowerment.* You have worked together cosmically on quite a few projects of the Intergalactic Councils, developing a deep friendship and actually agreed before arriving here, to meet up in this lifetime to work together, through your knowledge of how to bring sacred geometries, structures and cosmic forms into expanded being.

These actions will lay the foundations for the way of life of the *New Golden Age,* and an understanding that if the underlying structures and forms of whatever one creates are based on sacred geometries and formulas, you will produce an enhanced way of life and living. These constructions work with the bodily sacred geometries, and even with plants and food, to bring longevity and radiant vibrant health. Thus both agreed to work in tandem, but have forgotten the prime reason, as you shut down at an early age, because your full abilities were never understood. It is time to deprogram false beliefs, and redundant educational systems all geared to control and limit. Wake up to the truth of why you are on this planet – allow yourself to recall and be reactivated. So in essence there is nothing stopping or hindering you from having a beautiful and loving, lasting relationship, if you both are prepared to work on it, and to work in tandem."

SOUL GROUP: The Ones Who Serve

"Your Twin Flame has not incarnated with you, because the Lyrans have a different bodily form, and you could not both sustain such a low frequency body – the Lyran body is androgynous in form, and resembles those of the *angels.* You are an angel in disguise, so you need to understand that your sexuality will differ from others in many ways, and you really do not need sexual fulfilment in the way most do. You are **one** with your Twin Flame anyhow, in the androgynous form. In actual fact you are often confused about this, as you are both male and female, yes you are, and thus you can find balance deep within you, and really do not need to search for balance within a relationship."

———

SOUL GROUP: The Light Encoders

"So yes, your *Twin Flame* has incarnated, and she is transmitting the language of light, and also delving deep into its mystery. At the moment you would not even look at her, thinking that what she is doing is a little weird. However here is the mystery which technology cannot understand yet, because it has lost touch with the true reality on a cosmic scale. For in fact, they are one and the same. When you understand this, amazing things will trigger and prepare you to attract her into your life. For as long as you judge something you are judging yourself, and limiting your understanding of life. For the mystery is deeper than we will ever know, until we can span dimensions of time, and understand that the deeper we delve the more profound it becomes.

So, she has a specialized mission and is very creative. Through her **music** she triggers these light encodements deep in the heart and soul, for the heart has to open for the truth to sink in, and then when the truth is restored, the body's cells sing, literally. They tune into higher frequency bands of the cosmic cell and consequently start transmission inside, which in turn lifts the vibration of the body and form. That is the end of *dis-ease* for Humanity, *when the cells sing in tune with the cosmic cells.*

When you are reunited with her, it will be intense, for she will boggle your mind, and bring about a love like you have never felt before, as you teach each other, and the two will flow into one. This will require a deep cultivated trust, a profound knowing of each other, with that boundless commitment to love from the heart and soul, to work together for the greater good of Humankind – for that is why you are here. Your work will then flow into a single stream, and the effect on Humanity will be profound, for these light encodements when amplified, will bring about a truly insightful fine-tuning of all."

———

SOUL GROUP: The Keepers of the Platinum Ray

"You work with the *Intergalactic Fleet,* and in your sleep state you visit the abode of your husband, and are reunited with your children. He presently works in the Milky Way Galaxy at galactic core level, to help with the assimilation of the 7th Sun into this solar system, as it is now returning to Earth, which will soon have 2 suns. He also operates with the inner workings of the solar suns, directed by the Intergalactic Fleet, and constantly monitored by scientists.

Thus, in this lifetime, you have never met any man who can quite measure up to your husband – and the shared intense pure love. Subsequently you volunteered to return to anchor in the *Platinum Ray.* You do not really have karma to clear, so are here to help with this task and work in the inner planes with the energies in that area, and assist life forms. Sometimes you feel better able to cope with the animal rather than the human energies, but you do connect with both at a deeper level and can definitely understand what animals are saying."

———

SOUL GROUP: The Way showers

"You have been lovers in other lifetimes, and sometimes married. You are *Twin Flames,* in that you trained under *Lord and Lady Shiva* when they lived here, and practiced *sacred sexual union.* In that lifetime your bond was immensely strong, and you ignited the sacred fire between you.

However, in other lifetimes when male dominance reigned supreme, some of this intimacy was lost. Now it is a matter of remembering and learning to open yourself up to a much deeper and more profound manner of merging, which will be shown to you through the tantric path, if you both choose that. If you do, this will be a wonderful way to deepen the love, respect and bond, and it will serve you. Later on in life, you will be able to help so many other couples to practice this sacred sexual union as a blessing, with all the incredible benefits it brings, if there is a deep and profound honoring of each other, and a celebration of the Divine, the God and Goddess within, in total union."

———

SOUL GROUP: The Energetic Ones

"Yes, there is a *Twin Flame* and she is a highly spiritual woman, who is already doing energy healing work, and following the advanced path. She was your wife at the time of the Cathars and the Druids, and is a high initiate herself, a very beautiful woman with blond hair and greenish-blue eyes. The minute your eyes meet, you will both just know this is it. You have been contracted to meet in the next few years, when your work will combine as one. First you need to activate certain parts of this yourself, so that the two rivers or forces can blend with each other to then flow into one."

SOUL GROUP: The Harbinger Souls

"Your Twin Flame did not incarnate, not wishing to volunteer for duty here, and works rather in the inner realms of the Central Sun where he transmits the higher frequencies of light, to expand certain star systems, which are now coming into being. This is then the harbinger of immense changes in the Milky Way Galaxy and in being there, he is simultaneously assisting the full activation of the energy and dimensional shift. He often appears to you as a streak of light in the corner of your eye, but you shrug it off as a vision problem, or just something strange going on, when in reality it is him. You frequently also hear guidance in your head, and this is him. Most often this unnerves you, and then you shut him out. But in your sleep state you are always together in an immensely beautiful energetic union, way beyond anything you can experience on Planet Earth.

Yes, he was your lover in the two lives on Planet Earth. The first in the times when *Atlantis* was born, and when your soul sojourned here to assist with its creation and rising. You were the forerunner of changes needed to anchor it in, and worked with amplified energies and energy fields, as your soul transmits energies and you can literally beam energy rays into Earth energy systems, and intensify them.

In that lifetime you met a fellow scientist from the *Intergalactic Fleet*, as in those times there were space stations in Atlantis and craft from all over the Cosmos landed there, including those from other star systems and galaxies, who could immigrate and settle if so desired. He came from *Sirius*, and an intense love affair developed. However, he was not of the same cosmic race or soul group, and in those times, compatibility was carefully sought after, and you helped each other since your work sometimes overlapped. *In Intergalactic circles this is quite common place, for one does not marry, but rather has a life partner while a lover is normally chosen if far from home, working elsewhere in the Cosmos. This just sometimes happens, with the understanding that both partners know their life partner stays as that, for such unions are considered sacrosanct."*

SOUL GROUP: The Radiant Ones Who Emit and Exchange Light

"Her *Twin Flame* is not incarnate, he is still on her home planet, caring for their four children, two girls and two boys, as one parent always has to stay incarnated and be there, so that the family unit is not disturbed, and the love and support of a parent is constant. She does visit them though in her sleep state, and will often wake up feeling a heaviness or sadness that stems from this."

SOUL GROUP: The Ones who Communicate the Intent of the Divine

"Note that this goes back to the time when this soul was given away in an arranged marriage, as a peace negotiation to the man she was first involved with, and the father of her daughter. He had many other wives, and he desired her first for her beauty, but later on truly came to love her. However, she never wanted him as she loved another, whom she saw secretly, and who is her current lover. A love triangle formed, but when the prince discovered her affair, he was forced to banish her to another part of the country, as he nursed his hurt pride and heart.

There she lived a very quiet rural life, very soon channelling her own sadness into being of service to the locals. For the first time she used her beautiful and profound communication skills to help them in a diplomatic way, ensuring vital communication strategies were applied. Their lifestyles improved, and she became a mediator opening up her heart, and sharing their plight with her ex-husband. This won her the love of the people, and became her life journey, dedicated higher service. In this lifetime she has met both men once again, however, there is a third who is communicating with her telepathically. Just, stay there for a moment Little One, while we try to bring all of this into the equation."

———

SOUL GROUP: The Light Sounding Ones

"You do not have a *Twin Flame* incarnated here on this planet. You consciously requested to be one of the first volunteer souls from across the galaxies, who answered the clarion call of the Cosmic Masters, to help Planet Earth to move into the higher states of consciousness, and anchor in the *New Golden Age*. On your planet of origin souls are *androgynous*, and therefore the concept of *Twin Flames* is somewhat different, as there is perfect harmony in male and female within a single form."

———

SOUL GROUP: The Sacred Cantered Ones

"The man in question is her *Twin Flame,* but it is not necessary for them to be together, as this was not contracted in between them. Rather it was agreed that they would more or less walk the path next to each other for a while, as he had karmic ties to clear with his current wife, stemming from marriage contracts and dowry agreements in other lifetimes, where he sometimes abused his powers, and manipulated her. So this is his karma to clear, and he undertook to do just that. It is not to say that the soul is not a loving one, is just that he has had past life patterns to clear. So he is not free to have any relationship with you, and will not because of loyalty to his family." 368.

———

SOUL GROUP: The Divine Giving Ones

"The two halves of the same soul have had many challenges over many lifetimes wanting to be joined together again, alongside other marriages and partnerships with their karmic links and ties and cords, which attached themselves in her energy fields from men who had just used her, or had literally given her to other men. These need to be cut out, and severed, to deeply release the inner trauma involved in having being viewed as a chattel, to be used and abused at will. These are very deep soul scars preventing her from truly opening up her heart in this lifetime, and then deeply and profoundly opening up to her other half, although they are together now."

————

SOUL GROUP: The Radiant Solar Sun Ones

"In that lifetime in Atlantis you were with your *Twin Flame*, who worked in the *Halls of Records*, so you were both involved with *Temples of Higher Knowledge and Wisdom,* and lived on the premises, as ordained Priests. Twins were permitted to marry and experience sacred sexual union since the *Twin Flame* union amplified the energies, evoking immense activation of the life purpose and calling, and the energies released augmented this, and ensured both would be totally dedicated to higher service.

She was both very much like you, and also different, and in that lifetime, you often had to find time to be together, as you both were very involved and totally dedicated to living your life there.

You will meet this soul later on in life, when you are doing what you are called upon to do, back on stage, in one form or another. She is not an actress, but works with the *Enlightenment teachings,* and will be drawn by the content, to one of the shows, you are talking, singing, or acting in. It will be a combination of all these components, geared to opening people's hearts and minds to raise their consciousness through the performing arts, and you will immediately recognize each other.

You are hypersensitive yes, and very trusting, but you need to let go of the mother of your son. She entered your life for a brief time to unite with you, to conceive this child. He chose you as father, with your strong soul links through the *7th Central Sun and Galaxy and also because he has come in to anchor in the Christed-consciousness Rays as one of the Sun Children.* The woman agreed to be available for this for that short time, understanding that she would move on and out of your lives, as she was not on the same wavelength, and it could not have worked out. So thus it was a coming together, to create a window of opportunity for this little one to enter the world.

She was in a way preparing you for your *Twin Flame,* teaching you valuable lessons in love – in keeping your heart open, finding unconditional love for yourself, your son and for her, once you forgive and allow her to be and become, without the three of you being in the same location. It has in essence, given you the opportunity to experience fatherhood in a way that few men can, and has brought you many friends and acquaintances, so indeed nothing is damaged or missing. Change your inner perception, and you will see that all is perfect, whole and complete.

Learn to shield yourself. You radiate such a high frequency energy, which is wonderful on stage, or when addressing people, but not so beneficial when you leave yourself open like a sponge, absorbing negative energies. It would be best to put a huge golden orb around yourself, or bubble of blinding white light or golden energy, which will only allow that of the purest Christed light to enter your energy fields. It will help transmute all negative energy, as it cannot penetrate that shield."

SOUL GROUP: The Infinite Cosmic Ray Masters

"As he is a very highly evolved soul, only a fraction of this soul is here at the moment, and his *Twin Flame* did not incarnate, owing to the special assignment and mission, and since she is too highly evolved to be able to easily take on physical form in such a dense and very slow vibrational frequency. She meets up with him in his sleep state, and again when he is reunited with his soul family. She is a scientist, working aboard the *Intergalactic Fleet,* helping him to transmit the higher cosmic rays into the planet, so easing his sojourn here. He can tune into her, when he raises his vibrational frequencies. So, your *Twin Flame* in reality is not separate from you at all, but rather much part of you.

She is a beautiful soul and often holds you in her arms during times when you are severely tested and so forth. She guides and strengthens you, so just open yourself to the possibility of seeing, sensing and feeling her, do not shut down your faculties as you did as a child. You were always playing and talking to her then, but closed that all off. It is just a matter of remembering and activating what is within."

SOUL GROUP: The Life-Breathing Ones

"You have had other incarnations in Egypt, in Mesopotamia, in Israel, Greece, Northern Spain, UK, Ireland and what was Avalon, and Atlantis.

In all, you were connected to the *air element,* trained as a sorceress to use air, to bring into form what you intended to manifest or create, in the abodes of the Stonehenge area in Britain. You also worked with the wind forces, directing its course. You were under the apprenticeship of *Morgana,* and brought the wind element into being in times of war, when torrents of rain were urgently needed.

In those lifetimes you often found life on Planet Earth in a physical form an encumbrance, so just left it, when you did not wish to be here anymore, and not because your soul contract held you here. So, there is plenty of unfinished business, and patterns unravelling their strands – this is particularly predominant in relationships, especially with men. Thus, everyone who you have met, has had some karmic links and unresolved business with you, but with your being here to assist the planet through the shift, relationships will not be your first priority as a soul, though you often forget this, and get entangled with them again. It is best to understand that your soul is highly evolved, so very few men on Planet Earth will ever match you here.

Also, with your strong connection to the air element, you often tend to dance in and around the relationship, constantly out of anyone's grasp. This leads to bickering and frustration, as men can never quite tie you down. Your soul will not agree to being restricted, and if you do allow this, you will sink into depression, for this is not congruent with your own soul, and its ability to fly free and unencumbered, shape shifting into any form desired, (indeed your soul knows how to do this, even if you have forgotten)".

———

SOUL GROUP: The Exquisite Ones

"This soul is one of those rare souls who incarnated onto this planet in phases of integration, as her soul has never lived out a full lifetime here, and she wanted to be here with the raising of consciousness for the anchoring in of the new *Golden Age.* Therefore, as one of the first Crystal Children, she has a much higher crystalline form. *When she was about five years old, two of her soul flames fused together as one, shaping her life from that moment on.* The childhood self felt a little different in the beginning, amplified by the presence of two flames in one single body. This had not been noticed much by anyone, except by her parents who often wondered at her expansion, but kept their thoughts to themselves, as they supposed they were imagining things.

Sadly, this soul, later on in life, forgot her own uniqueness and why she had incarnated, not consciously, but she desired to fit into groups, crowds and follow trends and the norm, when in reality she should never have fitted into anything. *Inherently she is meant to bring the higher wisdom – those pearls of wisdom from the Divine Goddess herself back to the planet, an aspect of the Higher Divine Feminine, Sophia, the Goddess of Wisdom.*"

———

SOUL GROUP: The Intricate Web Beings who bring the Light quotient into All that Exists

"In this lifetime your *Twin Flame* did not incarnate as you are *androgynous* in form. However, you need to be extremely careful about who you allow into your home and *sexual energy fields*, for you are super sensitive. Passion and love have a place, but only with someone who is on the correct frequency band, coming from the state of pure love. The one you are considering has plenty of negative energy that he needs to clear, as he has absorbed too much – again your instinct for wanting to help lame ducks is active.

Your *Twin Flame* has not incarnated, and has no need to. He is very involved on Andromeda and elsewhere in the Cosmos as a landscape architect, creating the most amazing gardens and sceneries, and he loves cosmic travel. He is a beautiful and loving soul, and you have such a deep and intimate loving marriage, that no earthly man will ever be able to provide for you. You reunite with him every single night, and are therefore never apart. He acts as one of you higher guides, a very tall loving beautiful man with large blue eyes, with long white-blond hair, and he is strong. Meaning he is a Master in his own right.

You mainly incarnated in order to work through negative karmic patterns with your ex, and this man, and also to finally find yourself, in the sense that you live your highest soul calling and purpose, and love yourself so much that you will not settle for anything less than you are worth."

———

SOUL GROUP: The Blissful Ones

"You are having relationship problems because your male and female sides are very balanced, as an *androgynous* being, even in your other bodies, in other star systems, and this is what you are most comfortable with. You battle to truly be in a male/female relationship, because of the imbalance, so tend to shift from one to the other and get confused. The best is to honor the masculine and feminine inside of you, embracing them both and learning to accept and love yourself totally and unconditionally.

If you choose to have a relationship then do so, but the same patterns will repeat themselves, for this is not what your soul wishes at this moment – it wants rather to be free to express itself in bringing these gifts to Humankind. Any relationship depletes your energies, for you grow embattled with yourself, and your own *androgynous* being, and then wonder why you feel drained and ill-at-ease. So, breaking this pattern will assist you enormously, to allow you to be happy and content in your own skin. Friendships will work better for you, rather than someone living in your pocket all the time. It will give you the freedom to be and to become, and to grow into the truly beautiful being that you are!

Your twin or rather a part of your soul is helping you from the other side, for your whole soul has not incarnated. He/she, for it is both, is assisting you to remember so much more at this time. You are never alone, and you are being helped by a tremendous number of your own soul group. So do embrace all of this."

SOUL GROUP: The Inquisitive Ones

"You have your *Twin Flame* incarnated at the same time as you, hence the mutual recognition. However, there is karma to clear, and you will be challenged in this lifetime to do that before being reunited physically, and this was written into your soul contracts.

For in those lifetimes, he stayed true to the Light and never wavered. He is very much a lion that one, with the courage to stand his ground and defend his territory, if need be. In that Egyptian lifetime, you came into direct confrontation with him as a consequence of your actions, and even went so far in your love/hate for him, to kill him, because of his power to counteract you.

So, there is some forgiveness due here from both sides. You often sparked off each other, with immense love spilling over, which made for wonderful and passionate sex, but also for many disputes, and much drama in those other lives. You never listened to reason from him, and often did exactly what he cautioned you not to do. Thus, trust needs to be restored.

More than this, your *Twin Flame* will finally be open in heart and soul, in new ways, and you will romp and play together, and have fun like lions do when they mate. His fierce protectiveness of you will come to the fore, and you will want to love this man and make good what you were never able to show in those other lifetimes. This will be the first time you can love totally, no holds barred, for finally the shadow and light within you are in harmony.

So it is to *Egypt* then that we turn, in connection to the relationship mentioned, and here again you were a teacher Priestess, and the man in question was one of the most brilliant acolytes. He passed all initiations, before being referred to you for the final one These were normally overseen by the High Priest himself, but he was already ancient, and very ill at the time, so you assumed this mantle, after dice were thrown in all fairness, for all candidates. You were relatively speaking, much younger than the rest of them, and were very aware of their extreme jealousy, and that any mistakes made in this role would be used against you. For they were like vultures waiting for the High Priest to die, so that one of them could take over.

So, as this young man stood before you as a priestess, in that instant you experienced the most potent sexual energy charges ever coursing through you, catching you completely off guard. As an initiator, you had taken an oath never to become attached or sexually attracted, to the person being tested, as emotional attachment, or feeling sorry for the student, could prove fatal. So, this desire for him came as a complete and utter surprise, and momentarily, you let your mask fall. He stood there in the splendour of his manhood, a handsome and well-built man, ten to fifteen years younger, exuding the confidence of youth. He took no pains to hide his obvious attraction for you, as you were regally striking in your own right.

You had to hide your attraction, which turned into infatuation, as he haunted your dreams and you felt yourself under siege. You could not turn tail, for the priesthood was watching you, and pride would not allow you to bend, and ask to be replaced. So, to punish yourself for what you felt, and to show how well you performed your duties, and remove his insolence, you tightened the screws. Literally. You subjected him to unbelievably difficult tests, which in your heart and soul you knew were almost impossible to accomplish, and he came up trumps. That got under your skin, and your attraction only grew, so much so that one day while reprimanding him and being totally unreasonable, he lost his cool and shook you. That resulted in a passionate embrace, and almost in actual intercourse, only prevented because you willed it so, and somehow got yourself together. You also knew that if any temple spies had watched these goings on, it would be the end of your career.

As his final initiation loomed, he visited you in his other form, as he had been trained to do by you and others, and sexual intercourse was so powerful and unlike anything either of you had experienced before, began on that level, and you found yourself, for the first time in your life, hopelessly in love. You could have relinquished this and asked to be taken off the job, but your fierce pride prevented you. In that initiation, you further tightened the screws, wanting to punish you both, and in consequence he died. When you found his lifeless body deep down in the chambers, you sobbed hysterically.

He haunted you for the rest of that lifetime, and even though you rose to the rank of second in charge to the High Priest, who had recovered, you were miserable inside and never got over it, for you blamed yourself for this death.

So, in this lifetime you came together in that other energetic form in many ways, because both of you remembered. In this regard, forgive yourself for what happened, for it no longer serves your highest soul growth and good, and do forgive him. Neither of you, under the circumstances of such initiations, could let love flourish. As priests, you vowed not to become sexually involved with acolytes because of the potentially volatile repercussions, and in breaking that vow, even though not in a physical body, you also incurred karma, as agreed when you took these vows as a priestess at that specific temple. So, the vow needs to be released, along with the guilt in breaking it and causing his death, through being overzealous.

So, here old karmic debts are being paid off, and with him not being available, or this relationship not going as you felt it would, was really like his dying, and therefore felt like old patterns repeating themselves. However, the beautiful lessons in love were then mastered, as all of this is released.

Then with you meeting many acolytes, with whom you had strong bonds in later lifetimes – for the teacher-mentor role will replay itself for the same souls involved in these mystery schools, tend to come together again and again. This is especially apparent if there are bonds, some being those love bonds between teacher and student. In some these souls became lovers or husbands, because of these connections. You returned to bring back much of that knowledge, and to teach it in some form, but are reluctant to do so, because of the fear of the same old thing happening – the over zealousness. Your *Twin Flame*, who is highly trained in *Kabbalistic Sacred* law, will enter your life, coming to teach in your area. He is the High Priest of that lifetime and one who has always been your teacher and mentor in many lifetimes, as you also performed the ancient sexual rites together as *Twin Flames*, with him being your lover and consort.

He is a man fascinated by the mysteries, throughout this life, and a devoted scholar. As much as he teaches this, he is also a businessman and travels widely. So, you will attend a talk or class, and feel that he is of the same tribe or group as you. He is a rather tall and a slightly stooped man, with a prominent nose, wears round glasses, with a straggly beard. Yet, he is love – he will teach you about love in ways you never knew you could open yourself up to.

This will be a truly beautiful relationship, for you will at last meet someone who is at your level, and understands who you are at a deep level. You will feel a deep trust and respect for him that you have never felt for any other man. There will truly be a blossoming in your life, and although obstacles might appear to be preventing this relationship, they will sort themselves out, for the love ignited between you will be greater than the sum total of all else.

You have had many lifetimes together in what is the Middle East, Israel, and Egypt, also attached to the Mystery School, and the inner teachings. There were some lifetimes in Europe, and especially in Germany and Italy. So, this love has come over many thousands of years, and it was agreed that you would meet later in life, when both have worked through your karmic ties and debts, and are at last free to love on a much deeper and more profound level."

———

SOUL GROUP: The Loving Ones

"As far as the question of your *Twin Flame* is concerned, there has to be an understanding that sometimes souls are here on this planet to fulfil specific missions or tasks. You had to first find that path again, step into higher service, in order to work truly unencumbered, with no split in your energies in so many directions, as can happen when committed to someone. Women especially tend to sacrifice their own missions to please the men they are with. In essence your own soul is *androgynous*, male and female, as you hail from a part or parts of Creation that chose this specific form.

In Lemuria you were *androgynous,* and one of the very few who never split into male and female. It is good to remember this, and to cultivate the masculine and feminine within yourself, to be balanced. In reality when both are in balance, you are whole and complete on your own, not needing a man to fulfil you on those levels, for this becomes unnecessary, when you are really tuned in. However, there is the matter of a *Twin Flame – remembering that you have 11 flames within one soul, and therefore, other parts of you are still working and being, in different parts of the Cosmos.*

Your *Twin Flame* did not incarnate, as he/she is busy working on a special project in a new galaxy forming in the outer reaches of the Cosmos. Another part of you is working in Sirius, another in Venus and yet another part of you is busy with energy work in the Pleiades. So, all parts of you are very much engaged in working to the fullest."

———————

SOUL GROUP: The Crystalline Ones

"As for the *soul mate* – as said she is a companion at this stage, and someone you have a loving relationship with. Your soul is so highly evolved and your mission so very important, just how important – we cannot stress enough, so it is best to just flow with love, and activate yourself.

You do have not a Twin Flame here at this time, for the 11 other parts of your soul, hold the light for you from inside the Earth and the Milky Way Galaxy. This does not mean there are no soul mates out there, like her, who cannot connect deeply and profoundly with you, but all love relationships start first with you. Until you fully love and honour your soul and live your soul purpose, then true love is impossible. For you can only love another soul to the extent that you love yourself, and when you step into your soul mission, you cannot afford to be hampered anymore."

————

SOUL GROUP: The Resounding Ones

"Your twin has incarnated and is very involved in his creative work, traveling widely to find inspiration for his works of art. He paints oils on canvas, when not creating living spaces to beautify people's lives. He is a quiet, gentle man, and loves wide open spaces, so often needs to connect deeply with Mother Nature for inspiration. He loves using earthly colours to ground people, increasing their awareness of Earth's incredible beauty. Even in textile designs, or in his paintings, his earthly mix of colours is quite amazing, as he literally weaves different strands of colour together.

He is very deep this man – quiet and introspective. Yet, in those shared lifetimes you loved him precisely for this, for he grounded you in ways you could not. It is his gentle steadiness, which allows you to blossom and to be and become what you need to be. Your soul needs that. For in too stormy an environment or relationship, your soul will wither and shrink. You need that space to be, to weave together with gentleness and loving care, because when you feel yourself threatened at a deep soul level, you cannot grow and expand. Your soul feels caged in, you become depressed or filled with pain, in some way or other. You yearn to be set free to create from the depths of your heart, soul and being.

This man will appear in your life when you are ready, and at the moment there is no space, and he is also involved elsewhere. You are most likely to meet in places where your line of work intermingles, wherever that may be in the world. You are contracted to meet within the next few years, it will be like you just know or have known each other for ever, as you carry on from when you last left the planet. Both of you in a sense have reached that soul maturity where one just loves, because you can do and be no other, at your best, blending together exquisitely to create beautiful music and tapestries, and whatever else together.

The current relationship is just a stepping stone – a way to regain your own inner soul truth and live it, and dissolve what needs to be dissolved."

————

SOUL GROUP: The Crystal Conscious Ones

"Concerning the man in question, your soul knows him in a *higher state of being* from the Pleiades, and he often incarnates at the same time as you in all the outposts of the Cosmos, where there is work to do. However, at the moment he is so fulfilled in many ways that you would have to rise in frequency band and dedication, to truly be able to access and connect with him.

In your soul contracts you were supposed to meet each other for support in the soul mission work here, for this is the first time either of you incarnated. *You did help out from time to time, and sometimes used a fraction of an incarnation as a type of walk-in, but you were not here for complete incarnations. Star people sometimes do this, with the permission of the soul inhabiting the physical body, so that they can do much needed repair or rehabilitation or other work.*

In this regard, you were simply not ready for each other. He is a soul mate, not a *Twin Flame*. (Your *Twin Flame* has not incarnated because there was no need to. His higher frequency body cannot adjust to Earth, and there is too much work in the Cosmos needing attention).

You will meet up with him in a few months from now, as you tune your soul into the keys and codes you have to return to Earth. Some parts of his work and yours will overlap, when you find that you truly love working, and even living together. However, this is a matter of free will and choice. He is one who loves solitude (although he might say something different), not liking someone under his feet who could cramp his style, so prefers to do what he likes, when he likes. How this will work out then, is a matter of your own free will and choice.

Nonetheless there is another man entering your life, very tall and quite an interesting character, who loves to wear a cowboy hat and looks like someone who has just walked out of a Hollywood movie. He looks kind of rough-around-the-edges, and sparks will fly, as this is love at first sight which will literally knock you both out.

You have been lovers for a long time in other star systems, and parts of the Cosmos, and in regions where love has many expressions and forms. So, there is a deep remembrance here. He is into Earth healing and holds the keys and codes as you do, so you have much in common. He has an incredible insight and immensely astute inner seeing, and he can literally "see" where he needs to work on these grids. He has a beautiful sense of humour, with a constant twinkle in his eye, and does not take life on this planet too seriously – but what a magnificent light worker this is. He loves camping out under the stars, singing and playing his guitar, and most importantly loves to listen deep within.

He has had shamanic training, and incredible visions of what will happen to the Earth in the next few months and years. Therefore, he travels a lot in a 4x4, converted into a travelling home, and visits sites needing healing. You will find him in the regions of Arizona, where you will be asked to do some healing work. It is destined that you meet, and you will end up travelling with him. It will just feel right and you will do immensely important work together. For you will find that home is where he is, and you will not want to be apart.

One reason things never worked out with the other, is because deep down your soul knew this and you did not run away, but rather knew that things were not meant to be. Trust your inner guidance – it is always spot on.

You will do important healing work on Atlantis energies with this man, and this is as it is supposed to be. For you will travel the length and breadth of America and do *this vast work of repairing the Earth's energy grids*. That is why you need to be mobile. Even if this means becoming a gypsy – your soul will just love the freedom it brings, doing healing and sound energy work from wherever you are. Indeed, the pair of you will be like magnets, for people will soon discover your healing abilities and come for sessions. That will help to cover the travelling expenses and you will never lack for anything, in fact you will wonder how you ever got stuck in just one place. You will meet many like-minded souls along the way, and pull together a group of people to repair this grid. If this is not done, all of America will disintegrate into three separate pieces, and three quarters will disappear under the sea. That is how vital the work is that you have come in to do, especially **now** at this time."

SOUL GROUP: The Ones Who Transmit

"At this moment your *Twin Flame* is waiting in the wings for you to wake up to your own greatness and highest gifts for the planet. He has already been fully activated, and is known for his own ability to heal people. He is a *Master Shaman* working in Sedona, with a shop selling metaphysical goods. He was drawn there by the special energies present. He has longish hair, loves wearing Hawaiian shirts, is quite tall, with a beard turning grey and ginger, and wears round glasses. He drums and works with the Earth spirits, releasing of souls, and soul journeying work.

You will be drawn to him and meet up, once you open your third eye again, and start doing the real work, you have been called to do, stepping past all your own insecurities and fears, and stop using your hands to gather up all the soul problems of others.

Note here that some people are called upon to use their hands and others, their third eye hands so to speak, to assist those with a great need to be awakened. With you it is the latter. Your desire to use your hands comes from your teenage years, when you decided by using them and not opening your mouth so much, was the way to go to avoid ridicule. As you often said something (which was a form of channelling) which would happen, or prove to be true, and that scared the living daylights out of those around you, so they pushed you out of their circles."

SOUL GROUP: The Cosmic Joyous Ones

"As you have never experienced this before in your other lives (where souls have a committed partnership with their *Divine Other* happily for life, living in harmony and bliss), you will be challenged here on Planet Earth to find the same. Your *Twin Flame* has not incarnated, because you are both so highly evolved, but he is with you as a higher guide. So in your sleep state you are reunited with him, and receive all the love and attention and sexual pleasures there, that you cannot find on Earth. So, love is not absent in your life – it is merely that you know a higher state of love and being."

SOUL GROUP: The Ingenious Ones

"*You have locked up in your vast memory bank a memory of a beautiful soul who was and is your soul companion – your other half.* She is as fiery as you, and sometimes the opposite, tending to be deeply motivated by what is invisible, unseen, beyond physical perception. She is thus drawn deeply into the mystery, the essence of the life force itself. Hers is the inner vision, that inner knowing which sometimes is greater than the more usual understanding and limited seeing, and reflects the truth that she lives deep within herself. Initially in this lifetime she was drawn to the medical profession, became deeply depressed, and felt an inner prompting to break out of the mould, and wander far and wide, so off she went to the Himalayas, to Tibet, to Peru and all the great centers of the Earth, in search of her own soul. On this great journey she reached a deep understanding and reverence for the Nature Goddess herself, and then embarked on shamanic and acupuncture training, and these alternative healing techniques have kept her spellbound for some time.

This is a free spirit, and one who loves to roam between worlds, that inherent world where one is formless, yet all is one and the same. She has the deep understanding that unless people start reconnecting with this world, this greater and vast intelligent field, and the ancient knowing, nothing can heal.

So, she has wandered far and wide, whereas you have stayed put. She has broken through all the barriers of science, and paved a new way of understanding herself, which has greatly served her soul, for she has reconnected with that very aspect of herself that she was in the beginning, when she worked closely with you in the essence of co-creator. *The merging of your two flames brought this to the fore.* She remembers this and often yearns for you, and has connected with you in the other realms. You have forgotten all of that, but nevertheless do feel it at some level and are searching. She cannot manifest into your life, unless you start opening yourself to all levels of possibilities, and into that which is "out of bounds" – for she **is** that!

Your *Twin Flame* has had the guts to walk out of the narrow confines of the medical world into the unknown, to explore all of this, and that is where your own challenge lies. For as long as you cling to the limited prescribed restrictions, you cannot step into that inner world, where all the answers lie. So, if you decide to embark on this, it will pull you to new places and experiences you have never allowed yourself to explore. As a student, yes, but not since then. Something deep inside of you was buried in the fray, and it is clamouring for your attention now, and in that yearning for the twin, is also that deep desire to break free to finally reconnect with what is there within you, which has never really left, it is merely reconnecting with the vast knowledge held within your own soul.

Interestingly enough if your Twin would stand now before you, she would probably not even merit an extra glance, although something deep inside will recognize her immediately, as you peer into her deep blue eyes, and see her raven hair. She always has had that, and you remember. She also has that fey look about her, deep down at soul level, and so is quite beyond the norm. Now you would probably write her off as weird, and dismiss everything else, although the man in you would be stirred up, and she would truly fascinate you, even though you would still be closed to her, for you fear ridicule from colleagues and the repercussions which she has long since overcome. Therefore, there is much inner work to do before you can actually meet on the same wavelength and frequency band, because at the moment she has that inner knowing and has practiced healing techniques, shape-shifting and shamanic training that you cannot even relate to, at least not quite on the same level.

It comes with the opening up of the heart and soul, allowing whatever flows in guidance, in inner knowing to flow into you, and to be willing to explore this. You might feel drawn to places you do not normally visit, like oak groves, mountains, or just suddenly feel drawn somewhere. This is for a much higher reason, for those are places where your soul memory banks are triggered. It is good to write down whatever emerges, or to sketch or do something that will help that inner memory bank unlock.

For in essence this is an opening up of the sublime and immensely powerful energy fields, and these are the same cosmic and earth energies that the Druids worked with all the time. When unlocking these secrets, you unlock all the secrets of Creation, for everything is created to adhere to certain cosmic formulas. People have forgotten that, along with all ancient higher healing practices, working with the self-same energies and energy fields which have disappeared. One did not only study anatomy, but rather anatomy as related to energy fields! So, there is a vast knowledge pool and bank, which has been lost along the way, and humans cannot evolve further without this knowledge being retrieved and understood once again.

That is why your soul is here at this time, and why you volunteered to incarnate – for you wanted to return this knowledge, and therefore you and your twin incarnated more or less at the same time, with the understanding that at a certain time you would both merge your knowledge and energy fields into one single flame.

So, this will trigger a whole life change, and a reunion with your twin when ready, as something immense and totally different opens up a new way of loving and relating, turning everything, you ever understood about love and loving upside down, but bringing that inner happiness and experience of love in a profound and divine way. This union will be an immense blessing to the planet, and will bring about love and more love, if you are in harmony with one another and on the same frequency band."

SOUL GROUP: The Wisdom Keepers

"In that lifetime you worked with a man who has often appeared and disappeared, coming in and out of your life – not quite there, but present in his other altered form, often appearing in dreams or visions, or sometimes he is there somewhere in your energy fields, and yet not quite tangible. He had dark reddish blond to auburn (red) hair with a red beard, and was extremely tall – although you stood about 12 feet, he towered over you, with his booming laugh which had people spellbound. He worked mainly with acupuncture and meridians, but also had a wonderful gift of using his beautiful bass voice in chanting and playing crystal bowls to raise the vibrational frequencies, and you worked in tandem with him.

He was your *Twin Flame*, and your mutual love for each other, and devoted service knew no bounds in that lifetime. You were both blissfully unaware that your shared love and work caused envy and jealousy from others within the healing temples, with their perception that the High Priest and Priestess favoured you.

In those days, the Black Magi wished to break the power and stronghold of the temples, to spread disease and discomfort. So in order to control the population, they made it their business to infiltrate the minds and hearts of temple workers. One was a woman with red hair, who was extremely infatuated with your twin, wanting him for herself. She used all kind of illegal potions and spells to lure him closer, but failed, for he had eyes for only one woman, and that was you.

However, in the course of events, she spread rumours in the temples that she was having an affair with your twin, and having amazing magical sex that enhanced her powers. At first you paid no attention, but one day he went missing for some hours, and with doubts implanted in your mind, you demanded to know if he had been with her. However, it was soon revealed that indeed he had been called out on an emergency treatment, and the High Priestess cautioned you to be careful of this woman, and not to believe what she said, nor to allow doubt to enter your relationship, or else it would flounder. However, you went to a cavern, to get a special crystal needed for your work. Unbeknown to you, she was aware of this, manipulated things, and flooded this cavern with sea water. You tried everything to escape, but could not. You drowned there that day."

SOUL GROUP: The Wisdom Keepers

"Soul name: She who expresses the inquisitiveness of the Divine to know all things, and to understand the meaning behind all Creation.

When the Pleiades and her counter system were involved with the creation of Planet Earth, they were the first co-creators to introduce the plant and tree kingdoms, fish and some mammals. You were a *co-creator soul*, who in your Pleiadean Light body form, would not be visible here today, for it is of such a high vibration, a pure Light body. They act as custodians of life here, and all souls are first briefed in the Pleiades about life here, before incarnating and drawing up their soul contracts.

At a much later stage, Earth was not so pure and innocent any more, after the destruction of the first land masses, and the rising of Atlantis. As a young girl in that Pleiadean light body, you were playing in the gardens of a *Great Pleiadean Mothership*, created to be as much like the home planets and galaxies as possible, so that those acting as co-creators elsewhere in the Cosmos would always feel at home.

There was a boy, your other half, your twin who played with you there. There were ventilation shafts holding up certain tunnel structures, linked up with holographic systems on this vast Mothership, and some areas which were strictly off-limits to children. This was due to the dangers they presented, with the possibility of accidentally stepping into other dimensions, or forms of life that the Pleiadeans were creating, and also the possible dangers from other planets and galaxy species, as these Motherships served as huge laboratories.

Due to your inquisitive nature, natural in your soul group, you were exploring beyond the acceptable limits allowed on this ship. Your parents had shown you what life was like on Planet Earth, and you were fascinated by this beautiful planet, for indeed from the Mothership it appeared like a living jewel. You simply loved the colours and hues, and always claimed that one day you wanted to experience life there. At that time you were neither in the form nor the position to do so, and your parents knew very well the harsh reality of life here, so this was just considered a childish whim. So you told the boy, your twin, of this wish, and he knew where the connection or light tunnel was that linked this ship directly to the planet, and certain areas the Pleiadeans were working on, to return life to that part of Atlantis. Atlantis allowed galactic travellers to land on their vast space stations, and everyone enjoyed intergalactic travel. They also knew the *Pleiadean Motherships* were doing this work, so there was relatively little problem.

However, the boy showed you this tube or tunnel, and warned you to be very careful of what you wish for. He was trying to tell you that your fantasy of what life would be like with your natural inquisitiveness, implied that if you accidentally or deliberately explored this tunnel, you would fall into a *much lower dimensional state*, having to incarnate into that form, and separated from him forever, for he couldn't take on that form, by nature of his own soul calling and mission, within the Pleiadean creative team.

So, you often played in that garden, and he left for training. One day, bored and lonely without him, you remembered where that tunnel was, and it still intrigued and interested you. It was as if something about it fascinated you as much as Planet Earth, so you decided to find a way in, fully intending to return and brag about your exploits, and to impress him with your bravery. However, as you stepped into that tunnel, you were sucked up by a vortex-like energy, and your twin was immediately alerted that something connected to the tunnel was wrong, after you went missing. As he remembered, he understood that he could not rescue you, and nobody in the team could pull you out again, because of the nature of that energy and suction.

It was the tunnel for souls wishing to incarnate, and take on physical form on Planet Earth, and so you were literally transported into a physical baby form, without the preparation or soul contract your soul would have normally gone through before incarnating.

In that incarnation, as in the subsequent ones, you not only felt this intense loss of your Pleiadean light body, but also that intense loss of your *Twin Flame* as he never could incarnate here, as warned. Thus, if you incarnated onto Planet Earth, with its subsequent fall and loss of its original form, you would be subject to the laws of karma, and the cycles thereof. It was not that he was saying that you would be alone forever, but rather that if you took on lifetimes on Earth, he could never join you there, for he was called to work elsewhere. In your original created form, you were never meant to take on the denseness of physical form here, nor were you supposed to have taken on such a mission because your soul was unprepared. So, what essentially was inquisitiveness then cost you, for subsequently you were stuck and had to work through karma and karmic links and ties, returning repeatedly. This lifetime you have the opportunity to work these off, and once done you will be freed, and need not return.

That will allow you to be with your twin wherever he is in the Cosmos, and be within him, as you already are in your sleep state, and in your other soul bodies, where you are married in the inner planes, with three children in the Pleiades on board one of the Motherships of the *Intergalactic Fleet,* where he works. You visit them and your family when you sleep.

So you are in reality never separated from him – however you had to incarnate here from time to time, to work off karma. *One can never actually be separated from one's twin – no matter what form or dimension they are in.* Love is always there, and he helps and supports you as much as he can, and is one of your higher guides.

You have constant recalls of this, because you were quite traumatized during the lifetime in *Atlantis,* as your soul was unprepared, and experienced immense difficulty adjusting to life here. You subsequently got involved with people who did not serve your highest soul growth and good, thus creating karma, for you ended that lifetime by committing suicide.

So, then here and now, it is best to heed the lesson, work off karma to be free to resume your true soul life in the Pleiades, and to reunite with your twin forever, with no further need to ever return. There is immense love between the two of you, and your parents already knew at birth that he was your *Twin Flame,* for in the Pleiades these things are known at birth, so children grow up together, and then later are in partnership with their twin. That was why you were playing with him."

———

SOUL GROUP: The Infinite Ones

"In those Egyptian lifetimes she assumed the form of *Thoth*, and then later a female form, channelling *Isis* herself, and worked in the *Temples of Horus*, which were dedicated to the opening up of the third eye. She was first in a male, and then later in female form, and seems to use both forms and aspects of the Divine, for the purpose of bringing in infinite knowledge, wisdom and understanding. Thus her *Twin Flame* will also take on multiple forms, male and female, although in this lifetime she chose the female form again, and may find herself sometimes attracted to other females who resonate with her, as well as her lover, who in this case is a soul she worked with in the times of Thoth, when she had a male form, and he a female.

In fact, she very much embodies the male and female aspects of Creation itself, and this is for a higher reason, *as she brings in balance between the masculine and feminine, returning with the Divine Feminine, to equalize the masculine dominance after so many thousands of years.* She thus chose a female form as it brings with it the heightened ability to tap into the faculties of channelling, and the opening up of the third eye and pineal glands. Mostly though, because of her own strong connection to *Sirius*, as she can more easily communicate with the dolphins, whales, mermen and mermaids in this way – for they are of the same ilk, and chose to remain in that 7th dimensional body, to guard the undersea temples of those lands which sank.

She has fallen in love many times, but felt a distinct peculiarity, like half of her was engaged in the relationship and the other half not. The underlying reason was having lived in both forms in different incarnations, knowing that on Sirius the balance between the masculine and feminine already exists, with a higher understanding of unconditional love. Once experienced, earthly love is always challenging, for it is very difficult to understand deep down, where strife, lies, cruelty and inauthenticity originate. It is harder to love unconditionally, when the shadow appears in a partner, and is reflected within oneself.

Thus there is a tendency to withdraw at times, and just float along. There is in however a much higher perspective here. Not all souls are meant to be in partnership – some have a soul contract stating that their life's mission is more important than all relationships. Often, they have already been mastered in other planes of existence, and when such a soul is called into higher service, as is the case here, then higher service takes priority over any relationships. There was the decision to serve, first and foremost, then the relationship challenge is less of an issue, as long as she stays focused on her mission.

Understand this Little One, there is but one single fraction of your soul incarnated here, and the rest of your soul is working with the *High Lord and Lady of Sirius*, in order to reactivate the pyramids of Giza and the Halls of Records, which are in a different form than people generally understand. It is not in the form of scrolls, but rather in a crystalline form, accessible only to those who understand the keys and codes within their own soul, and can then unlock the doors there, and you are one of them. See, then the importance of your own mission, and the need to not get side-tracked.

This does not mean that you cannot love and have loving relationships. Yes, your twin soul is here, and you have met him, but remember you have switched male and female forms many times, and thus nothing is steady. It will challenge you both at times, but you are both here to complete a mission, and therefore understand that this is *but a tiny fraction of your complete soul incarnated – there are still 8 other pieces in Sirius*. Thus, although union is very desirable, and therefore serves a purpose, the soul mission and soul contracts take priority at a crucial time like this. The soul will be first of all drawn into completion and full activation of its mission, for it will constantly be reminded of this by its soul council, and in this case, it is the *High Lord and Lady of Sirius*.

First of all, then, ask them to assist you any time, and know *Thoth/Hermes* is here for you as well. Then go into deep meditation or visualization, and ask how you can serve. Doors will open and you will receive the necessary information. The minute you start asking, "How *can I serve?*" The tools will be given to you, as you grow more confident within yourself, to step into the higher purpose of your own soul. Also before sleep, ask to go to the *Ascension centers in Luxor* where *Lord Serapis Bey and Archangel Metatron* have their ethereal retreats. There you will meet these Beings who will assist you in remembering.

However, once you open this door, you will be taken through 7 initiations Into the inner planes, for only those worthy of this will be led through the *Doors of Amenti* into the true inner sanctuaries of the Sphinx. In contacting *this channel,* you already were aware deep down of your need to step into something, but had no idea where that may be. Here is your answer. *You have this work to do for the New Golden Age which can only dawn when certain information and infinite knowledge and understanding is returned to the planet. Understand this and surrender to this higher calling, and then the rest will happen."*

———

CHAPTER 10

Soul Mates and Twin Flames
(Part 4)

SOUL GROUP: The Creative Ones

"You often seek this magic, the extraordinary aspect in relationships, and then wonder why you are disappointed. You also have the idea that if you meet this Other, it will be as if a fairy Godmother waves a magic wand and you will live happily ever after, but that is an illusion. Until you delve deeper into your own soul, and reconnect with your magical soul, with its amazing abilities to communicate with trees, and all these creatures, magic will elude you.

This has to do with the lifetime, when the soul you eventually married, galloped into your life! He was an impetuous young man with fiery red hair, and a torque around his neck which proclaimed him a *prince*. As *Guardian of the Sacred Grove* you confronted him and asked him his business. He was unimpressed by your rank, and guardianship, but more by your fiery beauty, your raven black hair, blue eyes, and the majestic way in which you guarded the groves.

Anyway, you would not budge, and used your magic to keep him out, for he wanted to hunt there. In doing that you stirred his interest, and your refusal to bow to his rank and demands, irked him no end. So he told you straight that he would 'get' you and that no one refused him entry anywhere, least of all a comely wench! With that you lost your temper and then, just to spite him (and this is something you knew went against all you had been taught) used a little magic so that a lightning bolt flashed and spooked the horses and in the ensuing chaos, he was thrown off his horse, and lay there for dead.

You of course knew you had abused your power and would have to explain to the High Druid why, but you had a Prince on your premises with severe concussion! So you summoned help, and the Druids took him away to nurse him back to health, but forget you, he did not. Thus it came to pass that he was hell bent on breaking your powers, and wanted you obsessively, although he did know that he would be breaking a tribal taboo, and would have to pay the price. You were fascinated but also repelled which evoked a defiance, which knew no bounds. Since you had confessed your misuse of power to your Grand Master, you had been cautioned not to repeat this again. The Prince became high King, with far greater power then previously but he had not forgotten you.

So, he sent in armed men to take the forest by force, which provoked the Druids and Wizardry to stand together to defend what was theirs, in a mass confrontation. As the Druids could not bring this energy into their sacred groves, they had no option but to stand their ground, as wizardry was part of the Druids, indeed they were one and the same, mere branches of each other. In this confrontation, they witnessed the demented King who would see no reason, so they requested you give yourself up, rather than see the destruction of the sacred groves, and the slaughter of the Druids, due to a personal vendetta between you and the King. It was considered wiser that one druidess give herself up in sacrifice, rather than the entire community suffer.

At first you fought and rebelled, but then had a vision of the consequences if you refused, so you relented and were given a white horse, poison, in the form of a ring with instructions that should he try and rape you, rather than lose your powers, to drink it and so halt his revenge.

You surrendered, but to your surprise he courted you, and treated you well, for he was smitten, but when he could not make any headway, grew angry and planned to rape you, but you took the poison, and died in his arms. He vowed then that he would not let go of your soul, and that he would have you in other lifetimes, and he did. Interestingly, you had grown to love him before doing this, but you had made that vow to the teacher that you would not give your power to him in this way."

———

SOUL GROUP: The Sacred Healing Ones

Soul name: She has within herself the keys and codes towards that which activates the sacred geometries in the higher soul minds of those she meets, and therefore acts as a catalyst who brings about higher activations of soul purpose and mission.

"This soul is one of those first *crystal children* who volunteered to incarnate to assist the planet and Humanity through massive changes in vibrations and frequencies, as she triggers the *sacred geometrical programming* held within the higher mind in those whose lives she touches. This then activates their own remembering, so that they can step into highest service, and raise their own frequencies and vibrations and move into the *higher state of being*.

This is very important work, for in the next few years there will be a sorting of souls, and those who can move into the higher frequency bands will be separated from those who cannot, and this is a process of the whole rebirthing of the planet. Therefore she must experience this herself before she can activate this in others, as she has tended to be distracted from her soul mission and purpose by becoming entangled in relationships which have not always served her highest soul growth and purpose, and have more or less closed down her soul abilities.

Yes, her twin has appeared, and this has been a catalytic awakening for both of them, that there is still so much inner work needed – activations of the keys and codes, the sacred geometry within her higher mind, before she can truly do the work she has come in to do, and be with her *Divine Other*.

The *Twin Flame* has incarnated here before with you in Atlantis and Lemuria, and worked with the activation of people towards their highest potential. You worked together, you with the activation of the *geometrical keys and codes* in the higher mind, and him bringing that into fullest activation. Since meeting him your own inner keys and codes of your higher mind have been triggered, and in a sense, you have been catalysts for each other to remember this, and the vital work needed. *As the female part of this flame, you are the activator and transmitter of these patterns encoded in the left hemisphere of the human brain, and you work with the Goddess activations.*

In Lemuria you were *androgynous*, both inhabiting one single body, but you allowed yourself to be persuaded to be split into two bodies, male and female. This brought immense trauma for in this, you (female) felt this intense sense of separation from your other half, with an enormous inner void. Although you had sex (the reason why you split was because you wanted to experience the sexual energy), you felt you had been deceived. For the rest of that incarnation, you never felt having sex compensated for losing your other half, feeling rather that it was grossly overrated, and you withdrew emotionally from your other half. This was exacerbated by him experimenting with sex with other women, which resulted in an increased sense of intense loss. So you too engaged sexually with other men, causing you to drift out of each other's orbit.

When Lemuria sank, still reeling from the shock of losing your other half, you both sought solace in the arms of other partners. When incarnating in Atlantis you consciously chose the male and female forms, working together in higher healing temples. However, working together so closely, you often found that you were side-tracked by your work, while trying to make the partnership work. It did not work out as hoped, because as you activated people and he took over, he seemed to take all the credit, not acknowledging your part. You always felt that he dominated, and it will remain an issue in this lifetime, if not addressed and sorted out from the start.

In this regard it would be wise to look at how you can do things separately, rather than together – you do your work in a different timeframe and office or venue, so as not to be competitive, as you were in *Atlantis*. There is a fine line between partnership, having sex, and working together. Too much of the same will cause a rift between you, if not carefully balanced. You will also have to learn to be complete in yourself, and not to stand in his shadow, which you do so often, believing he is more advanced – this is not true. You might have been asleep and not fully activated yet, but your souls are on a par, and you both need to realize this. If one is too much and the other too little, then there is imbalance – that causes pain and dissension, for one cannot sustain any relationship that way.

Balance is both true partnership, and working together working towards a higher mission. You both are equally empowered and activated, and then your whole and his whole don't disappear into each other, but rather the unit enhances and brings out the best in each other, forming the greater or *third force energy field* that brings that empowerment from the greater whole. But if one is not fully empowered, one will be overpowered, with resentment growing in both – as one will feel they are giving too much, and the other that are not receiving in return. So be aware that this happened in Atlantis and Lemuria.

It is not that love is absent. Of course, it is present – for you were once in one single bodily form, with one single soul. However, the wounds of Lemuria, the split thereof and the void it created, the feeling of separateness must be addressed. In essence you must find immense trust and respect for each other, before you can merge into a true sacred union again, **equally** empowered and equally aware, consciously aware."

SOUL GROUP: The Ingenious Ones

"Soul name: The Ingenious Ones who bring in the higher understanding of the cosmic forces, and the wider cosmic formations.

This soul works throughout the Cosmos with the cosmic creative energies, bringing in technology and higher knowledge of the intricate workings of the cosmic energies and forces to build new technology, new structures, and are in a sense the administrators of the Cosmos.

He is always drawn to design, engineering, and admin structures, wherever he can use his inherent genius to bring structure, order and systems to seeming chaos. So this mastermind ability is amazing in itself, with a certain Midas touch in whatever he puts his mind to creating. In relationships this has not always been to his advantage however, because he attracts those that he wishes to be with, as he has a set idea of what a desirable physical female form is. Thus he attracts and meets her, but soon finds her boring.

Mostly because he often forgets that there is a soul in that body, and that a pretty face does not always match up with a beautiful inner nature. In the time of ancient Israel, you were a *son of King David*, highly trained in the art of governing, law and warfare. You had a rich lifestyle with plenty of adventure. Your administrative side truly surfaced when you laid out the temple foundations on the site of Jerusalem, which became the main *City of David*. As the King was old, you often spent hours in deliberation with him about construction. As was then the norm, you were married off when still young, to a plain cousin with a gentle and sweet nature who tolerated you seldom being at home, accepting that she had to tend to the hearth and children. When your father died, Solomon succeeded him, putting you in charge of administration, which included the design and building of these temples.

You travelled to Lebanon, for the master architects were there, and it was the source of most building materials. You took a detour through Damascus, and first saw her at a market place – the beautiful woman you are currently interested in. She was from a nomadic people, with an enchanting free spirit that lured you closer.

You paid her father a handsome sum of money to buy her, as she did not really want anything to do with you, being in love with another she planned to marry. By that time, you were already past your prime, so this proved to be a very challenging match. She resented your advances, and on numerous occasions tried to escape, so you stripped her of her freedom, and raped her. You were infatuated with her which later evolved into a love/hate relationship. It was not that you never loved her, for a part of you wanted to dote on her because of her sheer beauty, but another part was angry that she shunned all your loving advances and closed her heart to you. So, when she became more open and showed love, you did not know how to handle this.

As it happened you took her back to Jerusalem with you – not as a wife but as a concubine. The two women soon became best friends, which riled you. The children they both bore irritated you, because you were never or hardly ever at home, and the two women ganged up on you and rebelled. You had more problems in that lifetime than ever before. In subsequent lifetimes you have always been drawn to incarnate in that region.

Later you incarnated at the time of the Roman occupation in Jerusalem, Israel. She was a cousin and you played together as children. She was beautiful, head strong, always looking for adventure and you were the one always dutifully following her around like a lap dog, although she ignored you.

You were betrothed as the family considered it a good match, when this same trouble started all over again. As arranged marriages were then the norm, it was understood and hoped that the couple would learn to truly love one another, after a while, but you two always seemed to rub each other up the wrong way. So there was passion and fire, a type of truce, and then further eruptions. One day a merchant came along and the next minute, she ran away with this stranger, leaving you with the shame and children. You never saw her again in that lifetime. So, encountering her in this lifetime, of course there is a recognition, and a sense of owning her, which in other lifetimes you had. It is not that your two souls do not love each other – it is just that the accumulated baggage from those lifetimes when married or as lovers, was stormy, fraught with misunderstandings and challenges. So, these negative patterns will repeat themselves now if not resolved this time round, with both of you finally opening your hearts and souls to each other, and learning to love each other warts and all."

SOUL GROUP: Ascended Horse

"You have a great connection with the Planet *Lukema*, where horses and Unicorns originated. Your soul has always worked with them, so thus you can heal them and speak to their souls.

You stem from the *Constellation of Pegasus*, and like this Ascended Horse, have had lifetime after lifetime working with these horses, to bring in special energies and qualities. Indeed, you have so many horses, animals, fairies, gnomes and elementals around you, who simply love working with you. When you first incarnated in the *Celtic lands* you worshipped *Rhianna the Horse Goddess,* and worked with her and she is your protector and guide.

Chiron appears as the Wounded Healer and yes, he too has worked with you when you heal, for he knows their heart and innermost soul whispers. Then from the heavens with *oomph*, comes *Zeus,* and he stands there in all his glorified manhood smiling, his protective arms around you, as he tells me the story of *Persephone* and her relationship with *Hades,* the *Lord of the Underworld.* He shows me *Athena* and *Aphrodite's* Temples in Athens and the Parthenon, and then further afield the mountains of Athens and Greece...

You have had several incarnations in Ancient Greece, and before that in Atlantis, in Lemuria and in Elysium, the continent which came before all of them, having many of the same legends as Avalon.... for out of the mists of Avalon you rise... You were one of his many daughters, and roamed wild and free. Always the beautiful one, you became ensnared with some who were not in line with the rest. You fell in love with an unsuitable man, and your love for each other led you astray. *Zeus* saw your unhappiness and tears, and gave you his horses to take care of, and to help them to heal, which you did.

Then one day, out of the heavens and out of the blue, he came and kidnapped you and bore you off far, far away, to the lands at the end of the mists. He was uncouth and uncivilized, indeed as far as the Greeks were concerned, he was a barbarian. You married him, yet bore him no children and took lovers on the side, when he was busy with endless wars. Your incredible beauty lured other men in, and on many occasions, you betrayed him, for you were lonely, homesick and could not love him at all. One day Troy, a man with all the characteristics you adored, that made you fall hopelessly in love, arrived in your city port. You simply decided to pack up and leave on the boat, smuggled, and disguised as a servant girl. Yet, you had hardly left the safety of the harbour, when a huge storm broke out, the boat was tossed adrift, and smashed against rocks and sea, and your life ended.

In other lives in Greece, you acted as an oracle for the *Oracle of Delphi,* and those in the *Temple of Love* of *Aphrodite.* You were trained in the arts of sex, and pleasing men, not in lust or as a prostitute, merely as a vessel for their higher healing, almost like an initiation. As the Oracle you were simply asked to relay messages, which you did with great accuracy, and you carried that gift into this life.

Yet, in this lifetime, because of these previous ones, your soul decided that the best path to hone your inner soul strength, was for you to walk alone, using your skills to heal horses, to serve both your passions, and simply to have time to find yourself, before stepping into Higher Service – which is what Zeus meant by coming or going Home.

Men often approached you, as you enchanted and lured them, yet they simply could never break through certain barriers and walls of your heart, for in a sense you hid yourself there. Until your current lover came along, and then suddenly you felt love and opened up, yet he has not been able to choose between his other lover and you. He has fears and insecurities, and is threatened by your inner power, which he has glimpsed on occasion, and does not know how to handle. He is the lover who drowned with you in Greece, and you had to meet him in this life, to resolve your bond.

It is best to release this, for he needs healing himself, and to remember his own power and step into that – he is not ready to link up with you.

Do not be afraid little One.... Yes, the times are rough, but be willing to release **All,** knowing that whatever you lose will be given back to you in manifold ways. Look at your gift with horses, and then look at the Mexican and Latin American lands, and go there. You will be led to link up with certain horse people of the Spaniard lineage in Mexico and New Mexico, and will discover that your healing with horses is needed. They will also provide you with shelter. In the process you will be led to other people who will lead you to reunite with your *Crystal Keys*. You will find a High Priest, the Keeper of the Crystal Skull of Horse energy, and he has to give you the Keys.

Don't be afraid of adventure and venturing forth, for in finding the Keys, you will step into your Goddess and High Priestess Power once more – he will help and you will suddenly be able to use those abilities from Greece, Elysium, Atlantis and Lemuria – these are the gifts you bring into the world.

This is the time of *great rebirthing* for you and the planet, and you will find your way opens to go to *Machu Picchu*, and reunite with the *Feminine Portals* there. Indeed, during these journeys you will find your *Latin American Twin*, and he will read you like a book. He will not be the usual type you are attracted to, but completely different – that at first this will come as a shock. Yet, he will fascinate you and heal your heart and soul. He is that lover, the first one you had in Greece, and he is a beautiful shimmering soul... gentle and kind. He shares your great love for horses, and owns many himself.

You will be called in to do far more healing work, and you will find that once re-united with the crystal keys and your twin, you will simply love every single minute of being alive, and will heal lots of animals, plants, the planet and people, as all will come to you.

Zeus is smiling and nodding and saying, that one day, you and your twin will return to Athens and then, you will be doubly blessed. He loves you and blesses you, saying that you are never alone and that you have all those unicorns to help you and the fairies, angels and gnomes, and that you have Apollo watching over you as well."

SOUL GROUP: The Divinely Sounding Ones

"Coming back to your partner – he is a sensitive and beautiful soul, but also one who tends to get a little lost along the way. He sometimes feels profoundly and deeply, but does not quite know how express himself in words. Thus he is a good partner, but you both need to go through a purification process to return to your inner truth and core. If you introduce very high frequency vibrational sound and colours into your home, and truly start living from the heart and soul, then your relationship will change into something profound, with beautiful love and closer bonding. Your *Twin Flame* has not incarnated, mostly because, as said you have an *androgynous* body and he is keeping that space for you there. Only a fraction of your soul has incarnated here, so the other parts are working in space, and in your home galaxy. With you it is different to souls who have two aspects of souls, within the soul cluster. However, we will not go into details here, so as not to confuse you."

―――――――

SOUL GROUP: The Light Bearers

"This soul works with the frequencies and vibrations of light, as emitted by the *Central Sun, and therefore that of the Christed consciousness, or the highest consciousness states, the 12th Golden Ray, which is the Ray of Enlightenment in its highest form.* Therefore, it acts like a transmitter channel, or conduit for the Cosmic Sun's rays.

However, you sometimes allow yourself to be side-tracked from your mission by allowing others to run your life, especially where love is concerned. You need to be a tad more discerning about who you let into your energy fields, as you sometimes are drawn to those not on the same frequency band as you, allowing them into your most sacred energy fields, that of the sacred womb, they disrupt this and zap your power away.

This is very true with the man you were recently involved with, and deep down you know this. He is not of the same frequency band as you, and often pretends to be, because he feels threatened by your presence, and your powerful energy fields, so tries to somehow block them, or zap your energy away. So, just be aware of this, as he does this through your sexual energies. So know that one needs to have a crystal clear understanding that in a woman the womb area *is her power base*, and when someone enters, who is not of the same frequency band, then that person at some subconscious level will feel this, grow frightened, or feel that they can get or steal energy away from you to empower themselves, to make them feel better or more energized at some level.

It is sometimes better to allow yourself the freedom to truly be yourself, that which is really you at all levels, and not to compromise for anyone. It is better to understand that on a human level, not all are on the same high frequency band as you, so best to be discerning when searching for a match, so that he is heart and mind empowered. This is essential, as your body is supersensitive, vibrating at such a high frequency, amplified by your own soul, so be aware of this. You will only feel intense pain or get confused, the moment you feel that someone is zapping your energy.

So, it is best to keep some distance from him for a while, until he is sorted out, for at the moment his mind is trying to control you, while his heart is closed, because deep down he is frightened of your energy, as it is too much for him to handle. So allow each other some space, and if needs be, just give it a bit of a rest. In that way both of you can regain your space, and your full energy, and then from the space of truly being yourself, ask if this relationship is serving you and your own highest soul growth and good. If it is not, then no harm done, but rather move onto full empowerment of your life's mission, and put the intention out to the Universe to attract someone who is of the same vibration and frequency band as you, and who is in the heart-mind consciousness. This will serve you in the long run, and both of you will be far happier.

Also understand that it is necessary to put up healthy boundaries, as you are inclined to always wish to give, and not so open to receiving in equal measure. A soul mate will be entering your life in about three years, on the same wavelength and frequency band, and of the same profession, practising in France. You will meet at an international conference, and it will feel like you have known each other for ever. He is quite a handsome, dark-haired man, with a sense of humour and sparkling type of laugh, quite well-built and he does sports training. You will be like a dose of good-humoured medicine for each other.

Not that you need to be reminded to sparkle, that comes naturally to you, and you just love sprinkling laughter and good cheer on all you meet.

You have a beautiful soul sister and she is there to assist your process. You know in your heart and soul you have worked together in other realms and existences, in other life forms all over the Cosmos. Your soul knows this at some level although you have not always incarnated onto this planet – indeed she has more often than you. So cultivate the connection, and know that you will help each other greatly, when you both understand that you are that support in rough times, but also there as soul companion through the laughter and tears – for all of life is but one great journey of discovery of the infinity of life and love, and never just a destination."

———

SOUL GROUP: The Higher Healers

"Your *Twin Flame* has not incarnated at this time. He also works as a medical scientist on board the same Mothership with your children, for you agreed to not incarnate simultaneously, so that the family unit is not stretched too far as your children are still young. Another reason to often visit them in your sleep state. He is very tall, blond with beautiful blue eyes and a lovely smile. You love each other dearly. Here on this planet, you will never find that same abundance of love from any man, and deep down you know this. No one will easily match your own frequency, or love you as completely and unconditionally as him. No matter how hard you try, nothing is going to change this, while still here.

There is the knowing you have deep inside that this applies to you and of course there is the longing to be loved – yet, know this little one, you came to this planet as a member of a *Special Task Force,* and if you allow yourself to be side-tracked into just pleasing a man, while having a family, then you are stretched too thinly, and your soul cannot function at an optimum level. What the people think of as the completion of being and happiness, is very far from the truth in many cases, and when the soul gets stressed and distressed, then it cannot function, or tap into its own higher self, and the collective soul group knowledge. Sometimes it is better to work on your own, knowing that you will always be taken care of, and that you are immensely loved by your *Twin Flame,* and reunited every single time you go into a deep sleep state."

———

SOUL GROUP: The Radiant Ones

"As far as the man in question goes – yes, he is a highly advanced twin soul. It is his first incarnation here, and therefore there was instant recognition, as this was in the soul contract. Indeed, this is your first incarnation.

However, in the interim you have both slipped into the sleep of forgetfulness on this planet, and are not accustomed to such a dense physical form, rather to the higher frequency light bodies, so you both have a problem with being in such a body. You sometimes feel it is too slow, dense and also sluggish. With respect to you being involved with other partners, there is nothing wrong with this, it is just that when in such a relationship, it is best to be there wholeheartedly, for it to work. In meeting each other, this is going to be difficult, unless you *both decide to leave your partners.*

Meeting in the astral is natural for you both, accustomed as you are to union in this higher manner, due to your energetic origins, but it will not bring happiness, or work with your current partners, for you will want this other form of union, and not just a physical union with your partners.

It is really a matter of free will and choice, so although you are now contracted to meet up again, it does not mean that you will be together. That is always the risk souls take when they incarnate here, that they may fall into the sleep of forgetfulness, becoming involved with others along the way, as the physical urge on this very low vibrational planet ensures the desire to procreate. People very seldom feel the need to ask if this truly is the correct partner or not, as mostly the need to procreate dominates over common sense.

In that, little one, here is a time when it is perhaps better to do the inner work on yourself, asking what you really want in life.

If you wish to raise your family in the current relationship, then do so with all your heart, soul, mind and might, making a conscious choice. It is unfair to withhold love, so rather find renewed love for yourself and your other with appreciation, then the heart and soul opens up to love again. The twin is having the same experience, deciding to stay with his family, rather than risk losing them, and until he changes his mind, he will not connect with you.

It is therefore not fair to either of you, nor to your current partners, if you engage in astral sex, for then you not be fully present with spouse and family. That is living a lie, and something will give way somewhere. In most cases it will be the marriage, but it will be more likely be you suffering the consequences, as women tend to feel more from the heart space, and your soul does that naturally. So, until you both meet up face-to-face again, to discuss this clearly, you will be unable to make any decisions.

In the case of *Twin Flames*, it is not always necessary to be together after meeting. Sometimes the time is just not right and neither is ready for the other – as it is clearly shown here. Sometimes the meeting is contracted in, as here, but then both decide that they would rather focus on their mission, and to meet again at a later stage, when their children are older and both are free to pursue such a match and merge their power in Higher Service Work."

––––––––

SOUL GROUP: The Translucent Beings of Light.

"Soul Name: She is one who knows the ancient art of serving the Goddess and bringing in that beautiful translucent platinum light of the Divine Goddess and anchoring it into the Earth, and bringing new hope to the hopeless.

Your *Twin Flame* has incarnated as said, but he is a widower, and being open in mind and heart, is at the moment, more interested in western women, as they are more in touch with their own sexuality. It is just that he is wise enough to understand that if women are suppressed deep inside of themselves, they cannot open up, for half of them is missing. His wife was an arranged marriage and could never do that, because she felt inferior, and never complemented his intellect and his knowledge, so they had nothing in common to discuss and experience.

He does not want to repeat that, for he longs for a true soul companion, one there right beside him, equal in mind, body, spirit and soul, enhancing him. So in order to truly connect to such a man, you have to be his equal. This one is not even going to be interested if he feels that you are disempowered at any level – he is that enlightened, and not bound by convention or society around him. He is open minded and cosmopolitan. So take this time rather to empower yourself in all areas and levels of your own life, and stretch beyond the self-imposed confines, and into the greater version of yourself, and then teach others this higher way."

––––––––

SOUL GROUP: Ones who Serve with Higher Healing

"Soul Name: The One who brings Healing through Service and in Higher Service to the Divine. The soul has done immense inner work and therefore the loving healing light now flows through and within her. There is a great surrounding of appreciation from the *Lord and Lady of Arcturus*, and the *Arcturians* and those higher-ranking Masters within your own soul group.

We thank you for this, and for now truly stepping up into higher service. This is now living life in true alignment with your soul mission, where blessings will flow.

The soul group works mainly in the realms of the broader cosmic whole, so there are only a few souls incarnated here at this time. However, understand little one, that you can always request to be reunited with, assisted by, or to merge with the 11 other soul flames, or soul extensions of yourself. One does not have just one *Twin Flame*, but essentially 11 other flames, and in very rare cases one will meet up with all of them in a single lifetime – but not usually on this planet. However, it is still possible to ask for the merging in the higher realms, to assist you with your work in higher healing.

The man you were involved with and strongly attracted to, was indeed one of your *Twin Flames,* and you both still have much to work through. Until that happens, true and profound union cannot take place in the sense of you living together, but as said nothing is stopping you from having a relationship, if so wished.

Thus, if the *Twin Flame* is unavailable, and he is the only one incarnated at the time, then there is no reason to not love another, whether of the same soul group or not, if the heart stays open, and one understands that each soul group has their own higher calling and expression." 1328-2.

SOUL GROUP: The Purifying Ones

"During this time the soul you are asking about was *your twin sister,* and you chose to incarnate together (being of the same soul group) to work with the specific fire. During this time, you both worked for the highest good – you were known for the merging of your soul energies as taught, and carried out intense and massive purification work as needed. No details will be given, for it does not serve your soul to know them.

However *Avalon* was invaded with Priests, who were turning against Priestesses in their fear, so they in turn were forced to use their considerable powers in self-defence. The men often used their own knowledge against them which made them more vulnerable to being attacked by very powerful energetic forms, through the uses of fire, rather than by the brute force of the conquerors.

As twins you both had to defend yourselves against a very vigorous attack from one of the most dangerous defected alchemists from the same School, who had long since wanted to rule the Mystery Schools with total power. He used his devious skills, knowing that the two of you were nearly invincible with your combined powers, so he devised a plan to separate you, and then attack you both simultaneously.

As you were in the same location when attacked, and under siege, you called out to her for help, realizing you lacked the strength to hold the forces on your side, so she tried to merge her energies with yours. You had been trained never to risk this, as the repercussions were dire, and the fires would fuse you into **one**, creating trauma, with immense soul karmic residue, such as happens if you play with fire and get severely burnt.

But in that moment neither of you were rational, wanting to work a miracle in self-defence, so somehow merged your soul body fires to fend him off. In this moment you were struck by his fire ball, and both died instantly, but your merged souls were held there in the fire. You could not leave, which is what he intended.

The High Priestess was alerted to this, and witnessed events – the battle between you and this man. She succeeded in sealing off the Mystery School, with the help of other priestesses who rushed in to help, and he was killed. They were able to free your souls, enabling you to leave the planet. However, when back in your soul form, you were both briefed on events, and how it would now be necessary to spend a few lifetimes here, to allow your souls to work through this, and how you would both at times feel a deep merging between your souls, as if still in that fire.

It necessitated learning to separate yourselves to reclaim your powers, working with the fires to transform yourselves into your highest soul self again. Essentially when merging in that manner, you are not strong enough to hold your own soul fire. She has reappeared in your life through soul agreement to settle this, so neither of you will have to incarnate again. The lesson here is soul mastery. Of course, the sexual fire is related to the Soul fire and therefore sometimes the one may be confused with the other. In truth there is no *sexual fire here, but only the soul fire.*

There is another lifetime linked to this, during the two lifetimes where you were both once again were in the same mystery schools, but millions of years later. We find you in the *Mystery School of Alchemy,* in the school where *Mary Magdalene* was *Bishop.* You were cousins with a close bond, which often puzzled but knitted you together, and interestingly you were both always initiated and trained separately, as your teachers knew this to be best from soul readings which were done before entry to the school.

So, you really had little to do with each other in the training and initiations, only working together once ordained as priestesses. Now once again this school and all priestesses, were under a severe attack from men (the same ones who previously desired total power and feared women) and Mary Magdalene's school was stormed and burnt down. You were both working elsewhere when the news came, so in shock and dismay those survivors fled to the caves in the Pyrenees. You shared a cave, when the same happened as you describe. Neither of you understood what was happening, for the priestesses never engaged sexually with their own gender. It was forbidden for very powerful reasons.

However now this impacted on your ministries, and Mary Magdalene and the High priestesses were all murdered. Soon you were fighting for your lives, and to survive it was suggested you rather marry to procure protectors, and to safeguard valuables. You were separated, and never saw one another again. However during the times of the *Cathars*, this story more or less repeated itself, and interestingly you were both burnt together at the stake, after coming to each other's rescue when the crusaders attacked your village. You were both thrown in the fires, and your *souls merged again* as before.

You were never released from that, and now incarnated again to finally allow that soul power to be reclaimed, to free you both, so think of this as an act of unconditional love. In other words, you are both giving each other back the freedom as souls to work with your soul gifts, without merging to ward off an attack. The only way you can do this, is by releasing those soul memory banks, forgiving yourself for breaking the Order's rules, (albeit in self-defence and not understanding the underlying reason for them). Also forgive your attacker, and men in general. There is immense trauma there from all those lifetimes, when they were bestial in suppressing priestesses like yourself, with the distress of having to use your soul powers in self-defence. So forgive yourself and forgive the men. In this lifetime it is all about learning to reclaim your powers, and not allow anyone to take them from you – not even this woman."

———

SOUL GROUP: The Healing Ones

"Now, your soul has usually incarnated here before as a healer. You incarnated in the civilization of the Lion Kingdom, in an area now sunk under the sea, offshore from where you now live. You had a birthmark which identified you as a healer, and from the age of 3 were brought to the *Crystal Pyramid Temple* of the *Emerald Ray*, created from Emerald Crystals, and the highest healing temples. You were trained in energy healing, first learning to work with the energy patterns of plants, to bring out their best and most vibrant healing patterns, which in turn would be used for herbal remedies and potions, including trees. You learnt to work with their souls, for they have souls just like us.

You often swam with the dolphins, who shared their knowledge of the sea, and spent days and nights in the forest, so that you could communicate with the souls of the forest and all its creatures. You learnt about fungi, mushrooms etc., with the most profound visions and highest soul calling during such sojourns. Then you moved onto healing animals, who are very psychic, can read energy fields, and communicate telepathically with people.

You loved working with them, and they loved you. Then you trained as a human healer, using all the knowledge gained through plants, trees and animals, bringing it together to help the Human race. In these temples you were not allowed to have children, as this would distract from your mission, dispersing the energies in too many directions at once, and dissipating the power of the healers.

However, in that lifetime your twin incarnated, working at the same temples, but you only came together three times a year, according to the strictest of rules of *Hieros Gamos*. However these teachings currently practiced have lost half the potency, for the true sacred rites were removed from the planet, after people abused these powers, and controlled women as sex slaves. So, don't take all that people write about as truth. Question certain things. Your soul knows. Also understand that at the time, you shared sexual intimacy, but as **soul energy**, as the sexual energy does not need a physical body. The highest kind of sexual union, and merging of the sacred flames, can only be done in non-physical and energetic forms. Only the very high initiates ever knew and practiced it, for it never interfered with their soul calling and purpose, nor depleted their energies. Now, this is what your twin and you do in your sleep state, and no earthly man can ever do this with you."

———————

SOUL GROUP: Those who Blossom with Divine Love and Light

"Soul Name: She was born in the glorious blossoming of the Divine Love, and is that bourgeoning forth of the first spring flowers, that bursting forth with the exuberance of the beautiful life force itself, with that joy it brings to others, as they too feel this bourgeoning in their own soul, hearts minds and Being.

This soul came in to bring this flourishing forth of love and light into being, now that the Dark Ages and the veils of amnesia are lifting, with so many shifts of consciousness happening, as more and more souls wake up. That intense blossoming is called forth to become a way of life, where she literally allows this to bloom forth in others. She is like a Fairy Godmother with a magic wand, used with joy, love and light and when it touches anyone, it turns them on like a light, and opens the heart centre and pathways for the soul, to remember its highest soul truth and Being.

First of all, look deep inside to where your neediness lies. Is it loneliness, a feeling of deprivation, or that you have lost something, or that you are not enough? Are you blaming yourself for the break up, and then secretly wanting him back? Or are you just asking for another man to come into your life, who will take care of you and your children? These are fantasies – no-thing is missing. You are always being taken care of day and night, and love is never absent. For in truth there is the love for the children, and their love for you, there is Divine love for you, and hopefully, your love for the Divine, and the Angelic and Archangelic Realms, the Elohim and Elohim Councils, and your own highest ranking Ascended Masters. So you are held and surrounded by unconditional love, with no strings attached, and that love is constant. It can never be taken away from you, and neither can anyone kill it – it is always there.

As you grew older that elusiveness increased, so when you finally met your first husband, you felt this was it! This taught you one amazing lesson: that sex was not love, and nor was infatuation. One can be sexually involved, and in that moment feel as if you are light years removed from your body, just looking from above at yourself being encased by another human body, but your soul, your spirit was absent, as was his. A lonely, lonely place to be.

So, there was a need to have a new man in your life, and he appeared. Again, this was a passionate physical attraction, and to some extent a feeling he was a kindred spirit, but sometimes your intensity scared the hell out of him, for he was not ready for it. The soul itself is not of the same soul group, but you knew each other cosmically, for you sometimes work together with the co-creation of the *Divine Spark* in new planets which you create. So there is a type of soul recognition there, of having worked together and having fun, but he is not your *Twin Flame*.

Indeed, your *Twin Flame* does not want or need to incarnate. It was this part of your soul which wanted to volunteer and experiment, to find out what life was like in physical form here, and to bring to life the immense shifts – thus anchor in the love and light, and stimulate it into a much higher dimensional state of being. He is one of your higher guides, appearing often as light, or a light being to you, very tall, handsome, with long blond hair. He has very large blue-purple eyes, and a ready smile. Such love streams from his eyes and into you, love in its highest expression and form. You always are with him wherever he is cosmically, in your sleep state. So no earthly man will ever be able to give you that ultimate bliss, that ultimate sexual expression and union that he does.

In truth this is what you soul remembers here on Earth, and is so desperately seeking in a man, and not finding. You can't find it, for no earthly man can measure up to your true love and *Twin Flame*."

———

SOUL GROUP: The Expansive Songs of the Soul-heart

"Soul Name: She reaches the expanses of heavens with her soul songs, the songs of her heart, soul and being, and she is that love song sung within the Divine Heart and Soul for all it has created, ad infinitum.

Your soul songs are meant to be sung, and your soul wishes to express itself for the Divine sings through you. If you truly wish to empower yourself and your relationships, then start being true to the highest expressions of soul within you, empower yourself, and the rest will fall into place. There seems to be a reluctance at times to truly step out of the shadow of others and fully into the sunlight – the light of your own soul. Don't shrink yourself to suit others. Go and shine, sing those soul songs, and stop procrastinating.

As for your husband, yes, he has had a few lifetimes with you, and he is a soul mate, as your Twin Flame has not incarnated, but acts as a higher guide and is always with you. You reunite regularly with him in your sleep state as souls can traverse the Cosmos and be anywhere. Love is never absent. It is constantly there, and even if the Twin does not incarnate, it does not mean that love is absent. It is humans who have forgotten all of this, and then often spin fantasies around love, and loving relationships, forgetting that nothing is ever missing in the Greater Cosmic Creation – love can never go missing, or be absent. Love is everywhere. It may be in different forms and expressions, but it can never die – it is not like a tap which can be turned on and off. Love is omnipotent, omnipresent, and always there, 24 hours a day, 365 days a year, forever."

SOUL GROUP: The Infinite Cosmic Ray Masters

"However in order to assist you, as your soul's prayer and desire to help and love have been heard, a lovely younger woman will come into your life who is a *soul mate from your soul group*. She is quite tall with blonde hair, blue eyes with a ready smile and just radiates love and light. You will recognize her by her eyes, and from the moment you look into them, it will feel you have known her forever, and you have. She has worked with the *Master Rays*, anchoring them in with the angels and archangels, and is teaching this technique, and also transmitting the language of light. She sometimes uses this in combination with chanting and singing and has a beautiful voice. She is single, so free to form a relationship with you, if you both so wish, as suits your own free will and choice. We will not give you the name – for what is a name? Soul meets soul and remembers. That is enough!

You have repeatedly worked with her in the outer galaxies and star systems, with this love bond. As you are both master scientists of the cosmic rays, this work often took you to the very outposts of the cosmic whole, travelling in spacecraft and Motherships together.

In the Cosmos, one partners with one's Divine other, not through marriage as earthlings do. In other multi-dimensional existences of the 12 different flames of a soul, one meets other souls with whom one has love bonds, not just your twin flame. So you know this soul intimately. She is living in the same country as you – it is just a matter of you learning to trust your inner voice and guidance, and you can ask *Archangel Raphael* and *Mother Mary* to assist you, as they look after those who seek that ultimate love.

It is therefore of vast importance that you prepare yourself to be inspired, to step up fully into mission and power. It's important to realize that the next 10 years are crucial for Humanity and the planet at large, so you cannot afford to procrastinate any longer, and need to commit yourself 100% to this task. You are an immensely beautiful and loving soul when fully activated, and people sense this about you. Now it is a question of activating all 12 bodies, and your soul anchoring devices held in your third eye region to bring this work down to Earth. You often see colors and rays, remember that all cosmic rays have color, frequency and vibration, all merging into one single rainbow. It is a matter of understanding what each ray anchors in and enlightening people about this and how they fit in, for each soul will anchor in one or two of these rays, and you have the ability to anchor in all 12."

SOUL GROUP: The Sparkling One who reflects Divine Hope and Loving Being

"You will not be able to attract a child soul to you until you have entered into higher service, and become the truth of your own being. *For you have made a soul contract with a certain soul who wishes you to be her mother,* but this soul is highly evolved, and she cannot be born if you are not fully activated and living your true soul purpose. Only by doing that will you be able to raise your frequencies and vibrations to the level to become pregnant with her, as she is a very very special soul who needs you as mother, to be fully *present in soul.* This is the contract part. Hope in your heart for her to prosper and grow into the *beautiful being* she is, who will further anchor in the Divine Feminine. You cannot birth this child, if you are not prepared to do the inner work and reconnect to step into the truth, the mission of your own soul, and concentrate on that.

Your husband is a soul mate with whom you have been before, in the great continent in the North Sea area, which sunk there and is under the ice in Siberia. This part was previously the South Pole, and had a tropical climate and mammoths and other now extinct animals who still roamed there. You incarnated to bring in these animals and other species, to help settle them in there. You brought them in on the great Motherships, and you helped the volunteers to adjust to living here, in the experiment that was Planet Earth.

You had great powers of telekinesis, teleportation, levitation, and could literally appear and disappear at will. You could also shape-shift, working closely with the Goddess *Freya* and the God *Thor*, remembered in the Northern Myths. You were a part of all of that, and a Goddess in your own right. You were the *Goddess of Hope and Love*, and people called upon you – thus you did amazing work.

At that time this man worked alongside you as part of the team, as a Commander of a craft which transported the animals. You had a love affair in the Pleiades, so it is nothing new. You grew more and more attached to the physical and denser form of human life here, experimenting with sexual energies. This caused a rift between the two of you, so you decided to leave him, and to move closer into life here. This relationship will always be a challenge, in the sense that deep down you wish to have freedom, for your soul seeks freedom to fulfil your soul mission. So any man that you feel could bring this freedom will be attractive, but it is not really freedom from marriage you are seeking – but rather the keys and codes to full activation of your own soul mission and purpose. You are just confusing the one with the other, and make no mistake he knows this, and is aware of the other man. This is causing more distrust and challenges in this relationship.

The challenge for you will be to adjust to a new country and people. If you are not happy in your own soul and skin, then all the love in the world will not fill up the void deep inside of you. See this has happened before in a lifetime in which you lived for over a thousand years, becoming more and more attached to and infatuated with the human form, and eventually had to forfeit eternal life for the death of the human form, as Humanity sank into forgetfulness of who and what they were. At that time, he came from the Pleiades to assist, and you were delighted to have him and had a relationship and children. However, he soon found that the human female form was more interesting, and he too grew infatuated with these sexual energies and he enjoyed plenty of other women, which broke your heart. He deserted you completely, and you were left to fend for yourself. You had everything your heart desired, but the man you wanted by your side. In that lifetime you vowed that he would never do this again, and you would not be in a relationship with him until he loved you totally and unconditionally. In anger and despair, you then took your own life."

———

SOUL GROUP: The Emerald Healing Ones

"You incarnated mainly to do two things – to communicate with the dolphins, whales and sea creatures, and with the Mer people (who often appear next to you and communicate with you, but they appear invisible, because you closed your third eye down, sometimes without being aware of it, because you were afraid to see). You literally beam the *emerald green ray* into all whose lives you touch, and deep down you know this, and therefore the difficulty you are experiencing in completing your doctorate is because if won't help you much with your soul work. It would be more helpful to see how you could use your gift of healing, and the *emerald ray,* to open up communication channels with the Dolphins, Whales and the Mer People and then ask them how you could help to heal them, and how you can serve.

It is the same with shamanic work. You have been attracted to this work for some time, but then something deep inside says: This is not for me. I must do something which earns more money, or where I will have some security, like a piece of paper. However what value is a piece of paper, if your soul is unhappy? Your soul yearns to be of greater service, and to transmit the emerald rays into some comprehensive form of holistic work – whether this is to be healing, communication with sea creatures, or both.

You are a natural energy healing channel, transmitting the emerald ray without any effort, it happens naturally as part and parcel of your soul. You easily tune into people's energy fields. Even as a child, you often reached out to people and animals, to stroke the body part you knew was blocked energetically, and you healed them. Some people complained about this, and you were scolded, and thus stopped. It is time to remember this, and to do this work again.

The same applies to all forms of life, even marine life. You have a natural type of scanner in your brain, which scans and reads energy fields. You know instinctively, for sometimes in crowds of people, you shrink away when you read unpleasant or unsavoury energy and vibes. Just become aware of these extremely powerful gifts, and find ways to use them in higher service work.

This made you a very powerful healer, and you took these healing methods with you, before Atlantis sank, and went to what is now the Tenerife Island, where you practiced these healing skills, but as more of Atlantis sank under the sea, you were taken by aircraft to Mexico, to meet up with your Twin Flame. You both worked with the healing Emerald ray, and created the *Temples of the Emerald Ray* in Mexico (this is still buried under the jungle and rubble). You enhanced each other, and you had an emerald crystal key, which matched his emerald crystal skull. This emerald crystal fitted snugly into the palm of your left hand, and was used as a pure transmitter crystal – indeed it amplified your transmitting and healing powers.

Your crystal skull was stolen from you, by those who envied your powers, and you never quite recovered from its loss, although you did regain some of your healing powers.

Your main task in this lifetime will be to open up communication channels between the sea creatures and man – and to help heal people's energy fields, bringing them into higher alignment with the massive Earth changes. Some of this will come via the *Mer People* who are constantly monitoring the oceans. In the *Great White Lodge Healing Temples* on *Sirius*, you work with the emerald ray, and also the DNA and cell structures of dolphins, whales and other sea mammals. You are constantly monitoring their progress, beaming emerald rays into the oceans of Planet Earth, and other planets, for you are like a *Guardian of the Sacred Waters*. If you beam the emerald ray into water for instance, if will become energized and amplified in goodness, and it will act like an elixir of life, and bring rejuvenation.

The Sacred Waters are places where there is great energy and mountains, sea, lagoons and oceans, and there the emerald green rays are amplified by these massive expanses of waters, and the trees of the natural forests – all of these work with the emerald ray.

Your twin flame and you have worked together in many lifetimes, and in some both of you were severely persecuted because of your work, so in this lifetime there might be fear of stepping into the higher healing of the emerald ray. You work with *Archangel Raphael* and *Mother Mary*, and their healing angels. You also work with *Archangel Gabriel* and *Hope, Chamuel* and *Charity, Jophiel* and *Christine*. You also work in the inner planes with

Dr. Lorphan and his *Galactic Healers* on *Sirius,* and may call upon them any time to assist you with your healing.

By wearing emerald green on your person, you will enhance your powers, and amplify the energy within you. Also have this colour in some form in your living and working environments, for it will energize you and the people with whom you interact. You are here on special assignment – never forget this."

SOUL GROUP: Those who Align

"You incarnated in this lifetime to bring your own higher soul knowledge back to Earth. As long as this is your focus and your total dedication, and you do not allow yourself to be side-tracked, then blessings will rain down upon you and the work.

However, the karmic lessons of those days will haunt you. As a priestess you took an oath of purity, as did he, and in breaking those vows you incurred karma which you both were aware of, having been through all the initiation, knowing the consequences for breaking cosmic laws within the sacredness and sanctity of the temple. You knew this would bring you pain, and that you would be banned from this work. Nevertheless, both of you had free will and choice – you repeated this pattern in two different lifetimes.

So, you are drawn together, and are indeed prospering. However now you have free will and choice again, whether you wish to engage sexually or not. It is best to be crystal clear about what it is you wish to achieve. Is this for ego, and self-gratification, or even if it's love, then what is the reason?

If you want your paths to flow into one, and to dedicate your life to recreating the ancient sexual rites, then that needs total dedication and purity of intent. It also calls for higher service – for ultimately these rites were intended to bring heaven down to earth – yet if one does not know the higher pathways, or act with total integrity, then you will incur karma – this is unavoidable.

So, it is not that one cannot engage, or find mutual ground, or love one another – just be very clear what the higher service goal is, and what higher good you will bring to Humanity, and for the higher healing of the Human collective, if you engage.

There are other souls involved, to consider. With your current partner you had karmic debts to clear, because he gave you shelter and always loved you, in quite a few lifetimes, but you seemed to repeatedly shun his love and shelter. So deep down this is why you need to get crystal clear. This is a man with a huge heart and immense love, but he often feels that he has to compete with the other man for your time, devotion and interest. It greatly saddens him, for he loves you dearly. He is feeling left out, just quietly watching which way you are going, sensing that you are withdrawing from him emotionally and physically. Don't think he does not feel, for he is keeping it deeply inside, the memory of being deserted in other lifetimes is still there in his soul memory banks.

Do, you wish to leave him and your children and engage with the other, and in what way? If you engage sexually with the other man, your own soul will scream at you, because of the other lifetimes, and the sexual rites, and the rites of purity. If not done in a true way, the fire that is ignited will burn both of you, and cause immense pain.

So, here Little One, no one can help you. It is your own decision. You have free will and choice. So have both men.

The only way is to listen deep within, ask for highest guidance and listen intently to whatever comes. Inherently if you want to do healing work, you must set an example. Practise what you preach. If you cannot hold up your own ideals, how can you teach others? Integrity is a factor.

All of this is haunting you, for you need to resolve this once and for all on your own, and then do whatever you decide with all your heart, soul, mind and might, with no half measures, in your highest truth and integrity. What most people have never understood about the higher sexual rites since time immemorial, is that the sexual energy is not for playing around with, certainly not for entertainment, and most certainly not for self-gratification. It demands purity and totally pure intentions. It demands the highest pathways of the soul.

Anything less will hurt, burn and bring in immense pain.

Therefore only a few souls have ever managed to walk this highest of paths, without being burnt by the fires ignited. That is because their highest calling was greater than the sum total of self, and they were totally dedicated and devoted to each other, and a third party had no place. For this is a forging of souls, in a similar way as gold rock has to be melted down at extremely high temperatures, before the purest gold can emerge. If you are not prepared to give it your all, in total integrity with total dedication, and the same for the other, then it is best not to engage in it at all.

Let this be written.

Let this be heard.

Let this be understood.

For this is the truth of all time."

———

Epilogue

In truth, there is only love!
Love all-embracing.
Love infinite and eternal.
Love lived.
Love experienced.
Love loved.
Love received.
Love in action.
Love in being.
Love.
Love.
Love.

Love is in truth eternal.

It is not bound by earthly matter, not by the personas and egos a soul acted out in any lifetime, including the current one.

For when the soul is not in embodiment on Earth, it exists elsewhere in the Universe, and thus love carries on in many forms and multiple expressions.

The *Fountain of Love* never dries up, for love is omnipresent.

Before we incarnate, we agree to meet those we have loved in other lifetimes, and those with whom we have negative patterns to work through and dissolve. We will then meet them at preordained times, and whatever happens henceforth, is determined by our own free will and choice. Love however, will remain, whether we are consciously aware of this or not. Whether we are together, or not. For the soul is not bound in anyway.

We all have those loving souls who are not with us on Earth in embodiment, but who are eternally present, who we meet regularly in our sleep state at night. Such love is unconditionally present and indeed is there to support us, during our sojourns on Earth.

We are never without love. For Divine Love is present within us. It always has been and always will be there, even when we close our hearts, in various situations.

We all are now experiencing a greater and more profound heart opening on all levels as we will experience the Power of Love in its true magnificence.

For all love starts within oneself, within the soul itself, and then radiates forth like the Central Suns, touching the hearts of all those we encounter, and drawing to ourselves those souls we are meant love, in diverse forms and ways.

We are love in the deepest and most profound sense!

For our souls were created in love, through love and in truth **we are love** itself!

This book comes with all my love to you.

Judith Küsel